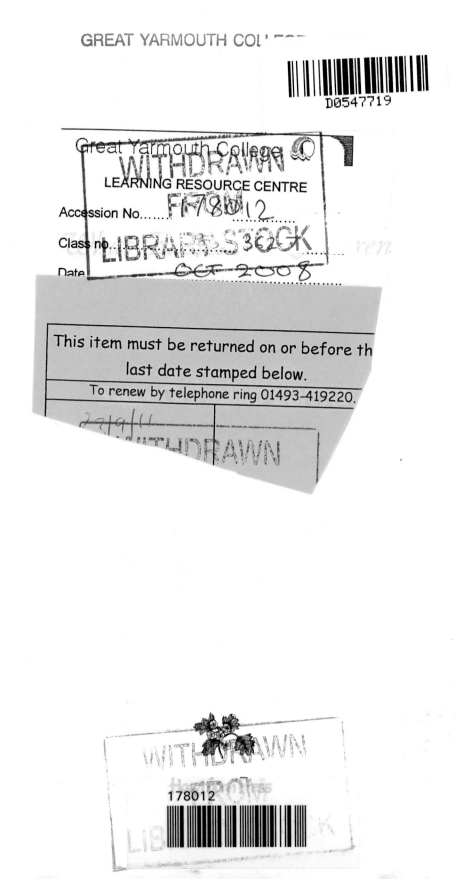

Published by Hawthorn Press, Hawthorn House,
1 Lansdown Lane, Stroud, Gloucestershire, GL5 1BJ, UK
Tel: (01453) 757040 Fax: (01453) 751138
Email: info@hawthornpress.com Website: **www.hawthornpress.com**

Illustrations by Marije Rowling
Cover photograph © Jupiter Images
Personal photographs of children reproduced by kind permission of their parents
Photograph of babies on page 161 © Getty Images
Photographs on page 161 and page 163 © Jupiter Images
Cover design and typesetting by Hawthorn Press, Stroud, Glos.
Printed by Cromwell Press, Trowbridge, Wiltshire

Mixed Sources
Product group from well-managed forests and other controlled sources
www.fsc.org Cert no. TT-COC-2082
© 1996 Forest Stewardship Council
FSC

Extract from *Gentle Birth, Gentle Mothering,* Dr Sarah J Buckley, reproduced by permission of One Moon Press, Adapted version of The Blythe-McGlown Screening Questionnaire for OBD, originally published in *An organic basis for neuroses and educational difficulties,* Dr Peter Blythe, by permission of Dr Peter Blythe, 'Screening for neurological dysfunction in the specific learning difficulty child', *The British Journal of Occupational Therapy,* Goddard Blythe, S A, Hyland, D, reproduced by permission of the College of Occupational Therapists.

British Library Cataloguing in Publication Data applied for

ISBN 978-1-903458- 76-1

Contents

List of Diagrams

List of Illustrations and Photographs

List of Tables

God could not be everywhere, so he created mothers.

Jewish proverb

This book is in praise of all mothers, past and present.
It is especially for mothers in the future.

DEDICATION

For my daughter

Acknowledgements

Sarah Buckley for permission to use sections from pages 133 and 134 of her book *Gentle Birth, Gentle Mothering* on the effects of caesarean birth.

Dr Peter Blythe for permission to publish an amended version of The Blythe-McGlown Screening Questionnaire for OBD (1979).

To Martin Large for time spent in discussion, his gentle suggestions, and faith in the proposal for this book; to Rachel Jenkins for her unending patience in answering all my questions and meeting my requests; Marije Rowling for drawing and re-drawing babies in different positions; to Richard House for his detailed attention to the content of the book and making it infinitely more readable; to all others at Hawthorn Press whose silent work has gone into the planning, design, and marketing of this book.

To all the children and their families who gave permission to use photographs from their personal albums to illustrate stages of motor development: Zoe, Gabriella, Natao, Valentin, Robbie, Julia, and James.

To Belinda Barnes, founder of the Foresight organization for pre-conceptual care, who spent only half a day with me nearly 20 years ago but who has influenced my thinking ever since on the importance of preparing the ground for every human life.

To Dr Ursula Anderson and Professor Mary Waller for taking the time to read the first draft of the manuscript, for their detailed comments, corrections, clarifications, and ideas and for additional information and reference sources, which have been inserted into the final version, and for the work they have each done over many years in making the lives of children better.

To Sue Palmer for writing the Foreword to this book, for her books and for being a tireless activist in bringing people together to help society recognize that children are our future and the rewards of a materialistic society are not necessarily what children need.

Foreword

It's not easy to be a twenty-first century baby. He or she is born into a world of bright artificial lights and sound-effects, an electronic global village that buzzes ceaselessly twenty-four hours a day. This high-tech world affects babies' development from the moment of conception, through the food their mother eats and the ways she spends her time. And once babies are delivered into it, the electronic global village will continue to affect the way they grow, body and mind, for the rest of their lives.

There's much to celebrate about our electronic village. Most of the developed world has enjoyed over half a century of peace and prosperity, universal education, and a level of material comfort that previous generations could only dream of. Old geographical borders, and the human prejudices that went with them, are beginning to break down, and the global nature of information technology offers the chance to share ideas and wisdom throughout humanity. Today's babies may live to see great wonders, and huge leaps forward in human understanding.

But there are also dangers. The ease of existence in the twenty-first century means we take the basics of life for granted – indeed, for many, 'lifestyle' now seems more important than the human context of daily life. Babies however are very basic creatures – since evolution is a long slow process, the blue-print for our species has not changed significantly since Cro-Magnon times.

So – as Sally Goddard Blythe so brilliantly describes in this book – our twenty-first century baby is actually the same creature as it was in Stone Age times, with the same, natural human needs that have characterised homo sapiens through the millennia. If he or she is eventually to become a fully-fledged adult member of the human race, with all the characteristics civilised humans have accrued through the ages, we must provide the right sort of environment and experiences. In some ways, material wealth makes this easier – we no longer have to go out hunting and killing our own food – but in others it makes it much more difficult.

The force keeping our global village afloat is competitive consumerism, so politicians and big business have to keep us constantly on our toes, ensuring money continues to circulate in an ever-expanding market. Today's global villagers have become trapped on a monetary merry-go-round – needing to earn more and more money in order to spend it on more and more goods. This means that the two most important commodities babies need are increasingly difficult to supply.

The first of these commodities is **time**. And in the quick-fire, quick-fix modern world, time is often in very short supply. Yet, as you will see in this book, babies need endless supplies of time … and not the high-powered highly-managed time we associate with twenty-first century multi-tasking either, but the slow, ancient rhythms of human time and the constant attention of a loving human carer.

This leads us to the second, and most important commodity of all: **love**. Fortunately, there's no shortage of love in most children's lives – parental love is still probably the most powerful force on the planet. Unfortunately, in a competitive consumerist climate, love can sometimes be perverted by the force of the market. Smiles, cuddles, closeness, communication, attention – the best things in any infant's life – are all free. But parents trapped in pursuit of a lifestyle may find this difficult to accept – surely love should come in an expensive package, ready-wrapped?

So twenty-first century babies, with their basic, old-fashioned, human needs, are in direct competition with the world into which they're born. And unless twenty-first century adults can resist the siren calls of the market and find a way of providing for these needs within our modern world, the development of the next generation could well be impaired. In fact, there's the distinct possibility that development will be so impaired that they won't be bright or balanced enough to keep the twenty-first century show on the road.

Fortunately, science is now coming to the rescue. Advances in psychology and neuroscience over recent decades mean we have a very clear idea of what babies really need for healthy development. Sally Goddard Blythe sets it all out with admirable clarity, providing the scientific evidence that empowers parents to resist the pressures of the market and concentrate on the realities of child development.

This comprehensive book provides parents with the information they need to raise healthy, balanced, resilient children. It guides the reader through all the factors affecting a child's development from conception to the teenage years, with particular emphasis on two critical elements within the first year – movement and communication – upon which children's social, emotional and educational development depend. Above all, it demonstrates that what babies really need is the time, love and attention of the loving adults in their lives.

Sue Palmer, author of *Toxic Childhood*

1.

Introduction

Since I completed the first draft of this book, two documents have been published reporting on the state of childhood in the United Kingdom and other economically advanced nations. The first, compiled by UNICEF,[1] assessed children's well-being across six dimensions: material well-being, health and safety, educational well-being, family and peer relationships, behaviours and risks, and subjective well-being. The report concluded that 'the United Kingdom and the United States find themselves in the bottom third of the rankings for five of the six dimensions reviewed'. Health and Safety was the only dimension in which the UK performed above the lowest level. The second report, produced by the UK children's charity NCH (formerly called the National Children's Home) found that a million children in the United Kingdom now suffer from mental health problems. One of the areas of growing concern was the increase by more than a third of the number of children being admitted to hospital suffering from eating disorders, probably fuelled by pressure on young people to look like a supermodel or celebrity.

The latter report was compiled from two other studies: one from the Office of National Statistics, which linked many mental health problems to lifestyle issues. They found that the level of mental health problems was higher amongst children from lone parent families (16 per cent) and reconstituted families with stepchildren (14 per cent); and youngsters with serious behavioural problems were twice as likely to be regular drinkers as classmates without problems, and were more likely to have used drugs, mainly cannabis.[2] The second study, from the Institute for Psychiatry, showed a twofold increase in the number of teenagers with emotional and behavioural problems between 1974 and 1999.[3] Possible reasons that were suggested included elongation of the transition from childhood to adulthood and increasing peer pressure fuelled by social networking sites. These reasons do not seem to be sufficient to account for the increase in the incidence and range of problems that we are seeing, however, not just in our young but through all levels in society. Lone parent families, stepfamilies, under-age drinking, use of drugs, and the power of the media to influence the minds of the young are a product of an existing sickness in society. It was in the attempt to find an explanation and a remedy for this sickness that I started to write this book.

First Love

From the moment of conception, mother is a baby's universe. Cradled inside a miniature ocean of amniotic fluid, the developing baby feels every movement she makes, experiences the sounds of her body, the food she eats, and the emotions she feels. This union between mother and child in the first nine months of life before birth led Russian paediatrician Michael Lazarev to describe mother and baby as one being, like a 'matrechska doll' – the traditional Russian wooden doll, which carries inside itself smaller and smaller versions of the original painted doll. When the physical union between mother and child is separated for the first time at birth, the baby, totally dependent on its mother to fulfil all its needs, embarks unquestioningly on the first love affair of life – unconditional love for its mother.

Animals also have an instinct to attach at birth. Konrad Lorenz[4] found that goslings are primed to 'attach' themselves to the first moving object they see upon hatching. Usually this is the biological mother, and the gosling will learn to follow its mother and approach her when in distress; but if the moving object first seen by the gosling during this crucial period for 'imprinting' is something else, such as a human being, the young bird will follow that object as if it were the mother bird. There are some wonderful photographs showing Konrad Lorenz going for a walk, being followed by a line of young goslings who mistakenly believed him to be their mother.

Imprinting is a fixed pattern of action or stereotyped behavioural sequence that is set in motion when the appropriate environmental stimulus or 'releaser' occurs. Some fixed action patterns can only be elicited for short periods of time during an animal's development. These periods are called 'sensitive' or 'critical' periods.

Not all human mothers feel the same rush of love in return towards their baby. Many factors in modern life have combined to impose stresses on the mother, leading to physiological changes and problems with the infant that can interfere with mother instinct. The purpose of this book is not to engender guilt in mothers and future mothers, but to explain what lies behind nature's design for human reproduction so that parents can harness the knowledge of generations to make environmental choices about when and how they bring children into the world, and what sort of world they provide for them to grow up in.

In my work as a psychologist investigating a physical basis for certain learning and behavioural problems, I have the opportunity to talk with many parents, teachers, and health professionals. Whilst for many, the problems they deal with have developed as a result of unavoidable events, I am also increasingly asked the question, 'why'?...

- Why are we seeing an increase, not only in behavioural problems that plague society, but also one in four children leaving primary school with inadequate mastery of the 3 R's (reading, 'riting, and 'rithmetic)?
- Why are we seeing so many children entering primary school unable to use a knife and fork or to dress themselves, so that they cannot change their own clothes for a physical education (PE) lesson?
- Why do so many children seem to be inattentive and unable sit still?
- Why are so many children entering school with poor language skills?
- Why is there such a rise in childhood obesity?
- Why is there an increase in childhood depression?
- Why do we see so much disaffection amongst young teenagers?
- Why does there seem to be so much substance abuse amongst the young?
- What has changed in the last 50 years such that, for example, the British have changed from being a nation renowned for its self-control (stiff upper lip) to being described in one of the

newspapers during the summer of 2006 as 'the most savage nation in Europe'?

Some 120 years ago, my grandmother grew up in a very different world from the children of today. A world in which she waited seven long years to marry my grandfather, during which my grandfather had to play billiards and drink with his future father-in-law for the entire evening in order to be allowed to speak to her for ten minutes. She and her sisters had to ask permission just to go out of the house to post a letter, and yet my grandmother was one of the least repressed or emotionally damaged women I have ever known. Despite losing twins in her first pregnancy and two of her four sons in their early twenties, she exuded an aura of calm, warm contentment. She had extraordinary self-control, was never angry, always interested in everyone around her and, as a small child, I can still remember basking in her company. She used to say that it was a nation's women that made it great.

Such stories are often dismissed as nostalgic sentimentalism, looking back to former times through rose-tinted spectacles and failing to embrace the progress of the present. All of life is about change. Survival, even in the technological jungle of today, is about being able to adapt to changing circumstances and meet the demands of new and unexpected events. Nevertheless, the strongest societies are those that hold on to values, customs, and practices that have served them well while being open to new, more efficient ways of living and learning. The example of my grandmother is to illustrate how different the experiences of childhood, men, and women are today compared with what they were in her time, and how some of those changes may be playing a part in the problems we are experiencing as a society today.

While society changes at breakneck speed, the physical processes of child development take thousands of years to change. A computer's brain can be assembled in less than a day in a factory, but the human brain takes some 25 years to mature, and in the early years, the innate process of maturation is dependent upon the stimulation of physical interaction with the environment and social engagement with a primary source of love, to unfold in healthy ways.

Starting in the late twentieth century and continuing in the present, the place of women in society has undergone a revolutionary change since the days when my grandmother was a young woman. Many of those changes have been for the better, and few would wish to return to the days when a woman was her husband's chattel; but there is another side to women's freedom to choose. In the swing toward personal freedom, pursuit of self-actualization (achieving the best we can) has almost overwhelmed the greater needs of society as a whole. In the technology-driven west, a woman's worth is often judged by what she does as a career rather than whether she has children, but in other societies a woman is not considered to have reached adulthood until she has become a mother.

The future of society dwells within its children, and a child's experience of the world begins with its mother. When a society ceases to value and barters the role of motherhood in exchange for materialistic gain, status and instant gratification, it mortgages its own future. Historically, society has never been very good at valuing motherhood[5] although it has idolized images of motherhood such as The Madonna and Child. In the money-centred culture of today, women and mothers are increasingly contributors to the gross national product and are not valued sufficiently (by themselves or by society more generally) for what they are contributing to family stability and society in their role as mothers.

A number of years ago, my husband and I were staying in a small country hotel in the Cerriog Valley in North Wales. As we sat having coffee after dinner, we started to talk to some of the other guests, one of whom was a famous biologist. When I asked him what his particular area of interest was, his answer was 'religion and behaviour'. In my ignorance, it struck me that this was unusual for a biologist, so I pressed him further. He said that nearly every religion carries within its belief system codes of behaviour, many remarkably similar to the Jewish (and later Christian) Ten Commandments.

At a fundamental level, these codes of practice are simply an attempt to sublimate the animal instincts of humankind to allow a greater society to flourish. Whilst man is capable of extraordinary acts of altruism, he is not a naturally altruistic creature. In the wild, it tends to be the selfish who survive. In order to create and sustain a society, it is necessary to curb the selfish instinct; to create rules and laws which society accepts and obeys, with lesser laws or codes becoming the social norms or manners of the day. The essence of good manners is consideration for others – being 'civil' – derived from the Latin 'cives', meaning citizens. A key component of civilization is self-regulation and self-control. The origins of self-discipline are rooted in the symbiotic relationship between mother and child. Mother is nature's universal teacher, and the nature of motherhood has a profound effect upon society.

Even in absentia, mothers have a lasting impact on the emotional life of their child. Children who have lost their mothers from an early age frequently suffer emotional isolation for the remainder of their lives, finding it difficult to form lasting attachments unless an adequate substitute can be found. This is particularly true for children who lose their mothers in the first six months of life.

Parenthood is not for everyone: some people choose it and repeat the experience over and over again; others become parents by accident, reluctantly adjusting to a role they had not planned; others look forward to being parents, only to find that the natural parenting instinct they had anticipated does not arrive with the birth of their child; some long to be parents but the much-wanted baby never comes. There is an abundance of books on pregnancy, baby care, and child-rearing practices, which vary from one generation to the next, and most of which offer advice from an adult's point of view. Over the last few months I have searched the shelves to find a book that approaches motherhood from the *child's* perspective. Literature which looks at childhood from the child's point of view tends

> to be submerged if not ignored by the over-riding power of the military industrial complex that has taken over society's mind as the centrepiece of existential importance. It is a commentary on values wherein society would rather pay for its mistakes than prevent them. Also pregnancy and the first years of life are, as it were, hidden from the general flow wherein money making and achieving status are considered to be the important things of life. The fact that you do not see too many of these books in bookshops is because there is a general devaluation of the role of mothers and the early nurturing of children, which we need to address in terms of how adults arrive at their belief systems, which dictate their feelings and behaviour.[6]

This is a book, which sets out to explain what *children need* from the adults and society that surround them, in order to grow into healthy, well-adjusted and happy individuals.

Study of child-rearing practices around the world shows how remarkably adaptable and resilient human beings are. Different traditions, customs, and cultures nurture their offspring in a myriad of different fashions, many of them developing as a direct result of the climate, landscape, and type of society as well as religious traditions under which the child will be expected to live. Despite the wonderful variation of traditions and practices, there remain certain underlying universal factors, which transcend codes of belief, fashions, and the politicization of society. It is some of these constant factors, viewed from a developmental perspective, that I shall explore in the following chapters; not to suggest that we should aim for a child-dominated society, or a de-liberation of women, but rather when society places the needs of its children first, the future for the next generations looks bright.

The following chapters will examine some of the changes in how and when fertilization occurs that have taken place over the last 50 years and the implications for children; why factors during the course of pregnancy can affect the development of the unborn child; the impact of events surrounding birth, early feeding practices, and why developmental milestones may indicate children's needs at different stages in development.

We will explore some of the physical foundations for learning and emotional regulation, mechanisms of movement control, development of vision and hearing, and why balance and touch are often the forgotten senses in the classroom. We will discuss why a child's physical experience of the world is often mirrored in his emotions or affect, and how we can help children's physical experience of the world to be a happy one.

There are no absolute rules for parenting. Every child is different and the parenting techniques that work with one child in the family will not necessarily work for others. The purpose of this book is to give parents and professionals who work with children an under-standing of the physical nature of child development and *what children need* so that they can solve problems when they arise, understand the language of children, and provide the best environ-ment they can for healthy, secure, and happy development.

Endnotes

1   *Child poverty in perspective: An overview of child well-being in rich countries. A comprehensive assessment of the lives and well-being of children and adolescents in the economically advanced nations.* UNICEF Innocenti Research Centre. Report Card 7, 2006.

2   Office of National Statistics, *Mental health of children and young people in Great Britain.* Palgrave Macmillan. Basingstoke, 2005.

3   Collishaw, S., Maughan, B., Goodman, R., and Pickles, A., 'Time trends in adolescent mental health', *Journal of Child Psychology and Psychiatry,* 45 (8), 2004: 1350-62.

4   Lorenz, K.Z., *The foundations of ethology.* Springer-Verlag, New York, 1981.

5   Anderson, U.M., 'Progress and virtue of non-adjustment. An historical insight into the origins of public health', *Journal of International Health,* Spring, 1967: 2-16.

6   Anderson, U.M., personal communication, 2007.

2.

Conception and Society: The Politics of Fertility

Evolution in Reverse/Retreat

When a female is born, her ovaries already contain all the eggs she will have for her life. This means that when a woman gives birth to her children, the viability of her eggs will already have been partly determined by the lifestyles of mother and her grandmother before her. In modern Western society, only a fraction of those eggs will ever be fertilized, and a smaller number still will go on to produce a baby. As a woman gets older, this finite supply of eggs gets smaller and the quality of the eggs deteriorates with time, as do the structures that house and maintain them. Nature designed women to reproduce in their late teens and early twenties from young healthy bodies with ripe healthy eggs.

Over time, there is a decrease in the quality of a woman's eggs. An increased proportion cannot be fertilized at all, or are so badly damaged they die soon after fertilization. The percentage of fertilized eggs that are discarded in this way in the general population is not known, as they are often flushed from the body with the menstrual period. In this way, nature practises her process of natural selection, sometimes without the woman ever knowing that, for a few fleeting days, she was a mother.

As women get older, the increased incidence of other health problems such as hormonal malfunctions, diseases of the reproductive tract such as endometriosis, blocked fallopian tubes, pelvic inflammatory disease or infection, particularly 'silent' or symptom-less sexually transmitted diseases such as clamydia, can all contribute to a general decline in fertility and increased risk to the developing child. Other problems associated with age such as diabetes and obesity can all reduce a woman's fertility.

Despite the potential problems associated with conception at a later age, modern Western society is part of a trend in which, at one extreme, motherhood is being progressively delayed until the 30s and 40s amongst the working population, and at the other end of the spectrum, teenage pregnancy is on the increase. Since the late 1970s, birth rates for women in their late 30s and 40s have increased dramatically.

A survey carried out by the National Centre for Health Statistics between 1978 and 1998 found that the birth rate for women aged between 35 and 39 had nearly doubled, and there was a 92 per cent increase of births to women in their 40s between 1981 and 1997 alone. Whilst the ability to delay pregnancy as a result of improved methods and choice of birth control (particularly the pill) has given women freedom and choice beyond the imagination of our grandmothers, these changes may not necessarily be in the interests of our children's health in the long term.

In the space of just 50 years, enormous changes have taken place in relation to women's role in society. These changes are accompanied by more insidious changes in the politics of society, so that what began as increased freedom of choice for women runs the risk of becoming an accepted pattern of education, taxation, and child-rearing practices which are at odds with nature's plan for the renewal of life and the survival of the fittest.

Only 50 years ago, it was the norm for a woman to be married in her early 20s and to have produced her family by the time she was 30. Today, children are encouraged to stay on at school until they are 18 and then proceed to higher education. As changes have been made in how higher education is funded, many of these students will enter their early 20s carrying a burden of financial debt, which will take them at least ten years to pay off. If they also wish to gain a rung on the property ladder, many are not in a position to provide a home and stable parenting relationship until they are well into their mid-30s, only to find that the longed-for and much-planned baby is not conceived.

These figures were confirmed by an editorial in the *British Medical Journal,* authored by a group of obstetricians and gynaecologists who issued a stark warning that women who delay pregnancy into their 30s and 40s were defying the natural progression of their biological clocks and risking heartache. Problems cited include infertility, higher rates of miscarriage, ectopic pregnancies, foetal and chromosomal abnormalities, and the increased likelihood of a premature birth, stillbirth, or neonatal death. Other factors such as difficult birth and low birth weight could be catalysts for later health problems such as diabetes and related developmental problems.[1]

More than a decade of contraception and sexual activity with more than one partner increases the risks of problems in conceiving and having a healthy pregnancy. There is also an increased likelihood of obstetric intervention at the time of birth. Each one of these factors can affect the subsequent development of the child.

According to figures published by the National Center for Health Statistics in the USA, the incidence of births to women in their late 30s and 40s has almost doubled in the last 20 years. Although most women over 35 have healthy pregnancies, the risks increase with age. Those risks include foetal and chromosomal abnormalities and a rise in the need for invasive tests such as amniocentesis, which are associated with risk of miscarriage. Although many invasive tests have been overtaken by use of ultrasonagrams (USG), the use of *multiple* ultra-sound scans may result in biological changes in the foetus. This is an area that is still subject to research.[2,3]

The risk of chromosomal disorders also increases with maternal age, the most common of which is Down's Syndrome – caused by an additional chromosome 21. The risk increases from 1 in 1250 if the mother is aged 25, to 1 in 1000 at 30, 1 in 400 at 35, 1 in 30 at 40, and 1 in 30 by 45 years of age.

Women over the age of 35 have an increased risk of developing high blood pressure and diabetes for the first time during pregnancy. They are more likely to have problems during the birth process, including foetal distress and a protracted second stage of labour, which increases the likelihood of obstetric intervention such as Caesarean Section, or use of forceps or ventouse extraction. Whilst such interventions are distressing for the mother, they can also have an effect on the baby.

During a normal vaginal delivery, mother and baby should ideally work together as cooperative partners. When labour begins spontaneously, it is *the foetus* that initiates the process by secreting a hormone into the mother's bloodstream, which stimulates the onset of contractions. Factors that influence the timing and onset of labour will be covered in more detail in Chapter 4.

The rate of miscarriage is significantly greater for older women, increasing from 9 per cent between the ages of 20 and 24 to 25 per cent between 35 and 39, and more than 50 per cent above 42. However distressing miscarriage is for the prospective parents, it is often nature's way of discarding an embryo or foetus that is not developing normally. As eggs grow older and the reproductive tract bears the scars of time, nature is ruthless in her desire to reproduce the fittest.

Fertility-boosting drugs and treatment can sometimes help to make up for lost time, but these same treatments and medications affect not just the parent but also the child.

In August 2005, figures were released revealing that 1 in 100 babies born in the United Kingdom are now born as a result of In Vitro Fertilization (IVF). As techniques to improve the outcome of IVF are improved, there is a very real danger that IVF will be seen as a natural option for women who wish to delay their child-bearing. In fact, the process of IVF is anything but natural and carries risks for the mother and the resulting baby/babies, as well as the embryos that are discarded during the process or who die in the first weeks following implantation.

IVF now accounts for 1.4 per cent of all UK births; 10,242 of them in 2004. While the UK pioneered the technology, it has contributed little to the long-term studies needed to establish just what is safe, wrote Jerome Burne,[4,5] a freelance medical journalist writing in the *Daily Mail* on the 12 December 2006. He quotes American researchers who in November 2006 revealed that

> by the time children born of parents with infertility problems were six, they had four times the risk of developing autism. They also had nearly three times the risk of serious disorders such as cerebral palsy and cancer.

> Last year Finnish research showed the toll IVF techniques take on the mother's health as well: 14% of women who had undergone IVF treatment ended up in hospital with serious complications such as

miscarriage, ectopic pregnancy and side effects from drug treatments.

However, he did emphasize that these figures should be viewed in perspective against the risks with natural births. 'With natural births there is less than 0.5% chance of developing autism and a 7% hospitalisation rate'; so even with the increased risk, the figures are still fairly low. Nevertheless, they indicate increased risk factors for both mother and child, and these figures do not take into account the toll that the process of IVF can place on a couple's relationship. Prolonged suppression of fertility for social reasons increases the probability of a woman needing to seek IVF when she wishes to start a family when she is older.

The effects on future fertility are not confined to women. A team of scientists from Rigshospitalet in Copenhagan compared the fertility of 1,925 Danish men whose mothers had needed help to conceive with those whose mothers had conceived naturally. They found that 50 per cent of men conceived as a result of fertility treatment were more likely to be infertile compared to men conceived naturally. Men born as a result of hormone-based fertility drugs had the poorest-quality sperm of all. While these results might be the result of genetics, with infertile couples passing problems on to their offspring, it also raises questions about the effects of drugs containing female hormones on the development of male sexual organs in the womb.

Results of a study presented at the Society for Maternal-Fetal Medicine Conference in San Francisco on the 9 February 2007[6] showed an increased risk of birth defects in children born as a result of fertility treatment. Although the number of children affected was still relatively small, amongst a sample of 61,208 births the incidence of a child born as a result of assisted conception having a birth defect increased from 2 per cent to 3 per cent. Not surprisingly, the chances of a defect increased with the complexity of the intervention, with IVF carrying the highest risk. The biggest difference was seen in the rate of gastrointestinal problems, such as defects in the abdominal wall or organs not being in the right place. Babies conceived through reproductive technology were nearly nine times more likely to have such problems – one in 200 births versus six per 10,000 for the others.

First-time mothers who have spent ten years in the workplace and are used to the financial, intellectual, and social rewards of being in the company of other adults during the day can find the adjustment to being alone with a small, dependent, and irrational baby for many hours in the week extremely lonely, tiring, and lacking in intellectual challenge. Some will opt to return to work within a few weeks and begin a second career of juggling childcare provision, work, and home, too exhausted to find much joy in either; others will find that in order to support the family finances, they have no choice but to return to work. The longed-for physical and emotional bond between mother and child is broken within a few short weeks of the baby's entry into the world. For the baby, the loss of its mother for just a few hours in the day can be like the loss of a love affair.

There are many different ways in which the young baby can be cared for. We will touch on some of these in later chapters when we examine issues surrounding breast-feeding, nursery care, childcare provision, and child-rearing practices in other parts of the world.

At the other end of the spectrum we see an increase in teenage pregnancies. These are no longer isolated incidents where a young girl finds herself pregnant, decides to have the baby, and vows never to place herself in such an isolated position again. Some of these children in women's bodies go on to have another two or three children with different fathers before they are 18 years of age, relying on the state or their own parents to support them in their premature parenting. It is my belief that, sexual gratification apart, some of these youngsters are seeking through sex and pregnancy the physical contact, reassurance, and a sense of belonging which are increasingly lacking in society and in the experience of our young.

The United Kingdom currently has one of the highest rates of teenage pregnancy in Europe. Recent figures showed that the rate of teen pregnancy in Britain was five times greater than Holland, three times more than France. and double the rate of Germany.[7] In 1999, the Government published the Teenage Pregnancy Report, which acknowledged that there was no single cause, but highlighted three major contributing factors. Many teenagers believe that they will end up on benefit anyway, so they do not see any reason to avoid pregnancy; despite sex education, teenagers have a poor understanding of contraception or what being a parent will involve; and teenagers are bombarded with sexual images which glamorize sex, but they do not feel able to talk about sex to their parents or other responsible adults.[8]

The spectre of sexual abuse has created a climate of fear and a host of forbidden practices amongst child care professionals, mostly associated with issues surrounding physical contact between secondary caregivers and children placed in their charge. Whilst, sadly, such restrictions seem to be necessary for child protection, they also deprive young children of some of the sensory and physical experiences which help to build the pathways in the nervous system, which are involved in emotional regulation and cognitive processing.

These are not presented as moral issues, but the unforeseen problems that can result from a society which puts materialistic needs before the needs of children.

In a Nutshell...

• In early life, mother and baby are interdependent.

• Modern living interferes with the natural cycles of fertility and conception.

• Pre-conceptual lifestyle, choices, and care are important.

• Children's needs are different from the needs, desires, and priorities of adults.

Endnotes

1 Bewley, S., Davies, M., and Braude, P., 'Which career first?', *British Medical Journal,* 331, 2005: 588-9.
2 Barnett, S.B., 'Intracranial temperature elevation from diagnostic ultra-sound', *Ultrasound Med. Biol.,* 27/7, 2001: 883-8.
3 Liebeskind, D. and others, 'Diagnostic ultrasound: effects on the DNA and growth patterns of animal cells', *Radiology,* 131/1, 1979:177-84.
4 Burne, J., 'IVF: Why we must be told the truth over birth defects', article featured in 'Good Health' section, *Daily Mail,* 12 December 2006.

5 Ibid.

6 El-Chaar, D., 'Fertility treatment raises birth defect risk', presented at a conference hosted by the Society for Maternal-Fetal Medicine, San Francisco, 9 February 2007.

7 Teenage Pregnancy; **www.dfes.gov.uk**

8 Teenage Pregnancy Report, **www.socialexclusionunit.gov.uk/ publications.asp?=69**

3.

Does Early Development Matter?

Prenatal Factors

Darwin's observations led him to believe that in nature, it is the fittest of the species that survive. This was certainly true in the days before modern medicine when, in the absence of anaesthetics, sterilization procedures, antibiotics, or vaccination, any form of surgery, or bacterial or viral infection, frequently heralded death. Child-birth was a particularly risky affair with high rates of mortality for mothers, newborn babies, and children under 5 years of age.

That our antecedents did survive and live into old age is a comforting reminder that we owe our existence today to the robust constitutions of our forebears. Our grandparents, and their great grandparents before them, were almost entirely dependent upon their own immune responses to protect them against dirt, accidents, pestilence, and disease. Modern medicine has enabled many more of us to survive than might have been the case even a hundred years ago, but every invention also brings with it an element of risk. It is tempting to be lulled into a false sense of security, believing that soon there will be a pill for every pain, a cure for every ailment, and a vaccination against all disease.

No matter how skilled scientists become at taming man's natural enemies such as viruses, bacteria, parasites, and natural predators, everything in nature has a purpose. God or Nature, through a long process of evolution, has devised solutions of ever-increasing complexity to develop *all* forms of life, many of which are in direct competition with humankind for survival and for the ecology of the planet.

In the process of its own development every human being mirrors the evolutionary history of its species (phylogeny) from its beginning as a single cell. A single cell is created from the union of two parent cells, the female ovum and the male sperm cell. The parent cells have two functions: first, the assembly of a living body out of a single cell of proteins, carbohydrates, and other biochemicals and the energy which drives them, which constitute the building blocks of life; secondly, the parent cells control the specific design of the baby, a design that will follow a pattern passed along a chain of inheritance, stretching back to the biological roots of the family:

> In this sense, each new life actually has no definite beginning. Its existence is inherent in the existence of the parent cells, and these, in turn, have arisen from the preceding parent cells. When any two parent cells unite, they bring together a blend of the attributes of all ancestors before them.[1]

The developmental history of the individual (ontogeny) will also have a significant influence on the outcome of development – this is where nature and nurture fuse together as interactive forces influencing the growth, health, and personal characteristics of the individual. At every stage along the way there are points of risk and times of potential for enhanced growth and development. If nature is the architect, then environment is the craftsman that fashions the design.

Prenatal Influences

Environmental factors have their greatest influence on an organism at times of rapid growth or cell proliferation. For this reason, embryonic, foetal, and child development are times of enormous potential for growth, but also for damage. The thalidomide tragedy of the 1960s provided a stark reminder of the vulnerability of organisms at such times.

Thalidomide was a sedative given to pregnant women to relieve some of the symptoms of nausea and early-morning sickness suffered by many women in the early weeks of pregnancy. Some mothers took thalidomide during pregnancy without adverse effect; others, who took the drug at the time when the foetal limb buds were developing, gave birth to babies without arms or legs, or with severely stunted growth of the limbs. Other developing organs were also affected. In other words, it was not the drug per se that was harmful but the *time* in pregnancy when the drug was taken – the difference between one week and the next could be devastating. One of thalidomide's effects is to slow down the rate of specific types of tissue growth. Paradoxically, thalidomide is now being investigated as a possible treatment to stem the growth of specific types of cancer.

The effects of early developmental factors on later development have been the focus of many years of research at the Institute for Neuro-Physiological Psychology (INPP) in Chester, a private research, clinical, and training organization.

The Institute for Neuro-Physiological Psychology was established by Dr Peter Blythe in 1975, to conduct research into the effects of immaturity in the functioning of the Central Nervous System on cognitive and emotional functioning. Over the years, INPP has established a link between developmental history and the later emergence of specific learning difficulties such as dyslexia, developmental coordination disorder, and attention deficit disorder in children, and emotional problems in adults such as agoraphobia, panic disorder, and physical symptoms such as motion sickness.

In 1979, Peter Blythe and David McGlown published the INPP Screening Questionnaires in the book An *Organic Basis for Neuroses and Educational Difficulties*.[2] The Questionnaires comprised a series of questions about early development, starting with family history and following the individual's development through pregnancy, birth, infancy, pre-school, school, and to the present-day symptoms. Specific developmental criteria were selected following an extensive search of medical and other relevant literature for factors which might either *cause* later developmental problems, or which might already be *symptomatic* of developmental deviation. Extensive use of the questionnaires revealed that individuals with low scores did not appear to develop later learning difficulties or emotional problems, whereas patients who presented with later problems all had relatively high scores on the questionnaire. These questionnaire instruments have now been used for more than 30 years as *initial* screening devices to identify children or adults for whom developmental factors might be playing a part in their presenting symptoms.

Use of the questionnaires indicates that negative or positive sequelae to factors early in development do not necessarily show up as major abnormalities at birth or even in the first few years of life, but can emerge in more subtle form as cognitive, emotional, or behavioural problems later on. The following three chapters cover *some* of the events before birth, surrounding birth, and following birth that can influence the later development of the child.

Family History

It is generally accepted that up to 50 per cent of specific learning difficulties carry a hereditary *tendency*. This tendency is by no means a certainty, however. The laws that govern genetics can be traced back for at *least* four generations, and one part of the genetic pool can cancel out the influence of another.

This same potential for genes to exert a positive or negative effect on the organism raises questions over future genetic engineering. While it is known that certain genes carry a tendency toward the development of specific diseases such as Huntingdon's chorea, breast cancer and so on, and that the elimination of these diseases can only be a positive development, the *precise* mechanism acting as the catalyst to switch on the gene to release its harmful potential is not always known.* One person can carry the gene and develop the disease; another will carry the same gene but never develop the disease. In addition to their harmful effects, the genes that carry a tendency toward developing a specific disease are also responsible for traits of personality and have exerted positive, protective, and in some cases creative influences upon previous generations. In seeking to eliminate the negative effects of one gene, we also run a risk of extinguishing the positive influences of that gene, many of which are still unknown.

Hereditary traits can pass down four generations, remaining 'silent' for several generations before appearing as if out of the blue. Certain hereditary characteristics associated with hypersensitivity of the nervous system can emerge as superficially separate disorders, which share a fundamental weakness or immaturity in the functioning of

---

*   Certain types of breast cancer are known to be oestrogen dependent and one of the mechanisms responsible for activating the gene is the presence of oestrogen or fluctuations in oestrogen levels such as occur at or around the time of the menopause.

Environmental stress is known to be a factor in the onset of disease, including cancer. For further information on the interaction of genes and environment see **www.Andersonbeyondgenome.com**

the Central Nervous System. This range of disorders includes specific learning disabilities, allergies, emotional hypersensitivity, and psychosomatic disorders. In a study carried out by Richard Eustis[3] in 1947, he reported that 48 per cent of children over 6 years of age who were part of a family tree covering four generations shared one or more of the following conditions: left handedness, ambidexterity, and body clumsiness, in addition to specific speech and reading disabilities. He suggested that these conditions were manifestations of a syndrome, hereditary in origin, which is characterized by a slow rate of neuro-muscular maturation, which probably implies slow myelination of the motor and association nerve tracts.

Heredity may therefore deal us a hand for life with the potential to develop specific diseases and problems. This potential may be either suppressed or expressed as a result of pre-conceptual factors, events during pregnancy, birth, and the early years of life.

Pregnancy – Factors Affecting Mother and Baby

Major sources of risk to both mother and child in pregnancy are well documented in the medical literature, and include:

Factors affecting the mother:
- Prolonged and excessive vomiting (Hyperemesis)
- High blood pressure
- Pre-eclampsia
- Gestational diabetes
- Incompetent cervix
- Stress

Factors affecting the baby:
- Threatened miscarriage
- Contact with diseases known to harm the foetus such as Syphilis, Rubella and Toxoplasmosis.
- Placental insufficiency or malposition of the placenta (placenta praevia)
- X-rays or exposure to radiation
- Alcohol
- Smoking

- Caffeine
- Administration of drugs (illegal substances) or medication
- Malnutrition
- Multiple ultra-sounds
- Amniocentesis
- Specific antibiotics taken by the mother (e.g. Tetracyclines affect enamel deposits of the teeth)

Other factors:
- Method of conception (e.g. natural, following hormonal stimulation, IVF, etc.)
- Age of mother and father

Prolonged and Excessive Vomiting (Hyperemesis)

Every generation brings with it new discoveries, new beliefs, and new explanations. While science often belittles the beliefs of folklore as 'old wives' tales', these same tales often contain grains of truth based upon years of observation in the absence of scientific verification. One old wives' tale associated with pregnancy maintained that early morning sickness was a good sign, indicating a 'safe' pregnancy that was likely to proceed to term. One explanation for the presence of morning sickness was that the levels of hormones needed to sustain the pregnancy (particularly progesterone) must be high, and that nausea was a mother's sensitivity reaction to these altered levels of hormones in her system. Over the course of the first 12 weeks she adapted to altered levels of hormones and the nausea receded.

More recently it has been suggested that the nausea, morning sickness, vomiting, and food aversions that often accompany early pregnancy evolved to protect the developing foetus from toxins, which are potentially harmful to the developing baby.[4] These symptoms should decrease as the major organs are formed, the placental barrier is established, and the foetus becomes less vulnerable. Nausea therefore has a function and should lead to avoidance of foods that contain substances more likely to interfere with embryonic and foetal development.[5]

Nausea and excessive vomiting may also be a response to maternal dietary deficiencies as well as potentially teratogenic substances. Teratogens are chemical substances that interfere with normal tissue development and can result in birth defects. Certain minerals and trace elements have a dual influence upon the biochemistry of the system. On the one hand, minute quantities of trace elements support certain functions and act as co-factors in the synthesis of hormones; on the other hand, they help to maintain a balance in the levels of other substances. Thus, for example, zinc helps to keep levels of aluminium down and to maintain a healthy ratio of zinc to copper; and calcium helps to rid the body of lead. In theory, a mother who has low levels of zinc or calcium may have elevated levels of aluminium, copper, or lead in her system. Continued vomiting in the early weeks may be one way whereby her body attempts to protect the developing embryo from the harmful effects of these potentially toxic substances before the placental barrier is established at 12 weeks' gestation.

Margie Profet[6] suggested that nausea and food aversions have evolved to impose dietary restrictions on the mother in order to protect the developing embryo. In an ideal world, dietary deficiencies or excesses could be corrected prior to conception, helping to minimize prolonged nausea through pregnancy and making pregnancy a more enjoyable experience for both mother and child. This is where organizations such as *Foresight*[7] – the organization for pre-conceptual care – aim to educate couples before conception to correct dietary deficiencies, balance hormonal status (particularly in women who have been on the contraceptive pill for a number of years), and screen for sexually transmitted diseases or other diseases of the reproductive tracts before conception takes place.

Prolonged and excessive vomiting is another matter, because it depletes the mother not only of nutrition but also of hydration, and upsets the electrolyte balance of her body. Electrolytes are substances that yield ions in solutions so that the solutions conduct electricity. They are dependent on the correct balance of salt to fluid in the solution and electrolyte imbalance can impair functioning of the heart and the nervous system. Prolonged and excessive vomiting can be harmful to both mother and child, and usually requires medical treatment. It may also predispose the baby to be born with mild deficiencies, which in theory could affect the child's ability to handle certain food types after birth. This may show up in the early weeks of post-natal life as colic, vomiting, unusual bowel patterns, or skin disorders (skin reactions such as eczema that are not a reaction to direct skin contact often indicate a problem with the gut in processing certain types of food*). Too often, such problems are treated as isolated symptoms instead of being investigated as part of a continuum, which might have its origins in earlier development.

High Blood Pressure

Maternal high blood pressure is important because it leads to alterations in many maternal organ functions, including a decrease in blood flow to the uterus and placenta. Renal functioning in the mother is impaired which, if it is allowed to progress, results in protein being excreted in the urine. Changes also occur in the functioning of the Central Nervous System such as a build-up of fluid in the brain (cerebral oedema) which can cause headaches and visual disturbances for the mother. If blood pressure continues to rise, liver functioning can be affected, and may ultimately lead to pre-eclampsia.[8]

Pre-eclampsia and Eclampsia

Pre-eclampsia and eclampsia are conditions which only occur in pregnancy. Both are serious and life-threatening for mother and baby if they are allowed to develop unchecked.

Pre-eclampsia seldom occurs before the 20th week of pregnancy. Its development can be slow and insidious, with clinical signs becoming evident before symptoms are felt. Blood pressure increases, and as a result protein is shed from the kidneys into the urine. The kidneys are unable to excrete fluid from the body effectively, resulting in a build-up of fluid, weight gain, and swelling. The causes of pre-eclampsia are still not fully understood. A recent study[9] has found that women who go on to develop pre-eclampsia have high levels of two key proteins in their blood. The proteins, which disrupt blood vessel formation, also suggest potential targets for treatment, but the reasons why these particular protein levels are raised is not known.

---

*   This statement is based on empirical evidence obtained from the use of the INPP Questionnaire followed by the analysis of vitamin and mineral status carried out by Foresight on children whose mothers had a history of prolonged nausea and vomiting during pregnancy.

Pre-eclampsia poses risks for the unborn baby. Maternal high blood pressure interferes with placental blood flow, resulting in a decrease in oxygen and nutrient supply to the baby. Premature labour is more likely, either spontaneous or induced. Small and immature babies are less likely to survive the first weeks of life, are at risk of respiratory problems due to immaturity of the lungs, difficulty with temperature control, and are more liable to infection, jaundice, and anaemia.

Gestational Diabetes

Diabetes can emerge for the first time in pregnancy. Stabilization of blood sugar levels, through diet and drugs if required, is essential because uncontrolled diabetes carries with it an increased risk of miscarriage, pre-eclampsia, polyhydramnios, problems with placental sufficiency, premature labour, giving birth to a baby with congenital abnormalities, a very large baby, or stillbirth. Babies of diabetic mothers show excess growth inside the womb, sometimes necessitating early delivery with all the associated problems. Size and weight do not compensate for lack of organ maturity; a baby born at 38 weeks weighing 2.5 kg stands a better chance of survival than a baby born at 34 weeks weighing 3.5 kg because the vital organs of the larger, less mature baby (particularly the lungs) have to provide oxygen and vital functions to a larger system. If the baby is allowed to grow too big before delivery, there is a greater likelihood of problems during the birth process or the need to deliver the baby by Caesarean Section.

Incompetent Cervix

An incompetent cervix will result in miscarriage at approximately 20 weeks. In order for a pregnancy to proceed to term the cervix must remain closed. Sometimes as a result of injury or surgery prior to pregnancy, the muscles surrounding the internal part of the cervix have been damaged and will start to open from 14 weeks, so that by 20 weeks the cervix is 1cm dilated. This allows the bag of waters to bulge through the cervix until they break, triggering the onset of premature labour and miscarriage.

In many cases an incompetent cervix can be treated effectively by inserting a small stitch around the cervix before or during pregnancy, which is then removed at 38 weeks in time for delivery. Some women also require bed rest to reduce tension on the cervix and supporting suture. Prolonged periods of bed rest or inactivity during pregnancy have implications for the developing baby's experience of movement while in the womb. Every movement or positional change a mother makes provides stimulation to the baby's developing vestibular system (balance mechanism), which will support the baby's own movements and postural abilities after birth (see Chapter 6).

Maternal Stress

One old wives' tale associated with pregnancy used to be that a stressed, anxious, or frightened mother would result in a fretful baby. As the whole process of motherhood became more medicalized in the West, this view went out of fashion for a number of years; but modern science is once again beginning to prove that the observations of the past may have had some basis in fact.

The physiological components of stress were initially proposed by Hans Selye in 1956.[10] In the preface to his book *The Stress of Life* he wrote:

> no one can live without experiencing some degree of stress all the time. Stress is not necessarily bad for you; it is also the spice of life, for any emotion, any activity causes stress. But, your system must be prepared to take it. The same stress which makes one person sick can be an invigorating experience for another.
>
> It is through the *general adaptation syndrome* (GAS) that our various internal organs – especially the endocrine glands and the nervous system – help to adjust to the constant changes which occur.

The general adaptation syndrome consists of three stages:
1 The alarm reaction
2 The stage of resistance
3 The stage of exhaustion

Initially, stress triggers an *alarm* reaction, which causes autonomic processes such as heart rate and adrenalin secretion to speed up. The resistance stage begins with some automatic mechanism for coping with the stressor, as the body attempts to make appropriate adjustments to restore equilibrium. If equilibrium is successfully restored then relaxation can occur. If, however, attempts to maintain equilibrium are extended or prolonged, exhaustion begins to set in, with effects upon general health. The primary indicants of the exhaustion stage are illnesses such as ulcers, adrenal enlargement, and shrinkage of lymph and other glands that confer resistance to disease.

Stress results in a change in biochemistry resulting not only in heightened secretion of corticosteroids during the alarm phase but also altered levels of catecholamines* including dopamine, epinephrine (adrenalin) and norepinepherine. Increased catecholamine and corticosteroid secretion affects a wide range of physiological processes such as heart rate, blood pressure, breathing, inflammation and other functions including hormonal secretion and activity in emotional centres in the brain such as the amygdala. The amygdala is involved in the making of memories, particularly those of an emotional nature. Increased activity in the amygdala has been found to be associated with decreased activity in the attention-focusing, organising and planning activities of the frontal lobes of the brain.

Why should such changes in the mother also affect the developing baby?

Studies carried out on rats have shown that high stress levels in the mother lower the level of the male hormone testosterone in the womb. Levels of testosterone at key stages in embryonic development can influence how the brain develops. Further studies on rodents reported by Anne Moir and David Jessel in the book *Brain Sex*[11] have shown that by manipulating hormones at critical times in gestation, behaviour could be changed from male to female and vice-versa. They also found that by manipulating hormones, they could alter the structure of the brain itself.

---

* **Catecholamines** – a group of physiologically important substances including adrenaline, noradrenaline and dopamine, which have various different roles (mainly as neurotransmitters) in the functioning of the sympathetic and central nervous system.
  Neurotransmitter – a chemical substance released from nerve endings to other nerves and across synapses to other nerves and across minute gaps between the nerves and muscles or glands that they supply.
  Synapse – the minute gap at the end of a nerve fibre across which nerve impulses pass from one neurone to the next

The word 'hormone' comes from the Greek word *hormao,* meaning 'to excite'. Biochemistry alters behaviour, perceptions, emotions, abilities, and self-control. Hormones are mind as well as body chemicals. Acting on the brain, they direct the body at key stages in the lifespan, such as puberty, pregnancy, and menopause, to make changes in the body. They also have an influence on the inter-connections and communication within the brain itself and on the regulation of energy.

Studies carried out on menopausal women found that there was an increase in dendritic* growth within 24 hours of administering oestrogen. This may account to some degree for the improvement in memory that menopausal women describe when prescribed hormone replacement therapy (HRT). In other words, changes in mood and performance that occur at times of rapid hormonal change are an expression not only of the hormone levels themselves, but also the influence they have upon connections within the nervous system and the brain as well as the biochemical balance of the body.

Adrenaline circulating in the mother's system also passes to the baby. Chemically, the baby feels what the mother is feeling. Whilst on the positive side, such symbiosis could be described as one factor in the origin of sympathy, on the negative side, sudden, excess, or continuous exposure to elevated levels of adrenaline while in the womb could, in theory, 'set' the baby's stress response for later life. The effects will depend on timing, extent, and duration of exposure to stress. In this way, a baby born to a mother who has suffered extreme stress during pregnancy could behave like a miniature stressed adult after birth – being more prone to crying, fretting, sleep disturbances, feeding problems, and hyper-sensitivity.

There is some evidence that psychological stress in pregnancy is connected to low birth weight and affects brain development in the unborn child, and may lead to mood disorders in the offspring in adulthood.

A four-year follow-up of the offspring from the Avon Longi-tudinal Study of Parents and Children found increased emotional and behavioural problems in the male offspring of women with high anxiety scores during pregnancy. 'An association between low birth weight and the development of adults' metabolic diseases has often

---

* **Dendrite** – one of the shorter branching processes of the cell body of a neurone, which makes contact with other neurones at the synapse and carries nerve impulses from the synapse to the cell body.

been shown. It is thought that exposure of the foetus to an adverse intrauterine environment may lead to permanent programming of tissue function.'[12]

Thomas Verny[13] in his book *The Secret Life of the Unborn Child* writes that 'the womb, in a very real sense, establishes the child's expectations'. Maternal, foetal communication is endocrine (hormonal) during pregnancy rather than neural: the foetus experiences the emotions of its mother through the biochemical changes that take place in her body and therefore also in his/hers.

One biological system that could be affected by foetal stress is known as the hypothalamic-pituitary-adrenal (HPA) axis – the main stress hormone system in the body. There is already evidence that psychological trauma, such as physical and sexual abuse during childhood, permanently alters HPA response.[14]

The potential impact of maternal stress in 'setting' the foetus's neuro-hormonal clock for later life is not a new observation. In the 1940s Dr Lester W. Sontag[15] published a paper following his wartime observations of the effects of stress on the expectant mother. He suggested that maternal stress heightened a child's biological susceptibility to emotional distress, and that this was a primary physical mechanism, of which emotional hyper-sensitivity was a secondary outcome. The theory of a heightened physical susceptibility to stress was independently investigated some years later by Dr Peter Blythe[16] in a paper 'A somatogenic basis for neuroses'. In other words, both authors, starting from different clinical and theoretical backgrounds, came to the conclusion that just as emotions can affect the body (psychosomatics), so biochemical and neuro-developmental factors can affect the mind (somatopsychics).

There is a difference between stress and trauma. At the extreme end of the stress scale are events that cause sudden unexpected shock. The possible effects of maternal shock on the developing child will be explored in Chapter 9 when some of the neurological and develop-mental factors in attachment and anxiety disorders are examined.

Threatened Miscarriage

At times nature can appear to be very wasteful. Of all the eggs present in a woman's ovaries at the time of her birth, even amongst women who by modern standards have large families, only a fraction of those eggs will be fertilized and a smaller number still will produce healthy babies. The ratio of natural 'wastage' is even greater for sperm.

If Darwin was right, Nature is ruthless in her process of natural selection and will discard anything that does not follow exactly the blueprint for healthy reproduction. Although nature can also make mistakes, miscarriage is one way in which she attempts to discard an embryo which is less than perfect, an embryo developing in a hostile environment, or a pregnancy in which there are compatibility issues between host and visitor (mother and child).

A study carried out on several hundred pregnant women by Dr Euan Wallace[17] of Monash Institute of Medical Research in Victoria, Australia, found that those who miscarried had significantly lower levels of a protein, microphage inhibitory cytokine 1 (MICI) that regulates the growth and development of the placenta. Very early in pregnancy the placenta invades the lining of the uterus and establishes a connection between the mother and the baby for the transfer of oxygen and nutrients to the baby, and excretion of waste products back through the mother's system. Placental functioning is crucial to the continued success of the pregnancy. It is hoped that in the future, a simple blood test may be able to identify women who have lower levels of the protein and manipulation of the protein may help the pregnancy to survive.

In many cases threatened miscarriage can be treated effectively if medical help is sought, and the mother goes on to give birth to a perfectly healthy baby, but the process/event gives rise to the question, 'why'? Why did the mother's body either fail to maintain the pregnancy or attempt to reject the foetus?

Teratogens Known to Cause Human Birth Defects

A teratogen describes any substance, disease, or event which can adversely affect the course of normal development. Specific diseases contracted by the mother during pregnancy such as Rubella (German Measles), if contracted in the first 12 weeks of pregnancy, can affect the growth of foetal organs, resulting in deafness, blindness, heart defects, and other abnormalities. Toxoplasmosis, a relatively rare disease in pregnancy contracted through contact with cat faeces, can affect the baby's subsequent eyesight. As the age of motherhood increases, so there is also a risk that the woman may have had a greater number of sexual partners. Sexually transmitted diseases such as Syphilis, which is caused by a thin motile spirochete, can be transmitted to the foetus if it is still present in the mother's body after the 20th week of pregnancy. Adequate treatment before the 20th week will prevent it being passed on to the developing baby.

There is some evidence to suggest that other viral infections can affect the foetus although they do not generally result in congenital abnormalities. Viral infections in the mother accompanied by a very high temperature can increase the risk of miscarriage.

Certain drugs used either for medical or recreational purposes are also known to result in abnormalities.

Preconceptually the use of alcohol amongst women has been linked to decreased conception rates, probably because heavy drinking can result in impaired ovarian functioning. Heavy drinkers are two to four times more likely to have a miscarriage between the fourth and sixth month of pregnancy than non-drinkers. Even small quantities of alcohol can affect foetal growth; larger quantities are associated with Foetal Alcohol Syndrome (FAS), intra-uterine growth retardation, and mental retardation.

Foetal Alcohol Syndrome (FAS) is one of the most common known causes of mental retardation, and it is also entirely preventable. Classic features of FAS include: babies who are abnormally small at birth and whose growth fails to catch up later in development; distinctive facial features such as small eyes, short or upturned nose, and small, flat cheeks. Certain organs, particularly the heart and brain, may not form properly; the brain is affected not only in size but also formation, with fewer convolutions resulting in a smooth appearance. Many children born with FAS suffer coordination, attention, and behavioural problems, which continue into later life. These may include problems with learning, memory, and problem solving. Adolescents and adults have varying degrees of psychological and behavioural problems, making it difficult for them to hold down a job and sustain meaningful relationships.

When a pregnant woman drinks, so does her baby. In the early weeks of pregnancy, sometimes before the mother even knows that she is pregnant, alcohol passes directly from mother to embryo. This is the most vulnerable period for organ development. Later in pregnancy alcohol passes swiftly through the placenta to the baby. Alcohol in the body is broken down much more slowly by the immature foetus, with the result that the alcohol level in the baby's blood remains elevated for longer. This, combined with the small size of the developing baby, means that the ratio of alcohol in the foetal bloodstream is higher than in the mother. In common with other teratogens, *timing* of alcohol consumption can affect specific systems, with birth defects such as heart defects being more likely to result from drinking in the first trimester, while growth problems are more likely to result from drinking in the third trimester. Drinking at any stage of pregnancy can affect brain development and no level of drinking can be considered entirely safe.

The most obvious signs of FAS usually occur in women who were heavy drinkers (more than 5 units per day), but it can also occur in women who have drunk moderately small amounts. Research carried out at the University of Washington in Seattle (2001) on a group of middle-class children up to age 14 years found that children whose mothers were social drinkers (1-2 drinks per day) scored lower on intelligence tests at 7 years of age than the average for all children in the study. At 14 years of age, these children were more likely to have learning problems, particularly with mathematics, and to have memory and attention problems.[18]

The teratogenic effect of alcohol is both structural in terms of brain development and functional. 'The infant is born not only with a brain smaller in size but with a reduced number of brain neurons, as well as altered distribution, resulting in mental deficiency in varying degrees from milder behavioural problems to obvious mental handicaps.'[19]

Animal studies have shown that while many areas of the brain are affected by maternal alcohol exposure, its effect seems to be particularly detrimental on the hippocampus[20, 21]. It has therefore been speculated that both the intellectual decrements and the behavioural deficits seen in infants born to mothers using alcohol during pregnancy may result directly from the specific hippocampal structural alterations.[22]

In the same article, reproduced for Foresight – the association for the promotion of pre-conceptual care – the author goes on to cite research, which has shown that the more mothers had reported drinking during pregnancy, the poorer the overall performance of the newborn and the pre-school child:

> On the second day of life they had a longer latency to begin sucking and had a weaker suck. They also suffered from disrupted sleep patterns, low level of arousal, unusual body orientation, abnormal reflexes, hypotonia and excessive mouthing. By 8 months and onwards, these infants continue suffering from disrupted sleep-wake patterns, poorer balance and motor control, longer latency to respond, poorer attention, visual recognition and memory, decrements in mental development, spoken language and verbal comprehension including lower IQ scores.

The sense of taste also begins to develop pre-natally. Taste buds emerge at around 7-8 weeks' gestation, and the amniotic fluid is rich with different taste experiences derived from the mother's intake.[23] These early experiences set the stage for later taste preferences, suggesting that the foetus quickly develops a 'taste' for flavours contained in the surrounding amniotic fluid. It is possible that the developing baby either develops a taste for alcohol before birth and/or receptors in the brain affected by alcohol are 'turned on' again in later life, predisposing the child to develop a taste for alcohol in adult life.

Smoking

In much the same way that the baby of a mother who drinks is also forced to drink, so pregnant women who smoke impose second-hand smoking on their unborn child. The most common outcomes of smoking in pregnancy are reduced length of gestation, low birth weight, and a slightly elevated incidence of deficiency in physical growth and intellectual and behavioural development. The effects are thought to be a result of exposure to carbon monoxide and nicotine. Carbon monoxide probably has the effect of reducing oxygen supply to body tissues, while nicotine stimulates hormones that constrict the vessels supplying blood to the uterus and placenta, resulting in less oxygen and fewer nutrients reaching the foetus.

Studies on both animal and human subjects have shown that both nicotine and the inhalation effects of tobacco affect the immune system, possibly contributing to a greater susceptibility to miscarry amongst women who smoke, as well as a greater incidence of respiratory problems in children born to mothers who smoke.

Cocaine

Cocaine, once the recreational drug of the rich, has become increasingly available at all levels of society. In addition to cocaine's highly addictive properties and their effect on the primary user, cocaine readily crosses the placenta, affecting the foetus. It constricts blood vessels, thereby reducing blood and oxygen supply to the foetus, affecting general growth and particularly growth of the bones and the intestine.

Cocaine and amphetamines are both psychomotor stimulants: they give the user a 'high' and in the early days of low dose usage they increase sensations of pleasure, alertness, sense of well-being, self-esteem, energy, and sexuality. They lower anxiety and social inhibition and in the early days of use, euphoria *appears* to be fairly consequence free. They are therefore highly seductive for those seeking pleasure and self-affirmation. However, users soon discover that the higher the dose, the greater the intensity of the resulting 'high' and that, over time, larger doses are required to maintain or increase the intensity and duration of pleasurable sensations. Animals given unlimited access to cocaine will compulsively increase self-administration until death follows, usually from cardiopulmonary collapse.

Approximately 31 per cent of women who use cocaine during pregnancy give birth before term and 15 per cent have premature detachment of the placenta – a potentially lethal event for the foetus. About 19 per cent give birth to small babies,[24] but the most devastating consequence for the baby is that it is born an addict. Newborns suffer withdrawal symptoms, they may be hyperactive, tremble uncontrollably, interact less with other people, and have difficulty in learning.

Characteristics of infants exposed to cocaine in the womb include: prematurity, low birth weight, smaller head circumference, and low Apgar* score at birth. The addicted newborn usually has a

---

* **Apgar Score** – a method of assessing the general status of the newborn immediately after birth.

piercing cry, is irritable and hypersensitive,e and switches from sleep to screaming for no apparent reason. They are often inconsolable. Feeding is affected, and physiologically they have high respiratory and heart rates. Startle responses are over-reactive and they are easily over-stimulated. They are unable to interact with caregivers and therefore miss out on physical and social interactions in the early weeks, which are essential ingredients of the normal bonding process between child and caregiver. Chasnoff et al. (1985, 1986)[25] observed that they were unable to respond to the human voice and face, that there was a higher incidence of cerebral infarction (stroke) and Sudden Infant Death Syndrome (SIDS). The latter may be a result of sleep pattern abnormalities associated with apnoea and deep sleep, resulting in increased susceptibility to primitive startle reactions.[26, 27]

Mary Bellis Waller[28] found that adolescents with social and behavioural problems who were born to mothers who had taken crack-cocaine (smoking) during pregnancy were unable to empathize with others, and that part of the frontal lobe of the brain normally involved in empathy had simply not developed. Their antisocial behaviour at a later age was not *im*moral: they had no under-standing of the effect of their behaviour on other people – they seemed to be unable to 'feel as someone else' and therefore understand the implications and consequences of their behaviour, either on themselves or others:

> What I learned in my work was that crack-affected children don't bond and don't have empathy because they are overwhelmed by normal stimuli and so instead of being attracted to touch and gaze, turn away from it. That means they never form the habit of watching a face and learning to pick up moods, information, etc. from the face of another.[29]

As with any form of addiction, receptors can retain an appetite for the substance for life. If the child is exposed to the substance again later in life, the chances of becoming addicted are increased.

Marijuana
The possible effects of maternal marijuana use on the unborn child are controversial. Animal studies suggest that it does place the

developing child at risk. Offspring of pregnant rats given a low dose of cannabinoids were found to perform poorly in learning tests throughout their lives compared to non-exposed offspring. The Italian research team[30] found that exposure to cannabinoids during gestation had an irreversible effect on chemical and electrical processes, resulting in hyperactivity during infancy and adolescence. In adult life, the offspring showed lower levels of glutamate in the hippocampus, a part of the brain involved in memory, visual ability, and learning.

Heroin

As recreational drugs have become readily available, there is a danger that an increasing number of parents have traces of these substances in their system at the time of conception or during the early months of pregnancy. The unborn child is particularly vulnerable to organ damage during the first weeks of pregnancy, but also to neurological damage during later stages of pregnancy as a result of disruption in neural migration – the process by which neurons reach their target addresses in the brain. As the categorization of certain drugs such as cannabis is downgraded, there is a risk that young adults, whilst accepting the consequences of use for themselves, will be unaware of the potential effects on their children in the future.

X-rays and Exposure Radiation

It is one of the ironies of radiological practice that X-rays can both cause cancer and be used to treat it. Nowadays, with the use of very small doses of radiation to produce high quality X-ray images, the risk of cancer after properly supervised X-ray examinations is extremely small. However, during pregnancy the developing baby is more vulnerable to the effects of even small doses of radiation. For this reason, as far as possible the use of X-rays during pregnancy should be kept to the absolute minimum. Any woman who suspects that she is pregnant, and who has been referred for an X-ray examination, should make sure that the radiographers and doctors caring for her know about her condition.

Exposure to other sources of radiation

Research carried out at the Institute of Oncology, Rabin Medical Center, Beilinson Campus, Petah Tiqva, Israel[31] examined the risk to the foetus of exposure to radiation during pregnancy. They concluded that provided the level of X-ray exposure to the foetus was sufficiently low, neither diagnostic radiography nor nuclear diagnostic examination posed sufficient risk to justify termination of pregnancy. Radiotherapy for breast cancer, Hodgkin's disease, and cervical cancer in pregnant women were all reviewed. Radiation therapy for breast cancer was not an absolute contra-indication for pregnancy, and the risk-benefit assessment should be discussed with the mother. The risk to the foetus during radiotherapy for supra-diaphragmatic Hodgkin's disease appeared to be minimal, provided special attention is paid to the treatment techniques and the foetus is adequately shielded.

Radiotherapy for the treatment of cervical cancer may be necessary during pregnancy, but the timing should be adjusted in relation to gestational age. Offspring of cancer patients who were treated by radiotherapy appear to be at little risk of childhood cancer or birth defects. Researchers concluded that cancer patients should not be discouraged from having children, and can expect a good outcome of pregnancy. However, in the non-pregnant woman, further to reduce any risk it is advisable to delay pregnancy for 12 months following completion of radiation therapy.

Multiple Ultra-sounds

Ultrasonography (USG) was originally developed during World War II to detect enemy submarines. The application of ultrasonography for medical purposes was pioneered by Dr Ian Donald in Glasgow in the mid-1950s, initially to look at abdominal tumours and later babies in utero. Ultra-sound has revolutionized investigative obstetrics because it enabled the clinician to see an image of the developing baby, reflecting details of soft tissue as well as bone outlines without involvement of invasive procedures. Ultrasonography is mainly used for two purposes:[32]

1 as a routine scan at round 18-20 weeks to check the size and integrity of the baby and to check the expected date of delivery

(this is only accurate to a week on either side);

2 to investigate a possible problem at any stage of pregnancy.

Ultra-sound pictures are formed using sound waves. A machine sends sound waves through the body, which are then reflected back and converted into an image on a monitor from where many aspects of foetal health, growth, gestational age, development, and abnormalities can be detected. Although ultra-sound is seen as safe, not enough is yet known about its effects on the developing foetus, and concern exists about the safety and usefulness of *routine* prenatal ultra-sound (RPU) as opposed to when it is used to investigate a suspected problem.[33] Some mothers notice that the foetus shows increased activity for considerable time following ultra-sound. Mothers who experience 'at risk' pregnancies tend to have an increased number of ultra-sound examinations.

A summary of studies which had investigated the safety of ultra-sound in human studies was published in May 2002 and concluded that

> continued research is needed to evaluate the potential adverse effects of ultra-sound exposure during pregnancy. These studies should measure the acoustic output, exposure time, number of exposures per subject and the timing during pregnancy when exposure(s) occurred[34]. 'Until long-term effects can be evaluated across generations, caution should be exercised when using this modality during pregnancy.'[35]

Nutrition

On the one hand the developing child is well protected by the environment of the womb, and is remarkably resilient to the many daily hazards of living – a resilience which stems from the power of 'life's longing for itself'[36] and which at times defies scientific explanation. On the other hand, the internal environment of the womb is closely governed by the mother's well-being. For the developing baby, the womb is its first world. A woman's nutritional status *before* as well as during pregnancy is one of the sets of factors that govern body processes affecting pregnancy.

Darwin observed that domestic cattle were more fertile than

those living in the wild, and deduced that hard living retards the period at which animals conceive. Under conditions of starvation, such as in times of famine or anorexia, when body weight drops, periods eventually cease as the body shuts down its reproductive capacities to conserve energy for survival. Epidemiological studies of periods of hard living during the Second World War in Leningrad, Holland, and Japan provided some of the first scientific evidence of the effects of nutrition on reproductive outcome.[37, 38, 39, 40]

In Leningrad and Japan, nutritional intake had been marginally adequate before the period of famine; in Holland, women were well nourished before the period of shortage. There was a dramatic drop in fertility rates in all areas following the famine period. In Holland, half of the women of child-bearing age developed amenorrhoea (cessation of periods). The birth rate in Holland dropped by 53 per cent during the period of food shortage. In Holland, where the population had been relatively well nourished prior to starvation, menses returned within six months of food intake returning to pre-famine levels. In Leningrad, where nutritional status had been marginal prior to the period of extreme shortage, fertility levels took longer to return.

Studies that have followed up the effects of famine in the Netherlands during 1944 suggest that if famine occurs at critical stages during pregnancy, it can have lasting effects on the unborn child. A team at Columbia University, USA[41] studied the physical records of women and their sons in the Netherlands, who had been subjected to the Dutch famine of 1944. They found that many of the group became severely overweight later on, but the degree of obesity was influenced by the stage of pregnancy when the mother had been malnourished. The greatest effect seemed to occur amongst women who had suffered severe hunger during the first four or five months of gestation. The team concluded that prolonged starvation during this critical period in utero could alter the setting of the hypothalamic clock for later life.

The hypothalamus is a part of the brain located below the cerebral cortex and above the primitive survival structures of the brain stem. It forms part of the ancient limbic system shared by all mammals. Situated beneath the thalamus but above the pituitary gland, the hypothalamus regulates the autonomic nervous system, maintaining homeostasis and influencing the body's moment-to-moment physiological responses to the environment. It influences blood pressure, heart rate, breathing, body temperature, appetite and thirst, and sexual desire, as well as movement of food in the gut. In addition to physical responses it plays a major part in emotional reactions, stimulating the release of hormones from the pituitary gland in response to emotional as well as physical stimuli readying the body for fight or flight. The Columbia team of researchers concluded that starvation in utero could set the hypothalamus and metabolic rate for later life. In theory this could either cause the body to be over-economical in its use of nutrients, predisposing the child to gain weight when fed a 'normal' diet after birth, or creating a 'hunger' for life that is never completely satisfied.

In the West, we tend to associate malnutrition with countries that are poorer than ourselves, with war zones, famine areas, and regions struck by natural disasters, but a life of plenty is not necessarily a guarantee of nutritional excellence. The last 20 years has seen an alarming rise in the rate of obesity, not only amongst adults but also in children. This trend is the result of a number of factors.

As technology has solved many of the physical problems of daily living, equipping us with an ever-increasing choice of labour-saving devices, levels of physical activity in daily living have declined. The amount of energy needed by the body to survive is directly proportional to energy expenditure. If we are less physically active, we need less energy from the food that we eat. This presents us with a number of choices.

We can increase our energy expenditure by taking more regular physical exercise; we can alter the food types we eat to provide suitable sources of energy for lifestyle; or we can reduce the amount of food we eat at each meal. One survey compared the eating habits of mainland Europeans, residents of the United Kingdom, and the USA. They found that there were major differences in the size of portions at mealtimes. The portions in France were approximately a third smaller than those in the UK, which were a third smaller than the USA. Portion control alone probably accounts for some of the differences in obesity rates between the three countries.

Foods that are high in fat, such as the traditional English breakfast of bacon, fried egg, and fried bread, may be suitable for a manual worker or in the days before the majority of homes were equipped with central heating, as fat helps to keep the body warm. However, a diet high in saturated fats is not needed in large amounts when heat is available at the click of a thermostat and eight hours of the day are going to be spent sitting in front of a computer. If diet is not adapted to lifestyle, we start to pay a price not just in terms of body weight but also in how the body uses nutrition. Activity assists in the utilization of nutrition by boosting circulation and helping nutrition to be pumped to the areas of the body where it is most needed.

It is also possible to have normal body weight while being deficient in vitamins and trace minerals, which play a pivotal role in fertility, pregnancy and pregnancy outcome, immune functioning, attention, and emotional stability.

It is known that supplementation with folic acid supplements can significantly reduce the risk of neural tube defects such as Spina Bifida. Zinc provides another example of the important role of minute amounts of specific nutrients for the development of the child and, perhaps more surprisingly, the mother's relationship with the child.

Animal studies have revealed that maternal zinc deficiency in rats can result in a range of malformations and increased postpartum fatalities amongst pups[42] as well as effects that are less immediately obvious at birth, such as behavioural abnormalities, and defects in pancreatic function, lung function, and immune competence.[43] The effects of zinc deficiency are not confined to the pups. Mother rats fed a zinc-deficient diet have shown changes in normal rat 'mothering' behaviour, such as failure to consume the umbilicus, failure to clean and/or nurse their pups, and failure to retrieve stray pups and build nests.[44] The increase in fatalities amongst pups born to zinc-deficient dams is probably related not only to the poor zinc status of the mother, passed on to the pup before birth and during lactation, but also to the lack of normal maternal behaviour.

Zinc deficiency in humans can be due to be a number of factors, including long-term use of the contraceptive pill, copper IUD (copper and zinc are antagonists – i.e. if the amount of one element increases, it suppresses absorption of the other), smoking, recent infection, burn, or injury. Zinc is necessary for healing. Recent infection or injury can temporarily deplete the zinc status of the body, as can emotional stress and certain food colourings. Tartrazine, the yellow food colouring added to soft drinks, is particularly potent in depleting zinc status in susceptible individuals.

The British charity for pre-conceptual care, Foresight, has noticed that:

> zinc deficiency is particularly common in little boys whose mothers have been on the contraceptive pill or IUD shortly before their conception. Boys need 5 times the amount of zinc in utero that girls need (for the formation of the testes), so commonly it is the boys who are grossly deficient. This may result in poor growth and general development both before and after birth, colic and diarrhoea, poor sucking, late teething and other milestones and generally retarded development both physically and mentally. Hyperactivity, dyslexia and behavioural problems will mar the school career and general growth and puberty may be delayed and/or incomplete.[45]

Analysis of vitamin and mineral status of children diagnosed with hyperactivity has shown that many children diagnosed with ADHD have low zinc levels. This may go some way to explaining why the incidence of hyperactivity is higher amongst boys from an earlier age than girls.

Signs of zinc deficiency amongst girls start to show up from about 9 years of age, when the ovaries begin to function in preparation for puberty some time later. Zinc is one of the co-factors required for the synthesis of female hormones, and problems in the regulation of hormones after puberty are sometimes related to zinc and other deficiencies. The work of Derek Bryce-Smith in the 1970s indicated that low zinc status was linked to anorexia and impaired sense of taste. Zinc levels are high in areas of the brain involved in food seeking and weight regulation.

The effects of zinc deficiency can sometimes be seen in the young child who is a faddy eater, either refusing food or insisting on eating only a narrow range of bland-tasting foods. Deficiency affects eating habits and poor eating habits further compound the deficiency. These are often the children who present with a range of 'minor' illnesses and problems such as being over-demanding, grizzly, never sleeping through the night, and suffering from repeated nasal and/or middle ear infections, food intolerances, allergic reactions such as eczema or asthma, and nightmares, making the child's life miserable and parenting more difficult. This is not so surprising when one realises that zinc plays a number of essential roles in the body, including assisting normal mental function and perception. Why choose zinc as an example? Changes in the modern diet, particularly in the young, have combined to make low zinc status more likely. The fast food culture imported from the United States in the last 40 years, combined with changes in the working status of women, has had a profound effect on the eating habits of the nation. A diet of refined 'junk' food (high in fat and refined carbohydrates) does little to maintain zinc status, whilst the regular consumption of soft drinks and confections containing food colourings will drain zinc from the system of individuals who already have a low zinc status.

More general changes in modern living may also have contributed. In the days when water was drawn from the well, it was often carried in zinc buckets. Even though it may then have been heated using a copper device, the method of transportation helped to maintain a healthy ratio of zinc:copper. Many factors in modern life, including intensive farming, over-refining, bleaching of grain, and a taste for refined, processed, and convenience foods, added to which are the effects of oral contraceptives, can all have an impact on the zinc status of men as well as women. The illnesses and behavioural problems that result are the products of lifestyle and are entirely preventable.

Zinc is needed for healing and is contained within many ointments for the treatment of skin conditions such as nappy rash (zinc and castor oil or fuller's earth cream), and zinc bandages are sometimes used for the treatment of severe eczema. Zinc is needed for sperm motility and zinc deficiency can therefore play a part in problems with conception for males as well as females. Zinc is needed in greater supply at times of stress, and it has been suggested that sudden or severe stress places a sudden demand on the body's zinc, stripping new hair growth of colour and playing a part in turning the hair white.[46]

Risk Factors in Perspective

The factors listed above have been included, not to frighten future parents into believing that all or anything they do will potentially harm their baby, but to help parents of the future to understand ways in which they can plan for a healthy baby and minimize the risk of avoidable problems. While the developing baby is vulnerable in specific ways, it is also extraordinarily resilient in others, and there is a high degree of plasticity in early development, whereby a problem in one area of functioning can be taken over by another. Some children have a very difficult start in life but grow up to be perfectly normal, healthy individuals. We cannot control all of life's events or nature's plan, but we can seek to provide the best possible environment for children to grow.

In a Nutshell…

- Human development is the product of evolution, both personal and trans-generational. Complex organisms require longer periods of physical development.

- The pre-natal environment can affect neurological development with long-term effects, both positive and negative, on learning ability, emotional regulation, and behaviour.

- Pre-conceptual awareness and pre-conceptual care can help to eliminate or reduce problems during pregnancy.

- The health and well-being of the mother during pregnancy is of prime importance.

Endnotes

1 Lux Flanagan, G., *The first nine months of life,* Simon and Schuster, New York, 1962.

2 Blythe, P. and McGlown, D.J., *An organic basis for neuroses and educational difficulties,* Insight Publications, Chester, 1979.

3 Eustis, R.S., 1947. The primary origin of the specific language disabilities. *Journal of Pediatrics,* XXXI, 1947: 448-55

4 Profet, M., *Protecting your baby-to-be: Preventing birth defects in the first trimester,* Addison-Wesley, Reading, Mass., 1995.

5 Horrobin, D., *The madness of Adam and Eve. How schizophrenia shaped humanity,* Corgi Books, London, 2002.

6 Profet, M., cited in J.H. Barkow et al. (eds), *The adapted mind,* Oxford University Press, New York, 1992.

7 Foresight; **www.foresight-preconception.org.uk**

8 Bourne G., *Pregnancy,* Pan Books, London, 1979.

9 *New England Journal of Medicine,* vol. 355, pp 992-1005; cited in: **www.newscientist.com.news.ns** 06 September 2006.

10 Selye, H., *The stress of life,* McGraw-Hill Book Co., New York, 1956.

11 Moir, A. and Jessel, D., *Brain sex: The real difference between men and women,* Mandarin, London, 1991.

12 O'Connor, T.G., Heron, J., Golding, J., and others, 'Maternal antenatal anxiety and children's behavioural/emotional problems at 4 years: report from the Avon Longitudinal Study of Parents and Children', *British Journal of Psychiatry,* 180, 2002: 502-8.

13 Verny, T., *The secret life of the unborn child,* Sphere Books, London, 1982.

14 O'Keane, V. and Scott, J., 'From obstetric complications to a maternal-foetal origin hypothesis of mood disorder', *British Journal of Psychiatry,* 18, 2005: 367-8.

15 Sontag, L.W., 'War and the foetal maternal relationship', *Marriage and Family Living,* 6, 1944: 1-5.

16 Blythe, P., *A somatogenic basis for neurosis and the effect upon health,* Institute for Psychosomatic Therapy, Chester, 1974.

17 Tong, S., Marjono, B., Brown, D.A., Mulvey, S., Breit, S.N., Manuelpillai, U., and Wallace, E.M., 'Serum concentrations of macrophage inhibitory cytokine 1 (MIC 1) as a predictor of

miscarriage', *The Lancet,* 363, 2004:129-30.

[18] Cited in: Medical References: Drinking alcohol during pregnancy; **www.marchofdimes.com**

[19] Tuormaa, T.E., 'The adverse effects of alcohol on reproduction', *International Journal of Biosocial and Medical Research,* 14/2, 1994; reproduced for Foresight, the Association for the Promotion of Preconceptual Care.

[20] Barnes, D. and Walker, D.W., 'Prenatal ethanol exposure permanently alters the rat hippocampus', cited in: *Mechanisms of alcohol damage in utero,* CIBA Foundation Symposium, 105/ Pitman, London, 1981.

[21] West, J.R., Dewey, S.L., Pierce, D.R. and Black, A.C., 'Prenatal and early postnatal exposure to ethanol permanently alters the rat hippocampus', cited in: *Mechanisms of alcohol damage in utero,* CIBA Foundation Symposium, 105/ Pitman, London, 1984.

[22] Tuormaa, T.E., 'The adverse effects of alcohol on reproduction', *International Journal of Biosocial and Medical Research,* 14/2, 1994; reproduced for Foresight, the Association for the Promotion of Preconceptual Care.

[23] McGaha, C., 'The importance of the senses for infants', *Focus on Infants and Toddlers,* 16, 1 (Fall) 2003.

[24] **www.merck.com**

[25] Chasnoff, I.J., Schnoll, S.H., Burns, W.J., and Burns, K.A., 'Cocaine use in pregnancy', *New England Journal of Medicine,* 313, 1985: 666-9. Chasnoff, I.J., Burns, K.A., Burns, W.J. and Schnoll, S.H., 'Prenatal drug exposure: effects of neonatal and infant growth development', Neurobehavioral Toxicology and Teratology, 8, 1986: 357-62.

[26] Kaada, B., S*udden infant death syndrome,* Oslo University Press, 1986.

[27] Goddard, S.A., *Reflexes, learning and behaviour,* Fern Ridge Press, Eugene, Ore., 2001.

[28] Bellis Waller, M., *Crack-affected children: A teacher's guide,* Corwin Press, Newbury Park. Calif.,1993.

[29] Bellis Waller, M., personal communication, 2006.

[30] Cuomo, V., La Sapienza University, Rome.

[31] Fenig, E., Mishaeli, M., Kalish, Y., and Lishner, M., 'Pregnancy and radiation', *Cancer Treatment Review,* Feb. 27/1, 2001: 1-7.

32 Buckley, S., *Gentle birth, gentle mothering*, One Moon Press, Brisbane, Australia, 2005.

33 Beech, B.L., 'Ultrasound unsound?', talk at Mercy Hospital, Melbourne, Australia, April 1993.

34 Marinac-Dabic, D. and others, 'The safety of prenatal ultrasound exposure in human studies', *Epidemiology*,13 (3 Suppl.), 2002: S19-22, S19 and S22.

35 Ibid.

36 Gibran, Kahlil, *The prophet*, Heinemann, London, 1972.

37 Antonov, A.N., 'Children born during the siege of Leningrad in 1942', *Journal of Pediatrics*, 30, 1947: 250-9.

38 Smith, C.A., 'Effects of maternal undernutrition upon the newborn infant in Holland (1944-1945)', *Journal of Pediatrics*, 30, 1947: 229-43.

39 Gruenwald, P., Funakawa, H., Mitani, T., Nishimura, and Takeuchi, S., 'Influence of environmental factors on fetal growth in man', *The Lancet*, 1, 1967: 1026-8.

40 Stein, Z., Susser, M., Saneger, G., and Marolla, F., *Famine and human development: The Dutch hunger winter of 1944-45*, Oxford University Press, New York, 1975.

41 Ravelli, G.P. and others, 'Obesity in young men after famine exposure in utero and early infancy', *New England Journal of Medicine*, 12/8/1976: 349-53.

42 Caldwell, D.F., Oberleas, D., and Prasad, A.S., *Trace elements in human health and disease. Vol. 1. Zinc and copper*, Academic Press, New York, 1976.

43 Apgar, J., 'Zinc and reproduction: an update', *J. Nutri. Biochem.*, 3, 1992: 266-78. Hambridge, K.M., Case, C.E., and Krebs, N.F., 'Zinc', in W. Mertz (Ed.), *Trace elements in human and animal nutrition, Vol. 2*, Academic Press, New York, 1986, pp. 1-137. Keen, C.L. and Gershwin, M.E., 'Zinc deficiency and immune function', *Annual Review of Nutrition*, 10, 1990: 415-31. Keen, C.L. and Hurely, L.S., 'Zinc and reproduction: effects of deficiency on foetal and post natal development', in C.F. Mills (Ed.), *Zinc in human biology*, Springer-Verlag, London, 1989, pp. 183-220.

44 Caldwell et al., op. cit. (note 42).

45 Notes on Levels given on Biolab Hair Chart; distributed by the

Foresight Association for Pre-conceptual Care.
[46] Barnes, B., personal communication, 2006.

4.

Events Surrounding Birth

A normal delivery confers long-term benefits on both the mother and the baby, although during the course of labour most mothers would reject this concept! Much of the discomfort experienced by the mother during labour is a direct result of the unique human combination of bipedalism (upright posture) and the growth of the size of the cranium, which houses the human brain.

> It is the price we pay for our large brains and intelligence: humans have exceptionally big heads relative to the size of their bodies and the opening in the human pelvis through which the baby must pass is limited in size by our upright posture.[1]

Karen Rosenberg and Wenda Travathen described how human birth has had to adapt to accommodate these two conflicting developments. Not only is the size of opening in the human pelvis limited by upright posture but it is also not a constant shape in cross section:

> The entrance to the birth canal where the baby begins its journey is widest from side to side relative to the mother's body. Midway however the orientation shifts 90 degrees, and the long axis of the oval extends from the front of the mother's body to her back. This means the infant must negotiate a series of turns so that the two parts of the body with the largest dimensions – the head and the shoulders – are always aligned with the largest dimensions of the birth canal.

Due to the different dimensions of the birth passage, a baby cannot be born simply as a result of being squeezed or pushed in a downward direction by its mother. The baby must also be able to turn, flex, and articulate different parts of its body as it moves down the passage.

Nature has designed the human baby to be able to do just this, provided the conditions are favourable. A baby's ability actively to assist in its own birth is dependent on a number of factors:

- Gestational age of the foetus at birth
- Position of the foetus as it enters the birth canal
- Strength and nature of maternal contractions
- Presentation at birth

The full-term baby (40 weeks gestation) is equipped with a series of reflexes, known as primitive reflexes, which help to facilitate extension and flexion of the head and rotation of the shoulders and hips in response to turning of the head and pressure applied to the head and lumbar regions. Primitive reflexes and their functions in early development will be the subject of Chapter 6.

Onset of Labour

During a normal vaginal delivery, mother and baby should ideally work together as cooperative partners. When labour begins spontaneously, the foetus together with the placenta influence the timing of the onset of labour.

Much of our knowledge of the mechanisms involved in the onset of labour has been based on animal studies in the past, particularly sheep. In sheep, the foetal lamb initiates the process of labour when the foetal brain releases a hormone (corticotrophin-releasing hormone) into the mother's bloodstream, which stimulates the onset of contractions. Shortly before the onset of labour there is an increase in activity in the foetal pituitary adrenal axis. The foetus signals its readiness to be born with a rise in the rate of cortisol released by the foetal adrenal. Cortisol acts on placental enzymes active in the biosynthesis of oestrogens from progesterone, affecting a change in the ratio of oestrogen to progesterone. Oestrogen levels rise, stimulating the release of a prostaglandin* from the maternal placenta and to a lesser extent the myometrium (muscular coat of the uterus). The prostaglandin enhances the responsiveness of the muscular layer

---

* **Prostaglandins** – a group of chemical messengers derived from fats, which are involved in the process of labour.
** **Oxytocin** – hormone released from the mother's hypothalamus. Oxytocin stimulates the uterine muscle to contract.

of the uterus to the hormone oxytocin**, which, after a latent period, stimulates contractions.[2]

Human babies release a different hormone in their adrenal glands (DHEA), which travels to the placenta, providing a vital ingredient for the production of oestrogen by the placenta. At the final hurdle there is a difference in the trigger to the onset of labour as between sheep and humans: the hormone that drives the human birth process does not come directly from the baby's brain but the baby's adrenal gland, which then elicits changes in the placenta and is not dependent on cortisol alone as the precipitating factor; whereas in the lamb the onset of labour is initiated from the foetal brain and is directly related to the increase in the levels of cortisol.

When all is well, the baby will not secrete sufficient quantities of the activating hormone to the placenta until it is sufficiently mature or 'ready' to be born (approximately 40 weeks gestation). Medical intervention is essential if either the mother or the baby is considered to be at risk, but induction of labour before term or the practice of 'elective' caesarean section for *social* rather than medical reasons may not be in the long-term interests of the child.

Benefits of a Natural Birth

Normal vaginal delivery is believed to provide many benefits to the baby. While on the one hand, birth is often said to be a dangerous and traumatic journey for the baby, on the other, it helps to prepare the baby to meet the world outside the womb. Maternal contractions provide possibly the deepest massage we will ever experience in our lives, helping to rid the lungs of fluid in preparation for breathing, priming the kidneys for effective urination after birth, and awakening the sensors of the skin and proprioceptors located in the muscles, tendons, and joints for control of movement in a gravity-based environment. Pressure applied to the head as a result of squeezing from uterine contractions stimulates the foetus to release thyroid hormones and adrenaline, which will help him to regulate his temperature after birth; and the same squeezing of the head also inhibits breathing until the head has emerged. This is important to prevent the baby from inhaling fluid or other substances present in the birth canal until the airway is clear.

Reflexes such as the foetal diving reflex probably protect the baby during birth. The foetal diving reflex, a response to stress,

> is inhibitory in nature while it is not so in postnatal life. While the adult generally reacts with a fight-and-flight response with increased muscular blood flow, increased breathing and tachycardia (rapid heart rate), the foetus becomes paralysed with decreased muscular blood flow, stops breathing and become bradycardic (heart rate slows down). This so called foetal diving response is probably a very adequate response to save oxygen consumption[3] –

and thereby protect the brain from damage during periods of asphyxia before and during birth.

This same mechanism, which has a protective inhibitory effect before birth, is reversed at birth, probably as a result of the surge of hormones (the catecholamine surge*) that occurs moments before birth in a vaginal delivery.

Lagercrantz suggests that reversal of this inhibitory mechanism at birth enables the baby to be, 'aroused, start to breathe continuously and become independent of maternal heating and nutrition by the umbilical cord'. He also found that vaginally born babies showed better lung function, higher levels of glucose and free fatty acids, and better pooling of blood toward vital organs when compared to a group of infants born by caesarean section.[4] Infants delivered by elective caesarean section were found to be less alert and to have a lower neurological score than vaginally delivered infants.[5]

Normal delivery is also thought to 'prime' the immune system as the baby is exposed to bacteria normally present in the maternal vaginal and anal tracts, which help to confer a natural resistance to exposure to the same or similar bacteria in life.

Various studies have indicated that children born by caesarean section experience a higher incidence of immune-related problems, including an increase in the incidence of allergies. A study carried out at the Norwegian Institute of Public Health in Oslo in 2005 found that out of 2,656 babies, those born by caesarean section were

---

* **Catecholamine surge** – sudden increase in catecholamine levels, particularly adrenaline, which occurs when birth is imminent. This surge of hormones is thought to activate the foetal ejection reflex – the final powerful contraction which expels the baby at the moment of birth and prepares the baby for the change from a state of inhibition before birth to arousal after birth.

twice as likely to develop an allergy to cow's milk compared to those delivered naturally. None of the children who grew out of intolerance to cow's milk by their second year had been born surgically. The same team had previously discovered a link between caesarean birth and egg, fish, and nut allergy.[6]

Time to be Born

The normal length of pregnancy is from 37 to 41 weeks. Babies are described as premature if they are born before 37 weeks gestation or post mature if they are born after 42 weeks, or 294 days, from the first day of the mother's last menstrual period. While the risks associated with prematurity are well recognized and are the direct result of immaturity in the functioning of vital systems, particularly the lungs in the absence of the placenta, long-term factors associated with prolonged pregnancy are less well recognized outside of the world of obstetrics.

Prolonged pregnancy can occur for a number of reasons: uncertain menstrual data, if fertilization has taken place at a late stage in the woman's cycle, or if the woman has an unusually long menstrual cycle; failure of the cervix to soften; lack of stimulatory factors such as oxytocin and prostaglandin, or if there is placental insufficiency and labour fails to occur.

The placenta is a unique organ, being the only organ to be shared by two people, mother and baby, other than in errors of nature such as conjoined twins. The placenta has many functions, providing oxygen and nutrients to the baby, processing nutrients from the mother to make them suitable for the baby, acting as a waste disposal unit and a barrier against many (but not all) substances that are harmful to the baby. In effect, the placenta acts as the lungs, kidneys, gut, and regulator of many hormonal functions including foetal growth.

The capacity of the placenta to support the needs of the growing foetus starts to decline as the end of pregnancy approaches. If conception occurred late in the cycle then the placental function will probably be sufficient to support the foetus beyond 40 weeks, and when the baby is born, typical features of post-maturity will be evident, such as large size, well calcified skeleton, long nails, well developed ear cartilage, genitalia and so on. If placental function has not been sustained, characteristic changes of growth retardation will be present: amniotic fluid is diminished and may be stained by meconium (the first stool passed by the baby), there is absence of subcutaneous fat, and the skin is dry and peeling. The baby is usually of normal length but is under-weight, and levels of blood sugar and blood clotting factors are often low.

Babies who have been subject to placental insufficiency are also at greater risk during the birth process from low glycogen stores, meconium aspiration syndrome – when the baby breathes in fluid containing the first stool – limp-cord syndrome, where the umbilical cord has lost some of its protective coating, rendering it more prone to entanglement, tightening, and shutting down of blood vessels providing vital oxygen and nutrients to the brain, and trauma-induced haemorrhage as a result of poor blood clotting factors. The need for operative delivery is therefore increased. Post-mature babies for whom the placenta has continued to function well face potential problems at birth due to their increased size, particularly the size of a larger and less mouldable skull (resulting from increased calcification in the final two weeks of pregnancy).

There may also be an additional factor, linked to the maturity of the foetus and placental capacity to support it. If it is the foetus who signals its readiness to be born by increased activity in the adrenal axis affecting hormonal levels in the placenta and if this fails to occur and pregnancy continues beyond 41 weeks, it might indicate that the foetus is immature in some way or that as a result of decline in placental function, the placenta cannot respond to the signals from the baby.

In the last ten years, use of the INPP questionnaire on older children (7 years of age and upwards) who are experiencing problems with reading, writing, coordination, and/or behaviour has revealed an increasing incidence of children who were post-mature at birth. Further examination reveals generalized immaturity in the functioning of the central nervous system confirmed by the presence of aberrant primitive and postural reflexes in the older child. Whether post-maturity is already a sign of neurological immaturity or whether the risks associated with post-maturity predispose the infant to being more vulnerable to subsequent immaturity is not known. Nor can it be said that *all* children who were post-mature at birth are likely to have later difficulties. However, post-maturity does appear to be one significant factor in a profile of early developmental factors, which might place a child at greater risk of having subsequent developmentally related problems.

Pre-term Birth

Prematurity is defined as childbirth occurring earlier than 37 weeks of gestation. The shorter is the term of pregnancy, the greater the risks of complications. Infants born prematurely have an increased risk of death in the first year of life. They are also at a greater risk of developing serious health problems as a direct result of immaturity in vital organs (such as the lungs), fragility of developing organs and systems (such as the nervous system), and injury during birth. Health problems associated with prematurity include cerebral palsy, chronic lung disease, gastrointestinal problems, mental retardation, and vision and hearing loss.

Due to the increased necessity for medical intervention and incubation, premature babies and their mothers often have to endure periods of early separation, and it can be difficult for the mother to establish successful breast-feeding. Mother's milk is produced on a demand and supply basis – the more an infant suckles, the more milk she produces. In addition to separation, and the emotional and bonding problems that can result, very premature babies are often too ill to feed from the mother, rooting and suck reflexes can be under-developed, and after a prolonged period of tube feeding, the baby can find it difficult to learn to breast-feed later on.

Factors Leading up to Birth

In order to understand why birth is a key factor in influencing the course of later development, it is necessary to understand something of factors leading up to birth, the process of birth, and how problems during birth can affect subsequent events.

The Lie
The lie of the baby describes the manner in which the baby is lying in the womb. *Longitudinal lie* describes when the baby assumes a

position with one end lying immediately above the pelvic brim. This usually occurs about the 28th week of pregnancy and is the most common (and favourable) position for both mother and baby. *Oblique lie* occurs in a very small number of pregnancies (approximately 1.5%)[7] and describes when the lower part of the baby lies just above the maternal groin with its spine lying obliquely in relation to the mother's spine. *Transverse lie* or shoulder presentation describes when the spinal column of the baby lies at right angles to the mother's spine.

Presentation

Presentation describes the position or situation of the foetus in the womb. The part of the foetus that is closest to the cervix is the presenting part. The cervix* or neck of the womb, which has remained closed throughout pregnancy, must thin out (efface) and open up (dilate) to allow the baby to pass through the birth canal.

There are various types of presentation, and the course of labour will be influenced by the presentation of the foetus. The most common and safest birth position is described as vertex or cephalic, where the baby's head is the presenting part and the head is flexed forward with the chin on the chest.

Breech presentation describes when the baby approaches the birth canal bottom first, with the buttocks presenting. Breech births account for about 3-4 per cent of all deliveries and are usually more difficult for a number of reasons. Firstly, the buttocks do not exert the same type of pressure on the cervix as the head, making cervical dilation a longer and more difficult process.

When the baby presents with the head down and flexed forward, the foetal head exerts pressure on the cervix, which stimulates secretion of oxytocin**, which then increases the amount of prostaglandin acting on the uterus. 'Nerve fibres carry impulses from the mother's cervix up the mother's spinal cord to her brain. The reflexive release of oxytocin by the mother in turn causes further uterine contraction. Likewise, this uterine contraction stimulates more oxytocin release.'[8] This loop is an example of what Nathanielsz

---

* **Cervix** – the neck of the womb is composed of tight fibrous tissue at the outlet between the uterus and the vagina.

** **Oxytocin** is the hormone that stimulates uterine contractions for the birth of the baby, delivery of the placenta and ejection of milk during lactation, parental bonding and the shrinking of the uterus after birth.

described as a 'feed forward loop' – a mechanism which is self-potentiating and therefore extremely powerful, difficult to control once under way, and suitable for limited processes, which reach a climax and natural conclusion.[9] 'The more pushing, the more oxytocin; the more oxytocin, the more pushing.'[10] Secondly, the most difficult part of the birth process in a breech presentation is birth of the head, which is left until the end, when both baby and mother are fatigued and the baby may not be able to assume a favourable position for safe delivery of the head. Where there are no other complications a vaginal birth is still possible, but there is a greater risk that forceps or a vacuum extractor may be required.

Where a breech presentation or transverse lie position is discovered during pregnancy, it may be possible to rotate the baby to an upright or vertex position using a procedure called external version. External version is performed under the guidance of ultra-sound. The physician manipulates the baby into a head-down position by applying gentle but firm pressure to the baby's head and hip through the abdomen. This procedure is generally most successful if it is performed at 36 weeks, due to the fact that after 37 weeks less amniotic fluid makes it more difficult to rotate the baby. However, there are risks involved in the process, including inducing labour, producing pain in the abdomen, and – although very rare – the risk of shearing the placenta from the uterine wall. Even after successful external version has been carried out, some babies revert to a breech position.

Foetal Position

The position of the baby refers to the direction that the foetus is facing. Most commonly the baby's position is anterior, where the back of the head is touching the mother's abdominal wall. The less common posterior position is where the back of the baby's head is against the spine. However, most posterior babies rotate to an anterior position before the second stage of labour.

The Process of Delivery

The process of labour takes place in three stages. *Stage 1* describes the time from the onset of labour (generally defined as the onset of regular, painful uterine contractions) to the time when the cervix or the neck of the womb is sufficiently dilated (an opening of between 9 and 10cm) to allow the baby's head to pass through.

The first stage of labour is usually the longest, lasting an average of 12 hours, but it can vary from 12 to 24 hours and is generally most protracted in a first pregnancy. Contractions of the uterine muscle cause the cervix to thin out or 'efface' and dilate. The degree of dilation is described in centimetres. The baby's progress is also described in terms of 'station', which follows the location of the baby's presenting part in relation to certain bones of the pelvis. This indicates how far the baby has advanced or moved through the pelvis, and is measured in centilitres above or below certain points on the pelvis.

Stage 2 describes the process from full dilation of the cervix to delivery of the baby. During this stage, the mother can start to help by using her abdominal muscles to bear down with each uterine contraction. Delivery usually lasts between 45 minutes and an hour, unless there are complications. When about 4-5 cm (1½ to 2 inches) of the head appears, the doctor or midwife may place a hand over the foetus's head during a contraction to control and, if necessary, slightly slow the foetus's progress. The head and chin are eased out of the vaginal opening to prevent the mother's tissues from tearing. Such manoeuvres aid the mother in the delivery of her child. Once the baby's head has emerged, the body rotates to allow the shoulders to come out one at a time (restitution). The rest of the body then usually slides out quickly.

Sometimes an episiotomy may be needed, which involves cutting the perineum, the area between the vagina and the anus, which must stretch enough to allow the baby to exit from the vagina. This delicate area will tear if it cannot stretch sufficiently. An episiotomy, if required, is usually after the administration of a local anaesthetic, rather than allowing the woman to tear or the baby to struggle.

Birthing position can help to ease the second stage of labour. The Western way of birth differs from positions used in other parts of the world and is one of the only places in which mothers are encouraged to give birth lying on their back. An upright (vertical) position or a lateral tilt, squatting, or four point kneeling during the second stage of labour give greater advantages as both gravity and muscular effort from the mother can work with the shape of the birth canal more efficiently. The upright position gives less discomfort and difficulty in bearing down, and relaxes the adductor and perineal muscles.

Stage 3 follows delivery of the baby and completes delivery of the placenta or afterbirth.

Complications

Occasionally problems occur during the course of labour. Complications can result from problems with the passage (mother) or the passenger (baby). There are various ways in which these problems can be dealt with.

Forceps

Before the development of anaesthetics, use of antiseptics, and modern surgical techniques, delivery by c-section was not a safe option and forceps were used to help extract a baby stuck in the birth canal. Forceps are designed to cradle the baby's head so that traction (pulling) on the handles helps the baby to be born. Forceps can only be used when the first stage of labour is complete and the cervix is fully dilated.

Indications for forceps to be used are:
• If the baby's head has descended but contractions have stopped or are not effective;
• Prolonged labour with a delay due to unfavourable position of the baby. Forceps can be used to rotate the baby's head;
• Foetal distress;
• To protect the baby's head in premature births or breech delivery;
• Maternal fatigue, or if the mother has a medical condition when prolonging pushing is contra-indicated;
• Administration of epidural or analgesics has rendered the mother unable to push effectively.

Effects on the baby

Forceps delivery can be distressing for both the mother and the baby. Local anaesthetic is usually administered to the mother before forceps are used. The forceps may leave temporary marks or bruising to the baby where the forceps have been applied. If the mother has been given increased analgesia immediately before forceps are used, the baby may be born suffering from the effects of analgesia, and be slower to breathe and to feed. There is always some degree of force when forceps are used. In rare cases this can result in damage to the baby's head, neck, or spine.

Occasionally a degree of torsion may occur, resulting in slight misalignment of the cervical area. Cranial Osteopaths and Chiropractors often see these babies when they are a few weeks old, suffering from poor sleeping patterns and difficulties associated with feeding. In Europe, a particular type of misalignment has been identified called Kinetic Imbalance of the Skeletal System (KISS Syndrome). Fortunately, if identified early enough KISS Syndrome can be effectively treated by a specially trained doctor of manual medicine. If KISS or related syndromes persist they can show up as postural, feeding, sleep, learning, or behavioural disorders later on. Not all babies who have undergone a forceps delivery will suffer from related problems, but there is a greater degree of risk when intervention of force of any kind has to be applied.

Vacuum extraction

Vacuum extraction is a slightly gentler method of assisting delivery when a baby has got into difficulties. A vacuum extractor (ventouse) or suction cup is applied to the lowest part of the baby's head. The cone-shaped cup is attached to a pump, which creates a vacuum, which serves as an external handle with which to gently rotate the baby's head and to apply traction.

Effects on the baby

Babies sometimes have cone-shaped heads for a couple of days when they have been born with the assistance of ventouse. A cephalhaematoma, or blood blister, may form on top of the baby's head, but this usually disappears in a week or the baby's head may be slightly grazed or bruised. Very occasionally the baby can suffer a degree of cerebral trauma.

Caesarean Section (C-Section)

A c-section may be planned in advance of the expected birth date (elective caesarean section) or if mother or baby starts to experience difficulties when labour is under way, and neither forceps nor vacuum extraction is suitable.

Medical indications for an elective c-section include:
- Head to pelvic incompatibility (cephalo-pelvic disproportion)
- Placenta praevia
- Multiple pregnancy with 3 or more foetuses

Possible indications for an elective c-section include:
- Breech presentation
- Moderate to severe pregnancy-induced hypertension
- Diabetes
- Intra-uterine growth retardation
- Antepartum haemorrhage

Indications for an emergency c-section include:
- Cord prolapse
- Uterine rupture
- Eclampsia
- Failure of labour – ineffective contractions which do not improve following administration of oxytocin
- Foetal distress, if delivery is not imminent.

Signs of foetal distress can be meconium in the water, changes in the foetal heart rate, and excessive movements of the baby. If these occur before the first stage of labour is completed, a c-section may be the only safe option.

Effects on the baby

The major risk for the baby following birth by c-section is breathing difficulties, which are four times more likely in a baby born by caesarean.[11] The first task a baby must accomplish at birth is learning how to breathe by itself. This involves replacing the shallow episodic breathing movements practised before birth with regular rhythmic respirations following lung expansion:

At term, approximately 110 ml of lung fluid is present within the respiratory tract. During delivery, compression of the chest wall assists in the expulsion of some of this fluid, the remainder of which is absorbed by the pulmonary circulation and lymphatic system after birth. Infants delivered by caesarean section are denied the benefits of chest compression and therefore expression of lung fluid.[12]

The authors go on to explain that

compression and decompression of the baby's head during delivery is thought to stimulate the respiratory centre in the brain which in turn maintains the stimulus to respiratory effort. Carotid baro-receptors sensitive to changes in pressure, may also contribute to respiratory stimulus by their response to the circulatory change which takes place when the placental circulation ceases.*

In her book *Gentle Birth, Gentle Mothering*, Sarah Buckley[13] explains why birth by c-section can affect not only the mother but also the baby, and in some cases the mother-baby relationship. An excerpt from her chapter 'Undisturbed birth – Mother Nature's blueprint for safety, ease and ectstasy' is quoted at length below. Readers who are interested in finding out more about the connections between hormones and emotions are recommended to read this book, which combines the author's knowledge as a medical doctor with insight gained from her own experience as a mother of four children.

With a caesarean, there is an absent or curtailed labour and the maternal hormonal peaks of oxytocin, endorphins, and catechol-amines are absent or reduced. The normal multi-phasic pattern of prolactin** secretion is abolished in caesarean section.[14]

Studies of babies delivered by elective caesarean also show significantly lower levels of oxytocin,[15] endorphins[16] and catechol-amines[17] and prolactin.[18, 19] Some of the well documented risks of caesareans may be due to these hormonal deficits – particularly, for the baby, to absence of the catecholamine surge. This means that babies born after caesareans are at increased risk of respiratory compromise[20, 21] for up to a week after birth,[22] as well as low blood sugar[23] and poor temperature regulation.[24]

---

*   i.e. when the umbilical cord is cut
** **Prolactin** – the chief hormone of breastmilk production. Levels increase in pregnancy but milk production is suppressed until the placenta is delivered

Brain oxygenation is lower immediately after caesarean versus vaginal birth,[25] possibly because of the lack of blood redistribution from the catecholamine surge and/or the loss of the placental transfusion with explain the caesarean delivery.[26] These changes may explain the slower neurological adaptation after birth in caesarean babies,[27, 28] which may in turn explain the caesarean baby's delay in adapting to a diurnal (day-night) sleep pattern.[29]

Recent research has found many more differences in the physiology of caesarean newborns. These include differences in levels of the hormones of calcium metabolism,[30] rennin angiotensin (fluid and blood pressure regulating) hormones,[31, 32, 33] human atrial natriuetic peptide (a hormone produced by the heart),[34] progesterone,[35] the muscle enzyme creatinine kinase,[36] dopamine (a brain chemical) pathways,[37] nitric oxide synthesis[38] (which helps with lung maturation) the insulin hormone IGPF-1,[39] melatonin,[40] thyroid hormones (which decrease during labour and surge after birth)[41] and liver enzymes.[42]

She goes on to explain how,

Gut function also differs for caesarean babies, whose stomachs are less acid after birth[43], and who secrete less of the gut hormones gastrin[44], and somatostatin[45]. Caesarean babies have an altered bowel flora (types of friendly bacteria present in the intestines) compared to vaginally born babies, which persists for at least six months and possibly life long[46]. This bowel flora abnormality (which occurs because the caesarean baby is not exposed to the mother's bowel flora at birth) may explain the increased susceptibility of premature caesarean babies to newborn gut infections[47] and possibly the increased risk of asthma[48, 49] and allergies[50] (including food allergies) for caesarean offspring later in life.

Midwives, Helpers, and Hospital Birth

Birth amongst most mammals is a private affair. The mother will seek a place of relative shelter and safety from surrounding predators (a nest) in which to deliver her young, but human birth is seldom carried out in private.

Most primates give birth with the baby monkey emerging to the front of the mother's body so she can reach down with her hands and guide it from the birth canal.[51] The size of the human brain and the shape of the human pelvis have resulted in changes in how the foetal head enters the pelvic basin and then rotates with the baby's face turned toward the mother's back (anterio-posterior presentation). This has made it very difficult for the mother to give birth by herself, as she cannot see or easily use her hands to help the baby to make its final exit, clear a breathing passage for the baby at birth, or unravel the umbilical cord if caught around the baby's neck. The difficulties associated with human birth have meant that most cultures consider it desirable for a woman to have assistance at birth. While assistance has helped to save many lives and to make the mother's job easier, assistance, particularly in the West, has also brought with it technology and interference which are not always in the best interests of mother and child. Too much interference during birth can affect the process in a number of ways.

The French obstetrician Michel Odent suggests that increased interference and medical mechanization of birth can render mothers less and less able to give birth naturally. He explains that giving birth, like making love, requires the temporary surrender of higher centres in the human brain to lower more instinctive functions.

> The enormous development of a part of the human brain (the neocortex) tends to inhibit activity of more primitive (instinctual) brain structures. When one feels observed the neocortex (the brain of the intellect) cannot take a back seat. A birth attendant interferes with the need for privacy and therefore tends to make birth more difficult, so that there is a need for more help.[52]

As technology has been developed to help overcome obstetric complications, mechanization has started to dominate the process of birth. The expectant mother is no longer a healthy symbol of fecundity but a patient awaiting the altar of medicine to ensure the safe delivery of her child. This is not to deny that medicine has conferred enormous benefits both in improving the safety, and in many cases the comfort, of child-birth, but medicine's role is to support or intervene when nature goes awry, not to *replace* some of nature's most positive instincts.

There has been a transformation in the way in which women give birth over the last century. Odent[53] traced some of these developments from the first months of the First World War in Germany when drugs such as morphine and scopolamine started to be applied to child-birth, promising an era of pain-free labour – an apparent 'miracle' for women who had endured the fear and pain of child-birth for generations.

Morphine was administered at the onset of labour, followed by a dose of the amnesiac drug scopolamine. Not only could women be relieved of the pain of child-birth but all memory of the process could also be erased. During the second stage of labour, ether or chloroform could be given inducing a 'twilight sleep' during which the mother was a passive patient and medical staff firmly in charge of the birthing process. In order to secure such comforts, birth, at least for the wealthy who could afford to choose, had to take place in hospital.

During the 1950s a new technique for delivering babies by caesarean section was developed. Hitherto, caesarean section had been a very risky operation which required making a vertical incision in the main body of the uterus. A new technique of low-segmental c-section involved making a horizontal uterine incision just above the cervix. The new technique, combined with modern advances in anaesthesia, plastic materials for making drips safe, blood transfusion, and the availability of antibiotics if required, made c-section a much safer option. However, until the 1960s most doctors involved in child-birth were not surgeons, and if a c-section was needed the skills of a surgeon had to be brought in. If the patient was not already in hospital, she had to be moved.

During the 1960s training of obstetricians extended to include specialized surgical training. As the number of surgically trained obstetricians increased, so the number of hospital as opposed to midwife-assisted home births began to increase. In this way, if a mother got into difficulties, the services of surgically trained staff were quickly accessible. As birth in a hospital environment increasingly became the norm during the 1970s, electronic foetal monitoring entered the birthing room on an industrial scale.

Formerly, the attending doctor or midwife would listen to the foetal heartbeat at regular intervals during labour (foetal heart rate provides an early warning of foetal distress). Electronic foetal monitoring meant that medical birth attendants could have a continuous record of the foetal heart rate, strength, and regularity of maternal contractions, and the foetus's response to contractions, printed out on a graph. The technology enabled birth assistants to view the state of labour and the passenger on paper, but it also meant the mother became increasingly confined to one position on a bed. The freedom of the mother to turn, walk, sit, go on to all fours, squat, or move became increasingly restricted. If the baby became 'stuck' at any point, the mother was equally stuck, and could not help the process by shifting her position and using gravity or postural change to facilitate renewed progress.

The development of epidural anaesthesia also comes with a hidden price tag. Its administration is a specialist skill carried out by injecting a numbing drug between two segments of the backbone through a fine plastic tube. The tube is left in place in case a 'top up' is needed later on. Whilst being a highly effective method of providing pain relief to the lower half of the body, it also numbs the mother's desire to push during the second stage of labour. Unable to respond *spontaneously* to the signals of her body, complications can set in during the second stage, necessitating the need for drip administration of oxytocin to sustain strong contractions and further obstetric interventions such as use of forceps and cutting of the perineum (episiotomy).

Induced Labour

Labour may need to be artificially stimulated (induced) for a number of reasons. Labour is also sometimes started off for social convenience rather than sound medical reasons. The inducing of labour without medical grounds is not a good idea, not only because the mother-baby dyad may not be 'ready', making the process longer and more difficult, but also because of hormonal factors that can affect the mother-child relationship after birth.

You will remember that oxytocin (from the Greek *okus* for 'swift' and *tokus* for 'birth') is the hormone that stimulates uterine contractions for the birth of the baby, delivery of the placenta, and ejection of milk (let-down reflex) during lactation. During a natural delivery, the mother secretes sufficient oxytocin to maintain uterine contractions. When birth is induced, physicians usually use prostaglandin – the chemical that drives the muscular contractions of the uterus and the softening of the cervix. If prostaglandin is not effective in bringing on and sustaining the process of labour, oxytocin may be administered as well.

Oxytocin functions as a natural opiate, reducing the experience of pain and fostering a feeling of general warmth and well-being. It also promotes affiliative feelings, and naturally increases during times of social as well as physical interaction. Levels of oxytocin and feelings of comradeship are raised when we sit down together at a meal table and during times of physical intimacy such as sexual intercourse, as well as being present in the potent cocktail of hormones in the mother following a natural delivery and when she breast-feeds her baby. This has led some authors to describe oxytocin as 'the hormone of love'. Odent[54] suggests that when oxytocin is administered artificially via a drip to induce or maintain labour, it sends a signal to the woman's brain to turn down the secretion of her own supply of oxytocin. Paradoxically, the hormone that should help to sustain labour to a successful conclusion is reduced, the amount administered through the drip is increased, and the mother's own supply is low when the baby is born. In theory, this could lead to greater difficulty in establishing breast-feeding and upset the chemical components of early bonding between mother and child. We will return to this theme when we explore the subject of attachment in Chapter 9.

Taking all these factors into account, whilst recognizing that the safety of mother and child is paramount, and that medical advice should *always* be followed, there is much to be said for allowing mothers to give birth as naturally as possible. Fear, stress, and too much intervention from well-meaning birth attendants can all interfere with a woman's natural instinct to give birth. Childbirth is one of the few remaining events in our modern world when instinct sometimes knows more than reason.

Separation at Birth

In the 1970s paediatricians Klaus and Kennell[55,56] pointed out that there is a sensitive period following birth. It lasts for about 30-60 minutes and is well developed in babies who have not been exposed to medication during the process of birth. The newborn is quiet, alert, wide-eyed, and ready to communicate and bond with its mother. The mother, who is also under the influence of the powerful hormones of birth, is primed to greet her child.

The effect of delivery-room routines on infant behaviour, particularly breast-feeding, was investigated by Righard and Alade in 1990.[57] They carried out a study observing the behaviour of 72 infants who had been born normally for the first 2 hours after birth. One group was placed on the mother's abdomen immediately after birth but removed after 20 minutes for measuring and dressing. The second group was left in direct contact with the mother for an hour without interruption. After about 20 minutes, the infants who had been left undisturbed began to make crawling movements towards the breast, feeling with their hands, nuzzling and exploring with their mouths (rooting) until they found the breast. Within 50 minutes of birth, most of these infants were spontaneously suckling at the breast, and more infants in the contact group than in the separated group showed the correct sucking technique. Infants born to mothers who had received pethidine during labour showed signs of sedation at birth and did not suck at all. The researchers concluded that, 'contact between mother and infant should be uninterrupted during the first hour after birth or until the first breast-feed has been accomplished, and that use of drugs such as pethidine should be restricted'.

The residual hormones of birth – adrenaline from the catecholamine surge – affect physiological changes in both the newborn and the mother. The baby's pupils dilate once it has adjusted to the light, making it wide eyed in wonderment and imitating one of the physiological changes that takes place during sexual arousal, making partners more attractive to one another. This same mechanism encourages mother and baby to gaze at one another, touch and stroke each other, affecting the hormone levels of both. If left undisturbed, the baby will not only find the breast but eventually start to suckle and feed.

This instinct starts to decline within a couple of hours of birth. At a lecture on 'The early expression of the rooting reflex', Michel Odent,[58] who had originally been in favour of father's being present and active throughout delivery, explained why he had modified his view. Mothers and babies are primed by nature in the first few hours after birth to attach to one another and to feed. Fathers who have patiently supported their partners through pregnancy and labour understandably want to share the first wonderful moments of contact with their child, but these first few moments are truly mother's moments – the time when mother and child still share a chemical bond which supports the process of attachment, helping mother and child to recognize (to know) each other and gaze for the first time upon the face of love.

When my first son was born in the beginning of the 1980s it was still normal practice for the baby to be removed from the mother and taken to the hospital nursery at night. The baby was brought to the mother by the night staff for 4-hourly feeds (if she was breast-feeding). The theory behind the practice was that it would give the mother a better night's sleep, an opportunity to recover from the rigours of birth, and help to establish a 'regular' feeding pattern for the baby in time for going home – all good ideas in theory. However, studies of both animal and human behaviour have shown that physical contact between mother and newborn in the first hours and days after birth is instrumental in forming attachment, reducing stress, strengthening survival functions in the infant, and establishing feeding.[59]

Newborn mammals that depend on the mother after birth need to be licked in the genital area shortly after birth. If not licked, the genitor-urinary and/or the gastrointestinal systems do not function properly and the animal is unable to urinate or defecate. These animals will die from oedema if they do not receive appropriate tactile stimulation from a surrogate source. Amongst goats, Blauvelt[60] showed that if the kid is removed from the mother for only a few hours before she has a chance to lick it, when the kid is restored to her she seems to have lost the behavioural resources to do anything further for her newborn. Hens also show a decrease in broody behaviour if they are physically removed from their chicks, even if they are still within visual contact.[61]

In humans, the sense of touch seems to fulfil the same function as licking in other mammals. Skin to skin is an intrinsic part of primal communication between mother and child after birth. It helps to improve temperature regulation, helps the infant to find, nuzzle, and suckle the breast, stimulating further production of oxytocin in the mother and also provides an additional chemical bond between mother and child through the powerful sense of smell.*

In his book on *Touching*, Ashley Montagu[62] writes that 'physical contact appears to act as a principal regulator of broodiness. Stimulation of the skin apparently constitutes an essential condition in causing the pituitary gland to secrete the hormone most important for the initiation and maintenance of broodiness, namely prolactin'. Prolactin is also the key player in the establishment and maintenance of breast-feeding.

Despite separation in the hospital nursery for the first few nights of his life, my first child and I were able to establish a cycle of successful feeding, but it took longer with him than with my second and third children, who were placed in my arms immediately after birth and from whom (as a more experienced mother) I was not separated.

In spite of all we know about the processes of conception, gestation, and birth, the birth of every child is still a small miracle. Human birth is a difficult process for mother and child, and mothers should not feel guilty if they have required medical assistance during labour. Mothers who are well informed about the reasons behind birth practices and interventions are in a better position to make choices about how they would like to give birth and avoid making decisions based on convenience or comfort rather than medical need.

Low Birth Weight

Birth weight tends to be regarded as the gold standard of pregnancy outcome, and an association between low birth weight and the development of adult medical and metabolic diseases such as cardiovascular diseases and diabetes has been repeatedly demonstrated.

In addition to the physical effects of low birth weight on health in later life, that low birth weight for gestational age, particularly at term, is also associated with adult psychological distress, which is not mediated by childhood factors,[63] suggesting a direct link between

---

* Smell is the only one of the main senses to pass directly to the cortex without first being filtered through the thalamus.

birth weight and adult mental health. As association has also been found between low birth weight and adult cognitive functioning.[64]

Early life factors such as birth weight influence cognition[65] and behaviour[66] in childhood and may be the result of a number of factors: premature birth with all the risks that accompany the immature infant; impaired foetal growth resulting from placental insufficiency, leading to a reduced oxygen and nutrition supply to the developing brain; structural changes to biological mechanisms such as the hypothalamic-pituitary-axis[67] (with its powerful influence on hormones, and emotional and cognitive responses), the growth hormone axis, and thyroid function. Low birth weight is not an absolute determinant of health or the development of adult psychological problems, but as with many events in early life, it carries slightly greater risks.[68]

Long-term Effects of Premature Birth

Links between children born prematurely and deficits in cognitive ability and school achievement have been established by numerous studies. The majority have found that the greater the medical complications at birth, the greater the cognitive and motor deficits, the lower the school achievement, and the higher the behavioural problems at school age. This paints a rather grim picture for the future of children who suffered medical complications as a result of being premature at birth. However, studies have also found that the early social environment of the child plays an important role in subsequent development; an enriched environment can often mediate between the effects of early traumatic events and the appearance of later development problems, while an impoverished or stressful environment is linked to lower cognitive abilities and delayed social development.

Birth in Perspective

The manner of a child's birth can affect many aspects of life in addition to the process of birth itself. The effects of major problems during the birth process will usually show up immediately after birth and require medical intervention, but more subtle problems and differences have less immediately obvious effects, and sometimes do not become evident until later in development. While medicine has made tremendous progress in reducing natal mortality, making birth safer for mother and child and more comfortable for the mother, *unnecessary* medical interference during birth can disturb the natural way of birth and nature's superb design for giving mother and baby the best start for their life together. Mothers should never feel inadequate if for any reason intervention has been required for medical reasons: the priority must always be the safety of mother and child, but there is a need for more longitudinal research to follow up the long-term effects of birth differences on development.

In a Nutshell...

- Complications associated with human birth are partly the result of evolutionary changes that resulted in upright posture.

- Birth takes place as a result of a number of biological processes in both mother and child.

- Many of the hormonal changes that take place during birth help to prepare both mother and baby for attachment and feeding after birth.

- Modern medicine has made birth a safer process, but should not seek to replace the natural processes of birth for social convenience rather than medical priorities.

- Natural birth strengthens survival mechanisms and primes the sensory systems of the baby for life after birth.

- If intervention is required for medical reasons, medical advice should always be followed.

Endnotes

1   Rosenberg, K. and Trevathen, W.R., 'The evolution of human birth', *Scientific American,* November 2001: 77-81.

2   Liggins, G.C., Fariclough, R.J., Grieves, S.A., Forster, C.S., and Knox, B.S., 'Parturition in the sheep', in: *The fetus and birth,* Ciba Foundation Symposium 47, Elsevier, Oxford, 1977.

3   Lagercrantz, H., 'Neurochemical modulation of fetal behaviour and excitation at birth', in E. Euler, H. Forssberg, and H. Lagercrantz (Eds), *Neurobiology of early infant behaviour,* Wenner-Gren International Symposium Series, Vol. 55, Stockton Press, New York, 1989.

4   Lagercrantz, H. and Slotkin, T., 'The stress of birth', *Scientific American,* 254, 1986: 100-7.

5   Leijon, I., Berg, G., Finnström, O., and Otamiri, G., European Congress in Perinatology, Abstracts, Rome, 1988.

6   Eggesbø, M., Botten, G., Stigum, H., Samuelson, S., Brunekreef, B., and Magnus, P., 'Cesarean delivery and cow mild allergy/ intolerance', *Allergy.* 60/9, 2005: 1172.

7   Bourne, G., *Pregnancy,* Pan Books, London, 1979.

8   Nathanielsz, P.W., *Life before birth: The challenges of fetal development,* W.H. Freeman and Company, New York, 1996.

9   Ibid.

10   Bainbridge, B., *A visitor within: The science of pregnancy,* Weidenfeld and Nicolson, London, 2000.

11   Statistic quoted on Birth Choice UK website: **www.BirthChoiceUK.com**

12   Bennett, R.V., Brown, L.K., *Myles textbook for midwives,* Churchill Livingstone, Edinburgh, 1989.

13   Buckley, S.J., *Gentle birth, gentle mothering,* One Moon Press, Brisbane, 2005. 'Ecstatic birth: the hormonal blueprint of labour', Online Mothering Magazine, Issue 111, March/April 2002; **www.mothering.com.articles**

14   Rigg, L.A. and Yen, S.S., 'Multiphasic prolactin secretion during parturition in human subjects', *American Journal of Obstetric Gynecology,* 128/2, 1977: 215-8.

15   Marchini, G. and others, 'Fetal and maternal plasma levels of gastrin, somostatin and oxytocin after vaginal delivery and elective

caesarean section', *Early Human Development,* 18/1, 1988: 73-9.

[16] Fachinetti, F. and others, 'Changes in beta-endorphin in fetal membranes and placenta in normal and pathological pregnancies', *Acta Obstet. Gynaecol. Scand.,* 69/7-8, 1990: 603-7.

[17] Jones, C.R. and others, 'Plasma catcholamines and modes of delivery: the relation between catecholamine levels and in-vitro platelet aggregation and adrenorecptor radioligland binding characteristics', *British Journal of Obstetric Gynaecology,* 92/6, 1985: 593-9.

[18] Rigg, L.A. and Yen, S.S., 'Multiphasic prolactin secretion during parturition in human subjects', *American Journal of Obstetric Gynecology,* 128/2, 1977: 215-8.

[19] Heasman, L. and others, 'Plasma prolactin concentrations after caesarean or vaginal delivery', *Arch. Dis. Child. Fetal Neonatal. Ed.,* 77/3, 1997: F237-8.

[20] Faxelius, G. and others, 'Catecholamine surge and lung function after delivery', *Arch. Dis. Child.,* 58/4, 1983: 262-6.

[21] Zanado, V. and others, 'Neonatal respiratory morbidity risk and mode of delivery at term: influence of timing of elective caesarean delivery', *Acta Paediatr.,* 93/5, 2004: 643-7.

[22] Richardson, B.S. and others, 'The impact of labor at term on measures of neonatal outcome', *Am. J. Obstet. Gynecol.,* 192/1, 2005: 219-26.

[23] Hagnevik, K. and others, 'Catecholamine surge and metabolic adaptation in the newborn after vaginal delivery and caesarean section', *Acta Paediatr. Scand.,* 73/5, 1984: 602-9.

[24] Christensson, K. and others, 'Lower body temperatures in infants delivered by caesarean section than in vaginally delivered infants', *Acta Paediatr.,* 82/2, 1993: 128-31.

[25] Isobe, K. and others, 'Measurement of cerebral oxygenation in neonates after vaginal delivery and caesarean section using full spectrum near infrared spectroscopy', *Comp. Biochem. Physiol. A: Mol. Integr. Physiol.,* 132/1, 2002: 133-8.

[26] Buckley, S.J., 'Leaving well alone – a natural approach to third stage', *Medical Veritas,* 2/2, 2005:492-9.

[27] Otimari, G. and others, 'Delayed neurological adaptation in infants delivered by elective caesarean section and the relation to catecholamine levels', *Early Hum Dev.,* 26/1, 1991: 51-60.

28 Kim, H.R. and others, 'Delivery modes and neonatal EEG: spatial pattern analysis', *Early Hum Dev.,* 75/1-2, 2003: 16-18.

29 Freudigman, K.A. and Thoman, E.B., 'Infants' earliest sleep/ wake organization differs as a function of delivery mode', *Dev Psychobiol.,* 32/4, 1998: 293-303.

30 Bagnoli, F. and others. 'Relationship between mode of delivery and neonatal calcium homeostasis', *Eur. J. Pediatr.,* 149/11, 1990: 800-3.

31 Broughton Pipkin, F. and Symonds, E.M., 'Factors affecting angiotensin 11 concentrations in the human infant at birth', *Clin. Sci. Mol. Med.,* 52/5, 1997: 449-56.

32 Fujimura, A. and others, 'The influence of delivery mode on biological inactive rennin level in umbilical cord blood', *Am. J. Hypertens.,* 3/1, 1990: 23-6.

33 Tetlow, H.J. and Broughton Pipkin, F., 'Studies on the effect of mode of delivery on the renin-angiotensin system in mother and fetus at term', *Br. J. Obset. Gynaecol.,* 90/3, 1983: 220-6.

34 Okamoto, E. and others, 'Plasma concentrations of human atrial natriuretic peptide at vaginal delivery and elective cesarean section', *Asia Oceania J. Obsete. Gynaecol.,* 15/2, 1989: 199-202.

35 Aisien, A.O. and others, 'Umbilical cord venous progesterone at term delivery in relation to mode of delivery', *Int. J. Gynaec. Obstet.,* 47/1, 1994: 27-31.

36 Malamitsi-Puchner, A. and others, 'Serum levels of creatine kinase and iso-enzymes during 1st postpartum day in healthy newborns delivered vaginally or by cesarean section', *Gynecol. Obstet. Invest.,* 36/1, 1993: 25-8.

37 Boksa, P. and El-Khodor, B.F., 'Birth insult interacts with stress at adulthood to alter dopaminergic function in animal modes: possible implications for schizophrenia and other disorders', *Neurosci. Behav. Rev.,* 27/1-2, 2003: 91-101.

38 Endo, A. and others, 'Spontaneous labour increases nitric oxide synthesis during the early neonatal period', *Pediatr. Int.,* 42/1, 2001: 340-2.

39 Hills, F.A. and others, 'IGFBP-1 in the placental membranes and fetal circulation: levels at term and preterm delivery', *Early Human Development,* 44/1, 1996: 71-6.

40 Mitchell, M.D. and others, 'Melatonin in the maternal and

umbilican circulations during human parturition', *Br. J. Obstet. Gynaecol.*, 86/1, 1979: 29-31.

[41] Bird, J.A. and others, 'Endocrine and metabolic adaptation following caesarean section or vaginal delivery', *Arch. Dis. Child Fetal Neonatal Ed.*, 74/2, 1996: F132-4.

[42] Mongelli, M. and others, 'Effect of labour and delivery on plasma hepatic enzymes in the newborn', *J. Obstet. Gynaecol. Res.*, 26/1, 2000: 61-3.

[43] Miclat, N.N. and others, 'Neonatal gastric PH', *Anesth. Analg.*, 57/1, 1978: 98-101.

[44] Sangild, P.T. and others, 'Vaginal birth versus elective caesarean section: effects on gastric function in the neonate', *Exp. Physiol.*, 80/1, 1995: 147-57.

[45] Marchini, G. and others, 'Fetal and maternal plasma levels of gastrin, somatostatin and oxytocin after vaginal delivery and elective caesarean section', *Early Hum. Dev.*, 18/1, 1988: 73-9.

[46] Gronlund, M.M. and others, 'Fecal microflora in healthy infants born by different methods of delivery: permanent changes in intestinal flora after caesarean delivery', *J. Pediatr. Gastroenterol. Nutr.*, 28/1, 1999: 19-25.

[47] Hallstrom, M. and others, 'Effects of mode of delivery and nectrotising enterocolits on the intestinal microflora in preterm infants', *Eur. J. Clin. Microbiol. Infect. Dis.*, 23/6, 2004: 463-70.

[48] Kero, J. and others, 'Mode of delivery and asthma – is there a connection?', *Pediatric Res.*, 52/1, 2002: 6-11.

[49] Hakansson, S. and Kallen, K., 'Cesarean section increases the risk of hospital care in childhood for asthma and gastroenteritis', *Clin. Exp. Allergy*, 33/6, 2003: 757-64.

[50] Laubereau, B. and others, 'Cesarean section and gastrointestinal symptoms, atopic dermatitis and sensitisation during the first year of life', *Arch. Dis. Child*, 89/11, 2004: 993-7.

[51] Bernard Bel; cited in W.R. Trevathan, O.E. Smith, and J.J. McKenna (Eds), *Evolutionary obstetrics. Evolutionary medicine.* Oxford University Press, New York, 1999, pp. 183-207.

[52] Odent, M., *The obstetrician and the farmer,* Free Association Books, London, 2002.

[53] Odent, M., *The scientification of love,* Free Association Books, London, 2001.

54 Ibid.

55 Klaus, M.H. and Kennell, J.H., *Maternal-infant bonding*, Mosby, St Louis, 1976.

56 Kennell, J.H. and Klaus, M.H., 'Bonding: recent observations that alter perinatal care', *Pediatrics in Review*, 19/1, 1998.

57 Righard, L. and Alade, M.O., 'Effect of delivery room routine on success of first breast-feed', *Lancet*, 3/336 (8723), 1990: 1105-7.

58 Odent, M., 'The early expression of the rooting reflex', paper presented to the European Conference of Neuro-Developmental Delay in Children with Specific Learning Difficulties, Chester, March 1991.

59 Biagini, G. and others, 'Postnatal maternal separation during stress hyporesponsive period enhances the adrenocortical response to novelty in adult rats by affecting regulation in the CA1 hippocampal field', *Int. J. Dev. Neurosci.*, 16/3-4, 1998: 187-97.

60 Blauvelt, H., 'Neonate-mother relationship in goat and man', in B. Schaffner (Ed.), *Group processes*, Josiah Mary Jr Foundation, New York, 1956, pp. 94-140; H.S. Liddell, ibid., p. 116.

61 Maier, R.A., 'Maternal behaviour in the domestic hen', *Laboratory Sciences*, 3/3, 1962-63: 1-12.

62 Montagu, A., *Touching: The human significance of skin*, Columbia University Press, New York, 1971.

63 Nilsson, P.M., Nyberg, P., and Östergren, P.-O., 'Increased susceptibility to stress at a psychological assessment of stress tolerance is associated with impaired fetal growth', *International Journal of Epidemiology*, 30, 2001: 75-80.

64 Toft Sørensen, H., Sabroe, S., Olsen, J., Rothman, K.J., Gillman, M.W., and Fischer, P., 'Birth weight and cognitive function in young adult life: historical cohort study', *British Medical Journal*, 315, 1997: 401-3.

65 Wiles, N.J., Peters, T.J., Leon, D.A., and Lewis, G, 'Birth weight and psychological distress at 45 – 51 years', *British Journal of Psychiatry*, 187, 2005: 21-8.

66 Kelly, Y.J., Nazroo, J.Y., McMunn, A. and others, 'Birth weight and behavioural problems in children: a modifiable effect?', *International Journal of Epidemiology*, 30, 2001: 88-94.

67 Thompson, C., Syddall, H., Rodin, I., and others, 'Birth weight and the risk of depressive disorder in late life', *British Journal of*

Psychiatry, 179, 2001: 450-5.

68 Gale, C.R. and Martyn, C.N., 'Birth weight and later risk of depression in a national birth cohort', *British Journal of Psychiatry,* 184, 2004: 28-33.

5.

Events Following Birth – Risk Factors

Chapters 3, 4, and 5 all concentrate on individual factors in early development, which the INPP Questionnaire has identified as possibly having an effect upon the course of subsequent development. In order to place these questions into context, before looking *behind* the questions covering events after birth, it is necessary to include the questionnaire itself.

The INPP Screening Questionnaire

The questionnaire was compiled to be used as an *initial* screening device to identify children and adults already suffering from specific learning difficulties, anxiety, or agoraphobia who *might* on further assessment be found to have a cluster of immature reflexes and balance, and problems connected to motor control.

Although certain factors in development carry more weight in terms of their potential impact on later development, only very rarely will a single factor be sufficient to predict later problems. The questionnaire is intended to gather information and compile a developmental *profile* of risk factors in the individual.

Over the many years that the INPP questionnaire has been in use, it has been found that if a child scores *more* than seven 'yes' answers on each *numbered* question (not including the sub-questions), it is highly probable that further investigations will reveal immaturity in the functioning of the central nervous system, which can be traced back to an earlier stage in development. In other words, it is perfectly normal to have a few 'hiccoughs' in the early years, and unless a single event was severe, it is unlikely to result in later problems. If, however, there is a cluster of factors in early development (seven or more), then the ability of the brain to compensate starts to become compromised. The higher the score, the more likely later difficulties are to emerge.

The Questionnaire
Devised by Blythe and McGlown. © 1979, 1998.
Amended Goddard Blythe 2006.

Part 1 – Neurological (Parts 2 and 3 are not included here; cover signs and symptoms of auditory processing problems, and nutritional factors).

Historical Infancy
What are the presenting symptoms?
Has a diagnosis been given at any time, i.e. Dyslexia, Dyspraxia, ADHD, ADD? If so, please state: …

Numbered Questions:

1. Is there any history of learning difficulties in either parent or their families?

2. Was your child conceived as a result of IVF?

3. When you were pregnant, did you have any medical problems? – e.g. high blood pressure, excessive vomiting, threatened miscarriage, severe viral infection, severe emotional stress; please state: …

   a) Did you smoke during pregnancy?
   b) Did you drink alcohol during pregnancy?
   c) Did you have a bad viral infection in the first 13 weeks of your pregnancy?
   d) Were you under severe emotional stress during the 25-27th weeks of your pregnancy?

4. Was your child born approximately at term, early for term, or late for term?
   Please give details: …

5. Was the birth process unusual or difficult in any way?
   If yes, please give details: …

6. When your child was born, was he/she small for term?
   Please give birth weight, if known: …

7. When he/she was born, was there anything unusual about him/her? – i.e. the skull distorted, heavy bruising, definitely blue, heavily jaundiced, covered with a calcium-type coating, or requiring intensive care.
      If yes, please give details: …

8. In the first 13 weeks of your child's life, did he/she have difficulty in sucking, feeding problems, keeping food down, or colic?

9. In the first six months of your child's life, was he/she a very still baby, so still that at times you wondered if it was a cot death?

10. Between 6 and 18 months, was your child very active and demanding, requiring minimal sleep accompanied by continual screaming?

11. When your child was old enough to sit up in the pram and stand up in the cot, did he/she develop a violent rocking motion, so violent that either the pram or cot was actually moved?

12. Did your child become a 'head-banger' i.e. bang his/her head deliberately into solid objects?

13. Was your child early (before 10 months) or late (later than 16 months) at learning to walk?

14. Did he/she go through a motor stage of:
      a)   crawling on the stomach, and
      b)   creeping on the hands and knees; or was he/she a 'bottom-hopper' or a 'roller' who one day stood up?

15. Was your child late at learning to talk? (2-3 word phrases by 2 years)

16. In the first 18 months of life, did your child experience any illness involving high temperatures and/or convulsions?
      If yes, please give details: …

17. Was there any sign of infant eczema or asthma? Yes/No
    Was there any sign of allergic responses? Yes/No

18. Was there adverse reaction to any of the childhood inoculations? Yes/No

19. Did your child have difficulty learning to dress him/herself?

20. Did your child suck his/her thumb through to 5 years or more?
      If so, which thumb? Right/Left

21. Did your child wet the bed, albeit occasionally, above the age of 5 years?

22. Does your child suffer from travel sickness?

Schooling

23. When your child went to the first formal school, i.e. infant school, in the first two years of schooling, did he/she have problems learning to read?.

24. In the first two years of formal schooling did he/she have problems learning to write? Did he/she have problems learning to do 'joined up' or cursive writing?

25. Did he/she have difficulty learning to tell the time from a traditional clock face as opposed to a digital clock?

26. Did he/she have difficulty learning to ride a two-wheeled bicycle?

27. In the first eight years of his/her life were there any illnesses involving very high temperatures, delirium, or convulsions (excluding any illness in the first 18 months of life?
     If yes, please give details: …

28. Was or is he/she an Ear, Nose, and Throat (ENT) child, i.e. suffer numerous ear infections, is a 'chesty' child or suffer from sinus problems?

29. Did/does your child have difficulty in catching a ball, i.e. eye-hand coordination problems?

30. Is your child one who cannot sit still, i.e. has 'ants-in-the-pants' and is continually being criticized by the teachers?

31. Does your child make numerous mistakes when copying from a book?

32. When your child is writing an essay or news item at school, does he/she occasionally put letters back to front or miss letters or words out?

33. If there is a sudden, unexpected noise or movement, does your child over-react?

Events after Birth – Looking *behind* the Questions. What Might the Questions Reveal?

Appearance at Birth

The medical condition of the child is assessed immediately after birth using the Apgar score, based on five parameters: heart rate, respiration, muscle tone, skin colour, and response to stimuli. Apgar scores are typically assessed at both one and five minutes after birth. A normal infant in good condition will score between 7 and 10. A score of below 7 indicates a degree of asphyxia and requires some form of resuscitation.

The need for resuscitation is significant because shortage of oxygen to the brain results in cell death and damage – the longer the period of oxygen deprivation, the greater the risk of subsequent problems.

In addition to criteria using the Apgar score, other physical observations provide information about the condition of the baby. Misshapen skull, swelling, haematoma, or bruising indicate that the baby may have had a 'rough ride' whilst being born. Stress or strain placed on the region of the neck and back of the head (atlanto-occipital region) can result in structural misalignment of the spine at the base of the skull. This can affect not only posture and muscle tone as the child grows up, but may show up earlier as a baby who is a poor sleeper, does not like being placed on either its back or its tummy, suffers from colic in the first 12 weeks of life, and, if uncorrected, may have postural-related learning problems later on.

Some research suggests that a difficult birth from a mechanical point of view can result in self-destructive behaviour later in life. Odent[1] described this as resulting from, 'an impaired capacity to love', in the cases of self-destructive behaviours such as drug and alcohol addiction, eating disorders, and the ultimate impaired capacity to love oneself – suicide. A study carried out on the female population in Sweden suggested that such behaviours were more common if there was a history of cephalhaematoma, which is more likely to develop as the result of a difficult birth, being present.[2]

The *pre*-term baby's appearance will vary greatly depending on the period of gestation before birth, and a special scoring system, the Dubowitz Score, is one method of assessing gestational age if carried out within 48 hours of delivery.

Small for dates babies may be identified from a combination of weight, length, and proportion. Some babies in this category are generally small and well proportioned – these are babies for whom brain growth during the second and third trimesters of pregnancy may have been affected; others appear long, thin, and scrawny with a disproportionally large head and little subcutaneous fat. Small for dates babies are particularly vulnerable to low blood sugar levels (hypoglycaemia) in the first few days after birth until regular feeding has become established. Hypoglycaemia at birth or in the first days after birth starves the brain of glucose and causes brain cells to die off.

Jaundice

The word 'jaundice', derived from the Old French word *jaunisse,* from *jaune* or yellow, describes the yellow discoloration of the skin and mucous membranes, which occurs when levels of a substance called bilirubin (from bile) are deposited in various tissues throughout the body.

Before birth, the foetus needs a high level of haemoglobin in order to attract sufficient oxygen across the placenta. This high level is no longer required after birth and the excess needs to be broken down and removed. The red blood cells of the newborn also have a short life span. These two factors combined result in an increased need for haemolysis (breaking down of blood corpuscles) and a higher production of bilirubin, which should be conjugated in the liver and converted to a harmless substance by bacteria in the gut. Early feeding of the baby stimulates motility in the gut and provides glucose for the manufacture of liver enzymes, which help the infant to metabolize bilirubin.

If the level of unconjugated bilirubin becomes too high and escapes into the basal ganglia of the brain, it acts as a highly toxic substance and can cause irreversible brain damage.

Most babies develop a slight degree of jaundice in the first few days of life. Mild physiological jaundice is common and is due to a temporary inability to deal with the normal metabolism of bilirubin. In full-term babies the jaundice always appears after the first 24 hours of life and reaches a peak on the fourth or fifth day. In preterm infants it usually begins within 48 hours after birth and may last up to two weeks.

Mild symptoms of jaundice are not a cause for concern provided that: it does not appear in the first 24 hours; the serum level of bilirubin does not exceed a safe limit and the highest level does not occur on the third or fourth day of life; the jaundice fades by the seventh day and the baby is otherwise well. If signs of jaundice *exceed* these limits, it becomes pathological and should be treated at the earliest possible stage to prevent damage to the basal ganglia. The most effective form of treatment is exposure of the infant to blue light, which converts bilirubin into the harmless blue pigment known as biliverdin. More serious causes of jaundice such as blood group incompatibility or hypothyroidism require special treatment.

Early Feeding

Infant feeding constitutes a dialogue between mother and child. Chapter 6 will explore early patterns of feeding and the advantages of breast-feeding in detail, but from a developmental point of view a baby's feeding provides evidence of its internal state.

The full-term baby is born equipped with a set of primitive reflexes to help it survive the first weeks and months of life before connections to higher centres in the brain have been wired up. These infantile reflexes are hard wired into the brain stem at birth and form part of the repertoire of instinctual behaviours that are characteristic of the newborn. At least two of these reflexes and related responses are instrumental in establishing early feeding.

If you stroke down one side of a newborn baby's mouth, for example, it will turn its head and open its mouth, instinctively searching or 'rooting' to find the breast or the bottle. If you touch the fold of skin above the centre of the upper lip, it will latch on to your finger with its mouth and start sucking. These two reflexes – the rooting and sucking reflexes – enable a baby to suckle within the first few hours of birth.

Nature has also provided a second 'fail-safe' mechanism by linking hand and foot movements to feeding movements in the first weeks of life. If a baby is unwilling to suckle, the sucking reflex can be stimulated by exerting gentle external pressure to the palms of the hands or soles of the infant's feet. Anyone who has ever tried to hand-rear a young kitten will recognize this response – as the young animal feeds, it also kneads with its claws. This is known as the babkin response, and links reflexive grasping and relaxing of the hands and toes to sucking movements.

Primitive reflexes emerge at different stages during pregnancy and continue to develop throughout gestation. Rooting and suck reflexes do not emerge until 24-28 weeks into a pregnancy, and babies born before 32 weeks are often born with under-developed rooting and suck reflexes. The rooting reflex is sensitive to the 'use it or lose it' law in the first hours after birth. We have already seen how, primed by the hormones of birth and if left undisturbed, the full-term infant will use a combination of the stepping, rooting, and suck reflexes to crawl up to the breast, root, and feed in the first hours after birth. This rooting instinct is particularly active shortly after delivery and appears to be reinforced by successful feeding. If feeding is delayed, and mother and baby are separated for medical reasons or due to extreme pre-maturity, the baby has to be fed by tube, the rooting reflex starts to wane, and feeding can be harder to establish at a later date.

Odent[3] noted that babies who are early or unwell when placed in an incubator can be seen 'rooting' in the first hours after birth. When their rooting attempts do not receive a reward, the rooting activity starts to decline.

The movements involved in successful suckling are also dependent on the alignment of the jaw and the palate. Skeletal misalignment resulting from a traumatic birth, torsion, or excessive use of force in the application of forceps can all result in feeding difficulties and discomfort. These babies may also find certain feeding positions uncomfortable and appear to be difficult or unwilling to feed unless a number of different positions are tried. These early difficulties with feeding in the first weeks of life can affect subsequent development of muscle tone, swallow pattern, and the resting position of the tongue in the mouth, affecting the ability to chew on solid food later on and, in some cases, translate into speech- and postural-related problems unless diagnosed and treated.

Some babies develop colic in the first 12 weeks of postnatal life. Colic is generally thought to be an attack of spasmodic pain in the abdomen arising from the presence of some indigestible matter in the lower part of the gut, which excites spasmodic contraction of the intestine. The reasons why some babies suffer from colic are not fully understood, but it is probably connected to problems in the immature infant gut being able to process food efficiently.

Most babies bring up a little of their feed towards the end of the feed. This is quite normal and is referred to as 'posseting'. 'Hungry' babies who gobble their feed, failure to 'wind' a baby regularly, or breast-fed babies of mothers who have abundant milk and for whom the 'let down' reflex releases a surge of milk are more prone to bringing up part of their feed.

Some babies vomit up a significant proportion of the feed on a regular basis. If this occurs in a bottle-fed baby without any other obvious cause being present, or develops when formula feed or cow's milk is introduced, it *might* indicate an inability to break down the proteins and fats present in cow's milk which are not present in breast milk. If a mother suspects this is the case, she should always discuss it with her health visitor or midwife before making any changes to the formula.

Regular or persistent projectile vomiting is a serious matter and advice should be sought from the doctor at an early stage. There are a number of medical conditions which cause projectile vomiting and which require treatment, but regular projectile vomiting can also result in dehydration, electrolyte imbalance, and mal-absorption syndrome, where the baby becomes depleted of vital nutrients. This can affect not only weight gain, growth, and immune functioning but also sleep patterns, activity levels, and mood disturbances, rendering the child more prone to allergies and related difficulties later on.

Empirical evidence from analysis of families where the INPP Questionnaire has been used indicates a trend whereby babies born to mothers who suffered from severe nausea and vomiting during pregnancy or who have a history of food intolerances are more likely to have feeding related problems in the first 12 months life. Allergic reactions of the skin such as infantile eczema, which are not the result of direct contact, sometimes indicate a problem in the functioning of the gut.

The problem in the baby may not be directly related to intolerance but be a secondary result of micro-nutrient deficiency during pregnancy. Foresight noticed that mothers who were zinc deficient were more prone to severe nausea and vomiting during pregnancy. Vitamin and mineral analysis frequently finds children who suffer from allergies also tend to have low zinc and essential fatty acid (EFA) status. In adults a particular type of colic can occur, known as lead or 'painter's' colic, which is directly due to the absorption of lead into the system. Although no connection has been made to infantile colic, it seems plausible that even slightly elevated levels of lead in the infant could lead to 'colicky' spasms. Vitamin and mineral analysis of children seen at INPP who have a history of feeding problems has found that a high percentage have low calcium levels and elevated levels of lead in the hair. Calcium and lead are antagonists – calcium helps to keep lead levels down; and in these cases it is not known whether the children have been exposed to polluting levels of lead which have then affected calcium, or whether low levels of calcium have enabled lead levels to build up, or whether there is a problem in the absorption of calcium arising as a result of inability to handle dairy products. Whatever the reason, where there is biochemical evidence of abnormality on analysis in the older child, it provides an indication that further specialist investigation should be recommended.

Demanding Baby

A baby has only a limited number of ways of signalling his needs to his mother. The most effective way of gaining her attention is through crying, and there is a vast range of what is 'normal' regarding the amount of crying a baby does across different cultures, with there being many reasons for a demanding baby. However, there are some babies who consistently cry more or less than others. The baby who cries excessively or the baby who rarely cries, demands attention, or engages with the people around him might provide an indication of existing and possible later problems.

Babies often cry and become restless before a feed and some will do so frequently (every 2-3 hours) in the early weeks of life. This is normal and is more common in small babies and pre-term babies who need a high milk intake to catch up their growth and weight and who take in less food at each feed. Breast-fed babies tend to want to feed more often than bottle-fed babies. It can take several weeks to establish a routine, which works for mother and baby, and babies who are fed 'by the clock' tend to cry more than babies who are fed on demand. This is all perfectly normal and should not be a cause for concern.

Babies also cry to gain physical contact and the experience of motion. Certain types of motion, particularly slow motion that mimics the rocking movements of the mother's walk, are especially soothing. In societies where infants are carried on the mother's body for the first months of life, children cry less. Observation of parenting practices amongst the San in the Kalahari, where babies stay with the mother at all times, found that San babies do not cry for long – more than 90 per cent of total crying events during the first nine months of life lasted less than 30 seconds.[4] If we could achieve a similar record for duration of crying in the West, we might have considerably happier, more energetic parents as well as more contented babies!

In the West, picking up the baby will often be sufficient to stop crying, only for the baby to start crying again as soon as he is put down. In societies where parents believe there should be 'separate' times for babies and adults, such behaviour can be very wearying, but the baby may simply be communicating its need to be held, to feel movement, and to socialize. Carrying the baby in a sling, rocking, singing, walking, or taking them for a short drive in the car can often fulfil the baby's temporary need. Non-nutritive sucking can also help to 'pacify' this demand.

Similarly, establishing a sleep routine can take several weeks and will depend on the maturity of the baby, weight, and mode of feeding as well as the baby's personality. The age at which infants sleep through the night and do not need a nightly feed varies, but it usually occurs when the infant's weight exceeds 5kg. Breast-fed babies tend to feed more often than bottle-fed babies and this can be accommodated in a number of ways, which we will explore when we look at breast-feeding in Chapter 6.

The baby who is a persistently poor sleeper, frequent waker, and/ or a baby who will not be consoled by feeding or being picked up may be trying to communicate discomfort of some kind. Babies who had a traumatic birth requiring forceps, ventouse extraction, or other complications affecting the atlanto-occipital area of spine (the uppermost portion of the spine where it enters the base of the skull) such as cord around the neck at birth, sometimes suffer from neck discomfort or headache when laid down. Practitioners of manual medicine such as Cranial Osteopaths and Chiropractors can often do much to relieve the discomfort if treated early.

Babies who have congestion of the upper respiratory tract (blocked nose, mouth breathers, and snorers) tend to suffer from more disturbed sleep. Pressure in the middle ear arising from an immature swallow pattern can result in pain, similar to the discomfort we experience when an aircraft descends too quickly. This type of middle-ear pressure does not necessarily develop into a middle-ear infection (otitis media) and therefore cannot be easily identified, but will nevertheless result in a miserable baby who does not like being put down.

Hungry, damp, and windy babies will also be unwilling to sleep. Children who are later diagnosed with Attention Deficit Hyper-activity Disorder (ADHD) often have a history of being poor sleepers and having sleep-related problems, which persist well into childhood.

Minimum Movement

Babies who exhibit little movement in cot or crib, or when they are left to play freely when awake, may be exhibiting early signs of hypotonia (poor muscle tone) or under-arousal.

Serious Illnesses

Most children suffer from a variety of minor illnesses in the first years of life. This is important in helping the developing immune system to recognize past enemies and launch a future defence. However, serious illnesses involving very high temperature and/or accompanied by febrile convulsions can in some cases result in lasting damage. Illnesses that might fall into this category include: Pertussis (whooping cough), scarlet fever, septicaemia, meningitis, encephalitis and bronchiolitis.

Commando Crawling and Creeping

There is often confusion between the terms 'crawling' and 'creeping'. Crawling precedes creeping and describes forward movement carried out with the tummy in contact with the floor (commando crawl). Creeping usually begins sometime between 7 and 9 months of age and describes movement carried out on hands and knees with the tummy off the ground. Both crawling and creeping develop in stages and not all children pass through the complete sequence of stages.

There are many children who did not crawl or creep in the first year of life and who do not go on to have later problems. However, amongst children who do have specific learning difficulties, the incidence of children who did *not* crawl and creep is higher. This may be important for two reasons.

1. Crawling and creeping act as integrating experiences in combining

the use of several systems involved in motor control: balance, proprioception, vision, and cooperative use of the two sides of the body (bilateral integration) which reflect active use of the two sides of the brain. The infant also gains a huge amount of tactile stimulation both from bearing its own weight in the prone position (when crawling) and dragging itself along the ground. These early tactile experiences assist in the internal 'mapping' of body awareness or knowing where different parts of the body are in the absence of visual cues. This is important for good coordination later on. Creeping on hands and knees may also provide early training for the hand-eye coordination at the same visual distance, which will be necessary for reading and writing some years later.

2. Some babies are so anxious to get on the move that they omit the crawling and/or creeping stages of development, preferring to be on their feet as soon as possible and walking before the end of the first year. Although they will miss out on some of the experiences described above, this is not necessarily a problem unless it occurs in combination with several other developmental factors. However, the baby who does not crawl or creep because he cannot seem to combine the movements necessary for crawling, or maintain the required position to creep on hands and knees, may already be showing that certain infant reflexes may still be active and later postural reflexes have not developed sufficiently. The significance of early reflexes will be discussed in detail in Chapter 7.

Crawling and creeping as landmarks of motor development are of interest in the context of the child's developmental history as a whole.

Age at Learning to Walk

Walking represents an important landmark in motor development because it signifies the successful acquisition of a series of infant voluntary movements, inhibition of infant reflexes, control of balance, and development of sufficient muscle tone to bear weight. Despite parents' desire to see their infant walking as soon as possible, gadgets and activities designed to encourage precocious walking are not necessarily in the child's interest if it means the child does not have the experience of crawling and/or creeping first. On the other hand, a child who is late at learning to walk (16 months or later) may be exhibiting early signs of delay in motor development.

Age at Learning to Talk

Children's language develops through a series of identifiable stages. Language in its broadest term describes the ability to communicate. Speech is not the only way in which humans communicate with one another but the ability to communicate with speech is unique to the human race. Children go through many phases of pre-speech in the first year of life, but the emergence of recognizable words used in a meaningful sequence is a milestone in a child's development.

The development of language will be explored further in Chapter 8, but for purposes of identifying possible early signs of developmental delay, children's spoken vocabulary starts to develop at about 12 months of age (at much the same time as the young child learns to stand on its own two feet). At this stage children can usually understand much more than they can actually say. This is described as receptive or passive language, which is more advanced than expressive or active language. Early babbling gives way to single-word utterances, usually beginning with 'naming' words and accompanied by gestures such as pointing or waving.

By 18 months, one or two words are often used to convey a more complex meaning such as 'cup' or 'drink', meaning 'I want a drink' or baby words such as 'cud' to say 'I want the cuddly or blanket that I take to bed with me'. Intonation is often used to compensate for lack of vocabulary.

At 21 months most children will start to string two or even three words together in short phrases such as 'Daddy home', 'socks off', 'want drink'. They may also start to use single-word questions such as 'where?' or 'when?'.

Development of speech depends on many factors: normal brain functioning; adequate hearing; fine motor control of the lips, tongue and swallow mechanism combined with breathing; exposure to the sounds of language on a daily basis; and receiving response for their own attempts at vocalization. The development of speech can therefore be delayed for a number of reasons.

If a child has not started to put 2-3 word phrases together by the end of the second year (24 months), it may be an indication of an existing problem with either hearing, motor skills, a more generalized language problem, or lack of environmental linguistic stimulation.

Persistent Rocking and/or Head Banging

Babies who develop a persistent rocking habit sometimes do so due to a lack of stimulation to the balance mechanism (vestibular system) or hypo-active vestibular functioning. Most babies love being rocked. The motion of gentle rocking, particularly from side to side, tends to be soothing, probably because it feels similar to the walking movements of the mother during pregnancy. More rapid rocking is arousing, and increases the infant's state of excitation. Self-rocking usually starts around age six months and disappears by age two. Many children rock for 15 minutes or less while listening to music, when falling asleep, or when learning a new postural or motor skill*. On the other hand, children who develop a violent or persistent rocking habit may be unconsciously trying to provide additional stimulation and/or increase their state of arousal.

A different kind of rocking has been observed amongst children abandoned in state orphanages in countries where they receive little contact or sensory stimulation other than basic feeding and changing. In the absence of neurological factors, some of these children develop a rhythmic rocking habit, often erroneously assumed to be an early sign of mental retardation. Confined in cots for most of the day, these children are probably providing themselves with sensory stimulation in the only way they can, by simulating the movements of being carried by another human being and providing stimulation to the vestibular system. Various studies[5] have shown that vestibular stimulation in the early years increases brain growth.

Adults will also develop a rocking habit under situations of extreme distress or during periods of mental illness. In this context, rhythmic rocking is sometimes referred to as 'institutionalized' rocking, because it emerges in situations of despair or confinement when there is over- or under-stimulation. It would therefore appear that rocking has a 'neutralising' function, helping to increase or decrease arousal

---

* The latter represents a normal stage of preparation in developing a new motor skill. For example, many infants rock rhythmically in the prone position just before they learn to crawl on the tummy, or from hands and knees prior to learning to creep on hands and knees.

and sensory awareness depending on the speed, direction, and plane of movement in which the rocking motion takes place.

Persistent or violent rocking amongst babies and young children, in the absence of easily explained factors, might suggest a problem with vestibular functioning, and it is more prevalent amongst children who are later diagnosed as being on the autistic spectrum.

Head-banging is sometimes seen amongst children who are more generally hypo-sensitive to sensory stimuli, and can be an attempt at self-stimulation.

Thumb-sucking up to and beyond the Age of 5 Years

For many parents, when a baby finds its thumb it is a source of parental relief, enabling the baby to comfort itself between feeds. Many children continue to suck a thumb or fingers beyond the first two years of life, and non-nutritive sucking, whether it is on a dummy or the thumb, is developmentally normal.

Some children continue to suck their thumb or fingers into later childhood (beyond 5 years of age). Apart from simply having established a habit, which is pleasurable and comforting, some children are unable to break the habit because the action of sucking is providing an additional 'feel-good' factor. According to Cranial Osteopaths, this can be true for children who had a difficult birth, which has resulted in a degree of intra-cranial discomfort. By exerting pressure with the thumb on the roof of the mouth using a cantilever action, the pressure and sucking movements help to relieve cranial discomfort. The child is treating itself!

Bedwetting above the Age of 5

Bedwetting or nocturnal enuresis occurs in about 30 per cent of children above the age of 4, decreasing to 10 per cent by 6 years, 3 per cent at 12, and only 1 per cent of the population at 18 years of age.[6] In about 1-2 per cent of cases there is a medical reason such as:
- Urinary tract infection
- Sacral nerve disorder
- Diabetes insipidus or mellitus
- Pelvic mass
- Psychological/emotional reasons
- Middle ear problems

- (Fatty acid deficiency)

The link between middle-ear infections (Otitis Media) and bedwetting amongst children is often overlooked. Otitis Media is common in young children and can occur as a secondary product of infection, resulting from inflammation of naso-pharyngeal cavities (nose and soft palate), allergy, unusually small ear canals or enlarged adenoids. Normally the middle ear is ventilated at least 3-4 times a minute by swallowing, which maintains a normal state of pressure in the Eustachian tube (the tube between the nose and the ear). If a child has an immature swallow pattern (possibly as a result of retained rooting or infant suck reflexes), small particles of food or liquid can enter the naso-pharyngeal cavity, increasing the susceptibility to infection.

Children who suffer from frequent ear and sinus infections, enlarged adenoids, and/or who snore are more likely to wet the bed. One theory is that breathing problems create a physical pressure in the abdomen that stimulates urination. Another is that the breathing problems can lead to low blood-oxygen concentrations, which can then affect the levels of hormones involved in urine production.

Researchers at Larissa University Hospital in Greece found that among children aged between 5 and 14 who were habitual snorers, 7 per cent wet the bed compared with 2 per cent who did not snore.[7] However, snoring was *not* a feature of *all* children who wet the bed, being present in only one quarter of the sample who were bedwetters.

The reason for the connection between ear and nasal congestion and bedwetting is believed to be partly due to the effect on breathing. Past studies have shown that when children have adenoids or tonsils removed, their bedwetting stops. Dr Derek Mahoney,[8] an orthodontist at the Prince of Wales Hospital in Sydney, Australia, said 8 out of 10 children referred to him for bedwetting problems have a narrow palate. If the roof of the mouth is particularly narrow, the tongue is pushed back and can partially block the airway during sleep. Children can be given a device, similar to a brace, to widen the palate.

Dr Dudley Weider[9] of the Dartmouth-Hitchcock Medical Center in Hanover, New Hampshire followed over 300 children with bedwetting problems who had surgery for airway obstruction. Bedwetting stopped in 25 per cent soon after the surgery, and 50 per cent stopped within six months.

In a case series report by Weider and others, 115 children between the ages of 3 and 19 with symptoms of upper airway obstruction, who were night-time mouth 'breathers' and bedwetters, were evaluated. Prior to surgery, children in the study had 5.6 enuretic nights each week. All children in the study underwent surgery to relieve upper airway obstruction; 111/115 had tonsillectomy/adenoidectomy. The children were followed for 12 months after surgery. After one month, there was a 66 per cent reduction in the number of bedwetting episodes each week; at six months, there was a 77 per cent reduction and this figure remained constant through the 12-month follow-up period. Some 12 children with secondary enuresis (onset of bedwetting coincided with the development of upper airway obstruction) had all stopped bedwetting at six months, and progress was maintained at 12 months.

Biologically, an association between airway obstruction and nocturnal enuresis could exist for several reasons. Obstructive sleep apnoea interrupts sleep and may limit normal arousal and self-alerting mechanisms. Hormonal change (obstructive sleep apnoea and lower levels of ADH) and increased intra-abdominal pressure have been suggested as possible factors.

There can also be developmental and neurological reasons for continued bedwetting. One of the baby reflexes is associated with urination in the neonate. If this reflex remains active in the older child, it can be elicited by touch or pressure to the small of the back. Children who still have a Spinal Galant reflex sometimes activate the reflex while wriggling and turning in their sleep. In a state of altered consciousness they do not have sufficient control to override the stimulus and end up wetting the bed.

Young children also go through sleep phases in a different sequence and rhythm to adults. Normal sleep consists of two types of sleep: rapid eye movement (REM) and non-REM (NREM) sleep. NREM comprises four EEG (brain wave patterns) stages associated with increasingly deeper stages of sleep and reduced arousal.

Newborn babies spend more time in REM sleep. Sleep disorders including recurrent night terrors, sleep-walking, and some cases of nocturnal enuresis are thought to be connected to differences in the way that the immature brain makes the transition from one sleep phase to another. In the waking state, brain-wave variants affect attention and short-term memory.

The newborn baby and the immature brain spend more time in REM sleep, and the transition from REM to NREM sleep is less well defined.

Mature patterns of sleep begin to develop over the first 2-3 years of postnatal life. Nightmares are particularly common from 3 to 4 years following scary stories, television, or computer games because this age group does not easily differentiate between fantasy and reality. Over-excitement, fear, stress, and changing routine are all factors that can affect sleep cycles in young children at various times, and are quite normal if linked to specific events. However, recurring sleep disorders such as regular night terrors, sleep walking, and bedwetting can occur when normal sleep cycles become disturbed or brainwave activity is immature in the older child.

Allergies – Eczema or Asthma

An allergic reaction occurs when the immune system identifies a normally harmless substance as a potential threat and reacts by producing antibodies. When an allergen (an irritant which stimulates the immune system to react) comes into contact with its antibody, it leads to the release of substances such as histamine, which are responsible for the allergic reaction such as asthma, hay fever, eczema, or dermatitis.

In inhaled allergic reactions such as asthma and hay fever, the individual produces large amounts of reagin antibodies, which stick to mast cells in the mucosa so that when the antigen is inhaled, histamine is released from the mast cell. There is a vast number of potential inhaled allergens from pollen to dust mites, feathers to pesticides, and in some children asthma only occurs when they have an infection or when they take vigorous exercise. Children who suffer from allergies also seem to be more prone to infection.

Allergies are caused by a combination of genes and environment, and may well be a throw-back to a time when we lived in closer proximity to creatures or substances that posed a real threat to life. Generations later, the immune system continues to react to relatively innocuous substances as if the danger is real.

Allergic reactions affecting the skin can either occur as a result of direct contact, for example washing powder, or can be symptomatic of problems in the gut. Inability of the gut to handle specific substances can result in damage to the hair cells (villi), which line the gut, helping to move food down through the system. Damage to the lining of the gut wall can result in 'leaky' gut when substances that should normally pass down the gut leak into the blood stream, acting as toxins and stimulating the immune system to react. Problems with the gut can develop for a variety of reasons from enzyme deficiency, inability to break down certain proteins (such as gluten or casseine), and absence of 'friendly' bacteria in the gut, to name but a few. Babies who are breast-fed are less likely to develop allergies even when there is a strong allergic tendency within the family.

Children who have a history of skin reactions, which cannot be explained by direct contact, sometimes have low levels of zinc, essential fatty acids, and other trace elements. Vitamin and mineral analysis can help to identify whether this is one source of the problem, and appropriate supplementation can often help to reduce the incidence of inflammatory reactions. Analysis and supplementation should only be carried out under professional supervision but can be a useful avenue of investigation for children who suffer the misery of dry, inflamed, and infuriatingly itchy skin.

Fitzgibbon[10] and others who specialize in the area of nutritional medicine also refer to the effect of biochemical problems on mood, energy, and behaviour. Over-production of histamine also results in the release of opiate-like substances into the blood stream, which have an effect on mental processes as well as producing physical symptoms. The effect of this potent cocktail on the child can be similar to an adult who is under the influence of alcohol or recreational substances, and may go some way to explaining why many children suffering from allergies are tired and 'below par' much of the time, in addition to sleep being affected by itching skin, snuffles, or wheezing. Poor sleep can also affect growth because growth hormone is secreted during sleep.

Michael Gershon[11] in his book *The Second Brain* describes the intimate relationship between the brain and the bowel as being one of an 'enteric nervous system'. He writes:

There is a brain in the bowel. The ugly gut is more intellectual than the heart and may have a greater capacity for feeling. It is the only organ that contains an intrinsic nervous system that is able to mediate reflexes in the complete absence of input from the brain and spinal cord. Evolution has played a trick. When our predecessors emerged from the primeval ooze and acquired a backbone, they also developed a brain in the head and a gut with a mind of its own.

He goes on to explain:

The enteric nervous system is also a vast chemical warehouse within which is represented every one of the classes of neurotransmitter found in the brain. Neurotransmitters are the words nerve cells use for communicating with one another and with the cells under their control... Nerves talk with a chemical language.

In other words, when we speak of 'gut instinct' we are referring to the other brain that does not reason, but which feels, reacts, and sets in motion a chemical reaction, which affects many other parts of the brain and the body. It may be one more reason why stress in both children and adults exacerbates existing allergic reactions. Not all allergies can be attributed to 'gut instinct', but some can and may directly relate to nutritional factors within the family, prenatal nutrition as well as feeding practices after birth.

This is just another reminder that what happens to parents matters, particularly mothers prior to, during, and after pregnancy. What we see as problems in our children today may be the product of the third or even fourth generation before us. The effects of a familial tendency to allergic conditions can often be minimized by ensuring that the mother is in the best possible health prior to pregnancy, has good nutrition throughout pregnancy, and, if possible, breast-feeds her baby for the first 3-6 months of life. The importance of pre-conceptual as well as prenatal care in our modern technological world cannot be over-emphasized.

Adverse Reaction to Vaccination

The childhood vaccination programme has virtually eliminated some of the past's most feared diseases of childhood. As we have lost first-hand experience of those diseases it is easy to become complacent about the very real risks they pose if vaccination is not maintained. In the United Kingdom all children start their immunization programme at two months of age:

Childhood immunization schedule (September 2006)

Age	Vaccine	Method of Administration
2 months	Diphtheria, tetanus, pertussis (whooping cough), polio, hameophilus influenzae type b (Hib) **(DTaP/IPV/hib)**	One injection
3 months	Pneumococcal **(PCV)**	One injection
4 months	DTaP/IPV/hib PCV Meningitis C **(MenC)**	Onc injection One injection One injection
Around 12 months	Hib/MenC	One injection
Around 13 months	Measles, mumps, and rubella **(MMR)** PCV	One injection One injection
3 years, 4 mths to 5 years	DTaP/IPV MMR	One injection One injection
13-18 years old	Tetanus, diphtheria and polio (Td/IPV)	One injection

The majority of children receive their vaccinations with little or no side-effects. In very rare cases a child may become ill following one of their vaccinations, exhibit marked change in behaviour, and/or regress developmentally. Further research is needed to identify common factors within the family and the developmental histories of the small number of children who are adversely affected by vaccination, to see if it is possible to identify susceptible children and avoid vaccine damage in the future.

Later Childhood – Developmental Indicators

Learning to Dress

Learning to dress oneself is quite a complex task, requiring both gross and fine motor skills including balance, the ability to use one limb independently of the other, a sense of direction, and in the case of items such as shoes and socks, the ability to see the difference between left and right. Added to this are fine motor skills of handling fasteners such as buttons, and eventually learning to tie shoe laces and a school tie.

Children learn to dress themselves in different stages, and may initially start with easier items such as pulling on a tee-shirt while sitting down: to do this while standing up requires balance and upper body control; and for very young children, the upper body is still involved in the basic task of maintaining upright balance. You can see this process in reverse when balance starts to deteriorate in the elderly, and they revert to sitting or using one hand to support themselves when getting dressed or undressed. Putting on a pair of trousers while standing up involves balancing on one leg, a skill which improves slowly over time. Mastery of each one of these small skills heralds a new stage in control of the body in space.

Putting clothes on the right way round depends on directional awareness – another spatial skill – and the tying of shoe laces requires the two sides of the body to be able to carry out separate manipulations, cross over, and reverse the final manoeuvre; in terms of brain functioning, this is a highly complex task involving bilateral integration, sequencing, and reversal. Tying of shoe laces becomes possible from about 7 years of age (assuming the child has had instruction and practice).

Travel Sickness

Motion sickness does not usually occur until the second year of life after the child has learned to stand and walk. Many theories have been suggested as to the cause of motion sickness, but it is generally accepted that it occurs when there is a discrepancy in the timing and synchronicity of messages passing from different sensors involved in the perception of motion to the brain.

Three primary systems are involved in the perception of motion:

the balance mechanism in the inner ear (vestibular system); feedback from the body via the muscles, tendons and joints (proprioception); and vision. Messages sent to the brain by these different systems inform the brain about the plane, direction, and degree of motion. Integration and coordination of information being sent to the brain from these systems is partly carried out by a part of the brain called the cerebellum or 'little brain'.

The cerebellum's role in the control of movements is rather like the job of mission control in Houston when an American spacecraft is launched into space. When a spacecraft has been launched, once it is airborne and before it enters orbit, control is taken over by the NASA headquarters in Houston, Texas. The cerebellum's function in the control and synthesis of centres involved in the perception of motion is similar to the job carried out by mission control in Houston: it sub-serves higher centres in the brain involved in coordinating and synchronizing the timing of messages being sent from different motion receptors to the brain.

If for any reason there is a mismatch in the timing of information being sent to the brain by the different motion receptors, we start to experience the unpleasant sensations of motion sickness – dizziness, disorientation, cold sweats, nausea, and eventually vomiting. Interestingly, these same physical sensations can also be produced by abnormal or inappropriate stimulation of the balance mechanism, implicating the vestibular system and its relationship with other motion sensors in the experience of motion sickness.

There can be many reasons for lack of integration in the functioning of these systems in response to motion, which can stem from specific receptors such as poor vision. People can be sensitive to movement in one plane of gravity only, being excellent travellers on land but as sick as a cat when they step on to a boat. This is because travel on water (and to a lesser degree by air) markedly increases stimulation of tilting motion. Many children experience mild degrees of motion sickness at some stage in middle childhood. It often settles down after periods of myelination, such as between 6½ and 8 years of age, and again around the time of puberty.

Dr Lawrence Beuret, who has specialized in the assessment and treatment of adolescents and young adults with neuro-developmental problems, has observed that a history of motion sickness that persists beyond puberty is often a reliable indicator of immature postural mechanisms as a causal factor in problems with higher-order learning processes and anxiety.

Schooling

Learning to Read

There is a big variation in the age at which children learn to read. Some children are able to make sense of words before their fifth birthday, while others may be approaching age 7 before reading really seems to click. The British national curriculum insists that all children are taught to read at the same age, and much of subsequent teaching and educational assessment is built upon the premise that chronological age is consistent with reading level. This policy condemns some children to under-achievement from the moment they enter the school room.

Rudolf Steiner, Maria Montessori, Louise Bates Ames, and other experts in child development and education have all recognized that chronological age is not the only deciding factor in reading readiness. Neurological and physiological development are of equal importance, and a number of people have suggested that true readiness for reading coincides with the timing of the shedding of the first milk teeth, which usually occurs at about 6 years of age.

Delay in motor development affects far more than coordination for catching a ball. Motor skills extend from control of posture and balance through to the eye control needed to maintain focus on one part of a page, for the eyes to follow along a line of print without jumping ahead, to the line below or the line above, and the ability to adjust focusing distance at speed. The visual system depends on postural mechanisms and motor skills to support the visual skills needed for reading. Children who are immature in control of their bodies frequently have not developed the visual skills necessary for reading. 'Children learn with their bodies before they learn with their heads',[12] and postural control is one prerequisite to reading readiness and writing success. Children learn postural control through a combination of neurological maturation *entrained* through physical interaction with the environment.

Reading is also connected to hearing. The English language in particular demands a combination of visual recognition and phonological decoding for fluent reading and comprehension. Unless a child can *hear* the difference between 'b' and 'd', 'm' and 'n', why should he understand that symbols that are the same shape have to face in the right direction to write 'bad' rather than 'dab', 'god', or 'dog'?

You will remember that a cognitive sense of direction is linked to secure knowledge of where our own body is in space. Children with poor balance and body control also often have poorly developed cognitive directional skills. The 'b' or 'd' dilemma can arise from directional and/or hearing discrimination problems.

In addition to intelligence, learning to read is therefore closely linked to developmental readiness in terms of physical abilities. If a child is still struggling to learn to read by the age of 7, physical factors should always be investigated.

Learning to Write

All of the developmental factors listed under reading also apply to writing: posture, balance, fine motor skills, visual functioning, and hearing. However, writing adds another component to reading – the need to use the hands and eyes together. Some children can compensate for immature eye movements as long as they only have to concentrate on controlling their eyes for reading. When they also have to use their hand, they cannot overcome the dual hand and eye coordination problem (visual-motor integration). We will return to some of the possible mechanisms involved when we examine reflex development in Chapter 7.

Learning to Tell the Time (Analogue Clock)

Most children learn to tell the time using an analogue as opposed to a digital clock at some time between their seventh and ninth birthdays. Using a clock to tell the time is a spatial skill – a child needs to be able to see the difference between up and down, left and right, before and after, big and little, as well as to recognize the numbers on the clock face. Spatial skills, like directional skills, are supported by secure knowledge of one's own position in space (postural control). Children who have immature balance and posture are often delayed in learning to tell the time.

Learning to Ride a Bicycle

Children usually master riding a bicycle without stabilizers, some time between their sixth and eighth birthdays. Riding a bicycle combines a number of physical skills. A child must find his/her centre of balance and be able to control it over a narrow base of support. He must be able to keep his upper body in one position, whilst getting his two legs to move from opposing positions. He must also be able to turn his arms in either direction without losing his balance, and look at where he is going. In the early stages of learning, balance is usually better once the child starts to move, but wobble sets in when he stops, sets off, or slows down. This is because speed helps to compensate for insecure balance, and children will often use speed at the expense of accuracy in other situations such as sports or when writing, to compensate or cover up poor control of static balance.

Children who find it impossible to learn to ride a bicycle or are extremely late (assuming they have had sufficient practice) may have immature balance, postural control, and motor skills, including difficulty in getting the two sides of the body to carry out separate tasks (bilateral integration).

Ear, Nose, and Throat Infections (ENT)

Most children will suffer from colds, coughs, and the occasional chest or ear infection in the first seven years of life. Minor illnesses are probably quite important in exposing the immune system to a range of germs, and in building up resistance so that when we meet the same or similar enemies later in life, the immune system can launch an effective defence.

This was made very clear to me when I was expecting my second child and both my husband and I succumbed to the worst bout of 'flu either of us had ever had. Both of us needed more than a week in bed and antibiotics for secondary infections, and it took several weeks to recover fully. My father, then in his later 60s, came to stay to help look after our first child while we struggled to get back on our feet. Neither he, nor my 18-month-old son, caught 'flu from us, and our doctor at the time said that this particularly virulent strain of 'flu had only hit the 20-30 year old age group, probably because we had not been exposed to a similar strain at any time in our lives.

My first son was probably protected having been breast-fed for the first nine months of life, my father because he had met the virus before. I was eight weeks into my second pregnancy at the time and my second son may well have paid the price in terms of mild to moderate hearing problems from birth – eight weeks is the time when the ears start to be formed.

Frequent ear, nose, and throat infections can have an effect not only on hearing at the time, but also on the child's auditory processing later on.

Otitis Media or infection of the middle ear usually occurs as a result of infection spreading up into the Eustachian tubes from the nose, throat, or one of the sinuses. In other words, it usually develops as a secondary consequence of a cold, enlarged tonsils (which are the first line of defence for germs entering the upper respiratory tract), sinusitis, or enlarged and infected adenoids. Ear infections are usually accompanied by throbbing or acute pain, deafness, and tinnitus, which either occurs during the acute phase of the infection or during the recovery phase. Treatment is usually with antibiotics, but persistent and recurring infections may require more radical treatment such as minor surgery to perforate the ear drum, relieve pressure, and drain fluid, insertion of grommets to improve ventilation of the middle ear and prevent future build-up of fluid, or in cases where infected, inflamed, or enlarged adenoids are thought to be contributing, adenoid and/or tonsillectomy.

Whilst treatment with antibiotics or surgery may solve the problem in the short term, the longer-term effects of repeated ear, nose, or throat infections can be more widespread. Hearing can be impaired for up to eight weeks after the acute period of infection has cleared up. In the first three years of life, children learn to 'tune in' to the sounds that are specific to their mother tongue – this is one of the 'sensitive periods' or developmental windows for learning and practising the sounds of speech. Frequent or prolonged periods of intermittent deafness resulting from congestion or infection can have an effect on the child's ability to discriminate between similar but different sounds later on. When tested on a standard hearing test, hearing levels are within the normal range, but the brain's ability to hear the fine-tuning differences can be impaired, particularly to sounds in the higher frequencies such as 's' and 'f', 'sh', and 'ch'.

It is also during the early years that children learn to orientate to sound (localization), 'switch off' from unwanted sounds, and focus attention on specific sounds. Paradoxically, some children who have had frequent ear, nose, and throat infections in the early years appear to be *hyper*-sensitive to certain sounds at an older age, presumably because they could not hear them during periods of infection or post-infection and did not develop a mechanism to shut them out or dampen them down at the time. Both hearing impairment and hyper-sensitivity (hyper-acuisis) can cause problems with effective listening, attention, and potentially speech and language later on. French ear, nose and throat surgeon Guy Berard said that, 'hearing equals behaviour'.[13]

The link between hearing and behaviour is illustrated in one case study.

The Case of Child C

C was born seven days late following artificial rupture of the membranes to stimulate the onset of labour. His mother had stopped gaining weight after the 27th week of pregnancy and there was concern that the baby had stopped growing after 36 weeks. He was born naturally after a seven-hour labour with a difficult second stage. There was slight bruising to the top of his head for the first few days and he was only 5½ lbs at birth. Apgar score was normal and breast-feeding was established within 2-3 days.

Due to his small size, C needed to be fed every 2-3 hours, day and night. He continued to gain weight but was a poor sleeper, and needed 1-2 nightly feeds for the first 12 weeks. His mother became tired and started to supplement with formula feed at three months of age. At three months, C had his first ear infection and course of antibiotics. He continued to suffer from frequent colds and ear infections every 2-3 months. When solid food was introduced at five months, he initially did well, but as the months went by he would not chew on any food that had not been puréed. As he entered his second year, he became a fussy eater, pouching food in one corner of his mouth, spitting it out, and only eating a bland and limited range of foods that were smooth in texture.

By two years of age, he had still not slept through the night, was a fussy eater, a persistent dribbler, and had a cough at night which never cleared up. He became a clingy child prone to bouts of inconsolable crying, and showed no signs of being potty trained. His parents sought help from their health visitor, and eventually a family therapist who specialized in children's problems, as they started to believe his behaviour must be the result of inadequacies in their parenting.

Shortly before his third birthday at the request of his mother, he was referred to an ear, nose, and throat surgeon. One look in his ears and throat and the surgeon recommended removal of adenoids and insertion of grommets. The operation was carried out on C's third birthday.

C slept through the night for the first time (his mother thought this must be the result of the anaesthetic). The next morning he got out of bed, sat on the pot, and ate a full cooked breakfast. From that moment he ate anything that was put in front of him without complaint. The dribbling stopped, his sleeping improved, and for the first time since he was a small baby he started to become a happy child. The family therapist was no longer required!

Prior to the operation, his speech had been immature. Behaviour will often regress when children (or adults as well) do not have the language with which to express their needs adequately, and they will revert to crying, whining, or manipulation. We have already discussed the inter-relationship between ear infections and bedwetting. C's spontaneous willingness to be potty trained immediately after the operation suggests that in his case, congestion and apnoea were affecting bladder control. Improvements in his sleeping and eating were probably also connected to being able to breathe, chew, and swallow more easily (hence the cessation of dribbling) and improved sense of taste through the nose.

His mother also remarked on how he was terrified the first time the lavatory was flushed when he came home after his operation. He had apparently not been able to hear it before, and could not understand where the noise was coming from. Thereafter for several weeks he developed a habit of repeatedly flushing the lavatory until the novelty wore off.

In addition to the immediate effects of pain, discomfort, and reduced hearing, repeated ear infections cause scarring to the ear drum, and some of the antibiotics used to treat ear infections can cause damage to the hair cells of the cochlea (the organ of hearing) if used repeatedly over a long period of time. Once damaged, these hair cells, each one responsible for detecting minute differences in pitch (frequency), do not re-grow.

As this case study indicates, hearing problems do not always reveal themselves as a straightforward ear infection. They can manifest themselves in sleep disturbances, feeding problems, and emotional behaviour as well as having an impact on speech, language, literacy, and functional listening, if they are not identified and treated at an early stage.

Catching a Ball

To many fathers, particularly sporty types, kicking and catching a ball is as natural as sleeping, breathing, and eating, and also seems to carry connotations of masculinity. When sons are unable to catch a ball or kick it in the right direction, fathers often think that more must be better and become very frustrated at their son's inability to carry out the most 'simple' of physical activities despite continued practice, demonstration, and instructions to 'keep your eye on the ball'.

To catch a ball, the eyes need to be able to track a moving object coming toward them at speed from one distance to another. This involves the visual skills of convergence, divergence, and accommodation. When we focus on an object at near distance, our eyes must converge on the object – this 'fuses' the two single objects seen by each eye into one, so that the brain can see one, clear, single image. If we then want to focus at far distance, our eyes have to break out of convergence (diverge) to take in a wider visual field, before converging again at the new focal distance. The ability of the eyes to converge/diverge/converge at speed is called accommodation, and is necessary to adjust visual focusing at speed. We need this for many activities – when driving, copying from a blackboard or a book, or tracking a fast-moving object coming toward us. Children who have poorly developed convergence cannot visually track an object at speed. By the time they have re-adjusted their focus as the ball comes toward them, it is too late to bring their hands together to catch it – they either miss it, drop it, or let it fly past them altogether. Some get such a fright when they manage to 'place' the ball at the final second before it hits them that instead of bringing their hands together to catch it they use their hands in a defensive action, repelling the ball and appearing to be a complete wimp. No amount of practice seems to help.

For slightly different reasons, kicking a ball can be a problem. Kicking requires that one can stand on one leg and swing with the other one without falling over. Remarkably simple, one might think; but only if a child has developed good control of static balance and independent use of either side of the body. As with all the other questions above, difficulty catching or kicking a ball might provide one indication that control of eye movements and balance are not commensurate with chronological age, and more advanced skills will be difficult to master because the foundation skills at a physical level are not in place.

Difficulty Sitting Still (Ants in the Pants)

The most advanced level of movement is the ability to stay totally still.[14] Stillness requires good control of balance, posture, and freedom from the need to use movement or other parts of the body to support posture. The soldier who stands motionless on guard in front of Buckingham Palace is demonstrating that all his months of training have achieved this ability – controlled centre of balance and the inhibition of extraneous movement. Children who cannot sit still may be fidgety for a variety of reasons: boredom, difficulty maintaining attention, distractibility, or immature balance and postural control.

The latter can make sitting still for any length of time almost impossible because they need to move in order to maintain control over their bodies. No amount of admonishment to 'sit still' or punishments to improve behaviour in the future seem to have an effect, because these children need movement in order to function. A psychologist reminded me recently that a number of years ago, such children were given a three-legged stool with legs of uneven length to sit on, meaning that they had to use continuous movement in order to remain sitting. With constant exercise, truncal stability started to improve and attention was markedly better. There are, however, less noisy and distracting ways of helping to improve children's sitting balance!

Mistakes when Copying

The most common causes of mistakes when copying are lack of attention or immature eye movements. As discussed in the sections above, both tracking and accommodation are necessary to adjust focusing and maintain visual attention on the correct place.

Letter and Word Reversals and/or Omissions

Many children reverse letters and numbers in the early stages of learning to write, and it seems to be more prevalent amongst left-handed children, probably because the direction of Western script (right to left) favours the right-handed child from a purely mechanical point of view. As children become more fluent at both the recognition and forming of letters, reversals and omissions decrease, so that direction and sequence of letters should be stable by about 8 years of age. If letter, number or word reversals, omissions, or mirror writing persist beyond 8 years of age, they are usually a sign of a dyslexic-type specific learning difficulty, and further assessment by an Educational Psychologist should be sought.

Although reversals and omissions can point to a specific learning difficulty at an earlier age, there is a neurological reason why they are not considered a definitive sign before 8 years of age. The nervous system of the child goes through periods of increased myelination at key stages in development: the first year of life, years 1-3, 6½-8 years, puberty, and again in the early to mid-20s. At the same time that myelination is taking place, the brain also goes through a period of neural 'spring cleaning' when redundant pathways and cells are allowed to die off while connections between others are strengthened. This pruning or clearing of neural clutter is similar to the neuro-logical equivalent of tidying your bedroom – the less you have, the easier it is to find what you need.

If children are still showing signs of difficulty above 8 years of age, it may suggest a number of unresolved problems which require further investigation:

1. *Directionality* – this is a spatial skill partly dependent on the efficient functioning of the vestibular-cerebellar loop and its related pathways.

2. *Immaturity* in the development of eye movements necessary for reading and writing. This can be the result of a specific oculo-motor problem, but is often connected to existing problems with balance and coordination, because balance provides the platform on which stability of eye movements depends.

3. *Phonological processing problems.* The child may have difficulty with auditory *discrimination* (hearing the difference between similar letter sounds), *speed of auditory processing,* which is a factor in being able to hear individual sounds within a word, particularly vowel sounds. Timing is also important because the difference between the brain hearing a sound as 'd' or as 't' is a difference of just 40-60 milliseconds in the timing of the first and second onset of sound. Children can also have problems with *locating* sounds (orientation), filtering out background noise and hyper-acuisis (hypersensitivity). Any one or combination of these can cause difficulty in the accurate decoding of auditory information or the translation of sounds into the correct visual symbol.

We will return to what can be done to try to prevent these problems occurring in later chapters.

Scoring the INPP Questionnaire

Although there are many sub-questions under each numbered question, when using the INPP Questionnaire as a screening instrument, a score of 0 or 1 is given to each numbered question (even if there have been several risk factors within a single question).

> 0 = No Abnormality Detected (NAD)
> 1 = Developmental Indicator Present

In other words, even if the birth process (question 3) was long and difficult, there was foetal distress *and* there was use of forceps or emergency caesarean section, the question about birth will only gain a score of 1.

The number of positive answers is then added up. If a child scores a minimum of 7 or more, it suggests that further investigation for neuro-developmental factors is indicated. The questionnaire should *not* be used in isolation as a diagnostic device. It should only be used as an initial screening device to ascertain whether further investigations or referral should be carried out.

In 1997 a study was carried out to review the validity of the INPP Screening Questionniare in identifying school-aged children for whom developmental factors were contributing to specific learning difficulties. The study compared the early developmental profiles of 70 children aged 8-10 years who had developed problems with reading, writing, and/or copying with 70 children of the same age who had no problems with reading, writing, or copying, using the INPP Screening Questionnaire. The study found that there were clear differences in the developmental history of the two groups.[15]

In a Nutshell…

- Developmental milestones in the first seven years of life can provide indications of 'missed' stages of sensory-motor development, which support higher cognitive functions.

- The INPP Screening Questionnaire can be used as an initial screening device to identify underlying physical factors in presenting symptoms.

- What can each stage of development tell us?

- Research supports the use of developmental markers as 'keys' to identifying 'readiness' for learning and resolving underlying physical factors in specific learning difficulties.

Endnotes

1 Odent, M., *The scientification of love,* Free Association Books, London, 2001.

2 Cited in Odent, M., T*he farmer and the obstetrician,* Free Association Books, London, 2001.

3 Odent, M., 'The early expression of the rooting reflex', paper presented at the European Conference of Neuro-developmental Delay in Children with Specific Learning Difficulties, Chester, March 1991.

4 Barr, R.G. and Elias, M.F., 'Nursing interval and maternal responsiveness: effect on early infant crying', *Pediatrics,* 81, 1988: 529-36.

5 Cited in Eliot, L., *What's going on in there? How the brain and mind develop in the first five years of life,* Bantam Books, New York, 1999.

6 The Merck manual of diagnosis and therapy. General medicine. Merck Research Laboratories, Merck & Co. Inc., Whitehouse Station. NJ, 1999.

7 Alexopoulos, E., Kostadima, I., Pagonari, E., Zintzaras, K., Gourgoulianis, A., and Kaditis, 'Association between primary nocturnal enuresis and habitual snoring in children', *Urology,* 68/2, 2006: 406-9.

8 Mahoney, D., cited in *Pediatric News,* 31 July 2003.

9 Weider, D., Sateia, M., and West, R., 'Nocturnal enuresis with upper airway obstruction', *Otolaryngology Head and Neck Surgery,* 105, 1991: 427-32.

10 Fitzgibbon, J., *Feeling tired all the time,* Gill & Macmillan, 2002.

11 Gershon, M.D., *The second brain,* Harper Collins, New York, 1998.

12 Paynter, A., cited in: 'Summary of reports from schools using the INPP schools' programme', INPP, Chester, 2006.

13 Berard, G., *Hearing equals behaviour,* Keats Publishing Inc., New Canaan, Connecticut, 1993.

14 Rowe, N., personal communication.

15 Goddard Blythe, S.A. and Hyland, D., 'Screening for neurological dysfunction in the specific learning difficulty child', *British Journal of Occupational Therapy 61/10, 1998.*

6.

Breast-feeding

No farmer, gardener, pharmaceutical company, or food manufacturer has ever produced food more perfectly designed for its purpose than human breast milk.

Mammal means 'breast', and as one of the many species of mammal, humans are designed by nature to suckle their young. Whilst there are 4,000 species of mammals that produce milk for their offspring, the only source of milk specifically designed to provide all the nutrients a human baby needs is human breast milk. Before the invention of formula feed, a baby would almost certainly have died if the mother was unable to feed it herself or find a substitute in the form of a wet nurse.

Problems associated with feeding a baby 'by hand' were twofold. First, there was the problem of finding a method of getting food into a baby's mouth and down its throat. There is evidence from classical times[1] that hand-feeding was attempted, as feeding vessels have been discovered in infant graves, but such attempts were largely doomed to failure as no viable alternative to the nipple could be found. Attempts were made to fashion teats from linen and sponges, or to pour or spoon-feed from vessels made of pottery, but spoon-feeding did not take the infant suck-and-swallow mechanism into account.

Secondly there was the problem of finding a comparable food source that was suited to the infant's immature digestive system, which could be kept clean and given without risk of contamination or infection. Until recent times, one of the major causes of infant mortality was diarrhoea. When the combination of the rubber teat, safe formula feed, and adequate sterilization practises was developed, infant mortality was dramatically reduced and the advantages associated with the development of a safe, alternative to breast-feeding, when breast-feeding is not possible, cannot be over-emphasized.

However, the advantages of bottle-feeding were chiefly for babies where the mother was unable to breast-feed her child. Over the last century there has been a complete reversal in much of the Western world, with women opting to bottle- rather than breast-feed for a variety of reasons, many of which have more to do with social changes than with benefits to the child or the long-term health of the mother.

Nature in the form of human breast milk designed a source of food which, provided the mother is well nourished and in good health herself, is instantly available, requires no additional preparation, equipment, or washing up, and is carried with you wherever you go. Whereas in less-advanced societies, breast-feeding is normal practice, in more complex societies it has become harder for mothers to establish and maintain breast-feeding.

Advantages of Breast-feeding for the Baby

Breast milk is easy for babies to digest and helps to 'prime' the infant gut by providing the correct ratio of flora and bacteria that prevent the growth of harmful organisms, and which will enable the digestive system to process a more complex diet later on. Babies are very rarely allergic to their mother's milk, and in cases where a reaction does occur, it is usually connected to something in the mother's diet or medication that she may be taking (see contra-indications, below).

Breast milk naturally contains substances not available in formula that help protect babies from illness: antibodies, immunoglobins, active enzymes and hormones, because human milk transfers to the infant the mother's own antibodies to disease. These antibodies are specific to the immediate environment of mother and child. They were provided by the placenta before birth and are passed on through breast milk after birth. Sarah Blaffer Hardy describes these antibodies as being

> tailor made to protect the infant from precisely those bacteria, viruses and intestinal parasites that are present in the environment

and that the baby is in greatest danger of contracting. Like the cellular equivalent of a pharmacy, the mother's mammary glands deliver secretory immunoglobins that work like specialised prescriptions.[2]

Human breast milk also carries natural protection through the mother's own immune response, against allergic tendencies, which run in the family. These may include food allergies, skin conditions such as eczema, rashes and airborne reactions linked to inhaled allergens (asthma, hayfever, allergic rhinitis), and infection-induced reactions such as bronchial asthma.

Breast-fed babies are less likely to develop infections of the ear or digestive system. While breast-feeding does not provide total protection, many instances of infection of the ear and digestive tract or skin allergy can be traced back to when breast-feeding was first supplemented with formula, or mixed feeding was introduced. There are a number of reasons why there can be an increase in the incidence of ear infections following the introduction of mixed feeding.

1. *The position from which the baby feeds.* In order to take milk from the breast, the baby needs to be positioned with the head slightly raised. There is often a tendency when bottle-feeding to allow the baby to lie with the head lower and the neck more extended. In this position, milk can enter the naso-pharyngeal cavity more easily, providing fertile ground for the development of infection.

2. *The part of the mouth used to suck.* The breast-feeding baby needs to take a surprisingly large portion of the nipple into the mouth so that it sits near the back of the throat. The baby's tongue then squeezes milk from the breast by massaging with the tongue against the ridges on the roof of its mouth. The ridges help to keep the breast in place. Rather than sucking, milk is extracted using rhythmic pressure applied, which strips milk from the ducts.

   Bottle-feeding uses a different mechanism. Sucking takes place nearer the front of the mouth with pressure applied to the frontal portion of the palate. It has been suggested that this can affect subsequent development of the palate and the position of the teeth, as well as the swallow mechanism. Breast-fed babies have to work harder to extract milk, which helps to strengthen the jaw and associated muscles, and encourage the growth of straight, healthy teeth. Development of the jaw and muscles at the front of the mouth will influence the later feeding patterns of chewing and grinding when solid foods are introduced. The mechanisms involved in feeding also provide practice for the actions of many of the fine muscles needed for clear speech and articulation.

3. After the first ejection of the 'let down' reflex, breast-fed babies also have some control over the flow of milk, so there is less danger of milk entering the nasal cavity and of harmful bacteria setting up infection in the middle ear.

4. Some children are intolerant of the higher protein content present in cow's milk products. As the young body lacks the enzyme to break the protein down, the immune system can be compromised and the baby is more prone to various types of infection.

Breast-feeding and Fatty Acids

Breast-feeding is also associated with possible enhanced brain development. One of the reasons suggested for this is the relatively high ratio of omega 3:6 fatty acids contained in human breast milk, which is not present in the same ratio in formula milk. Omega-3 fats are necessary for the complete development of the human brain during pregnancy and the first two years of life:

> The Omega-3 fat and its derivative, DHA (docosahexaenoic acid), is so essential to a child's development that if a mother and infant are deficient in it, the child's nervous system and immune system may never fully develop, and it can cause a lifetime of unexplained emotional, learning, and immune system disorders.[3]

The human body cannot manufacture essential fatty acids – they have to be obtained from a food source. One source is alpha-linoleic acid (LNA or ALA). This is an Omega-3 fatty acid and can be found in walnuts, unrefined wheat germ (white flour has had much of it removed), and canola oil, and is present in small quantities in dark green, leafy vegetables. The best food source is flax seed, flax oil, and *human breast milk*.

The second essential fatty acid, Linoleic acid (LA), is known as an Omega-6. It can be found in many types of seeds such as sunflower, safflower, sesame, pumpkin, soy and corn oil, and in most nuts. The ratio of Omega-6 to Omega-3 should ideally be no higher than 3:1, and in less-developed societies such as hunter-gatherer cultures where they eat a wide range of unrefined foods, nuts, and plants, this balance is usually well maintained. On the other hand, the modern Western diet uses larger proportions of linoleic acid not only in vegetable cooking oils but also in margarine, baking, and processed foods. The ratio of Omega-6:3 fatty acids in the American diet has been estimated as being 20:1.

A third group of Omega-3 and Omega-6 fatty acids is termed 'non essential' because the body is able to manufacture them from the other two essential sources. The term 'non essential' is misleading because their role in development and functioning is far more essential than the term 'non essential' suggests.

The Omega-3 fatty acid alpha-linoleic acid (ALA) is converted by the body into two other (non-essential) fatty acids:

1.   DHA (docosahexaenoic acid) and
2.   EPA (eicosapentaenoic acid)

DHA and EPA are abundant in oily, cold water fish. These are the fatty acids needed by infants and children for proper brain growth, and the primary source (ALA) must be obtained from their diet. The best source of ALA, which was provided to the foetus via the placenta before birth, is supplied by nature to the developing infant after birth in the form of *human breast milk*. Fish oil can provide a supplementary source of the *non*-essential omega-3 fatty acid DHA and EPA, while flax oil can be used to provide an additional source of the precursor to DHA and EPA, (ALA), if required.

The Omega-6 fatty acid Linoleic Acid (LA) is converted into two other (non essential) fatty acids:

1.   AA (arachidonic acid) and
2.   GLA (gamma-linolenic acid)

Sometimes conversion from ALA to DHA and/or EPA is not sufficient. This can be the result of inadequate intake of the raw material ALA, or if there is a deficiency in vitamins and co-factors such as vitamins C, B6 and B3, zinc, and magnesium, which are required for the body to convert ALA to DHA to EPA. This is another reason why a woman's nutritional status prior to and during pregnancy is so important. If she is depleted in vitamins, minerals, trace elements, or fatty acids herself as a result of an over-refined Western diet, her baby may be born with a greater need for fatty acids to be supplemented by external dietary sources in order to ensure optimum brain and nervous-system development.

If the ratio of Omega-6:3 is too high, as is often the case when the maternal diet is heavy in trans-fatty acids normally found in foods like French fries, margarine, crisps, and processed foods, then the conversion is slowed down. Meat and dairy products are high in Omega 6 fatty acid but low in Omega 3. Modern food-processing techniques have tipped the balance even further in favour of Omega 6 fatty acids, altering the availability of a basic building block of the brain and interfering with fatty acid metabolism. Trans-fatty acids become incorporated into brain cell membranes, including the myelin sheath, replacing natural DHA, which then affects the electrical activity of neurons (the power houses of the nervous system).

The problem can be counter-acted by eating flax, and other sources of DHA and EPA such as oily cold-water fish like salmon, trout, sardines, herring, and mackerel, provided the mercury content is not high.

Fatty Acids and Brain Development

Animal life first originated in the sea, where there was an abundance of Omega-3 fatty acids. These are the same fatty acids that now form the essential components of the photoreceptors of our eyes and our brain's cell membranes. The membranes of neurons are made up of a thin double layer of fatty acid molecules, which the brain uses to assemble the special types of fat it incorporates into its cell membranes. Myelin* is also made up of at least 70 per cent fat, of which the most common fatty acid is oleic acid. Oleic acid is abundant in *human breast milk*.

---

* **Myelin** – the white cells composed of lipids and proteins that form a protective sheath around some types of nerve fibres and help facilitate electrical impulse transmission. Myelin also acts as an electrical insulator, increasing the efficiency of nerve conduction and preventing interference or 'cross chatter' from neighbouring pathways.

Anomalies in the availability and metabolism of fatty acids have been implicated in lower educational performance, hyperactivity, depression, Alzheimer's and Parkinson's disease, and schizophrenia. Interestingly at least three of these conditions have also been linked to abnormalities in the availability of dopamine – a neurotransmitter involved in the regulation of motor movements and reward centres in the brain. We will discuss the functions of dopamine later on when we examine the effects of electronic media on the developing brain.

David Horrobin in his book *The madness of Adam and Eve*[4] goes as far as to suggest that fats, particularly fatty acids found in abundance in coastal regions where inhabitants have a large proportion of marine food in their diet, played a major role in human evolution:

> We became human because of quite small genetic changes of the fat inside our skulls…. The brain is an organ which is mostly made of fat and requires a lot of energy to run. Although by weight it is only about 2% of the body, it uses about 20% of the energy. I believe that the rich food supplies of the aquatic/marginal environment, together with mutations of lipid metabolism which enabled the brain to change and become more effective, were the prime causes which allowed the development of hunting and all its associated skills. These food supplies also allowed our guts to become smaller as our brain grew.

In his work as a neuro-endocrinologist (the interactions between hormones and nerve function), he found that one of the functions of prolactin was to release fatty acids from cell membranes. In other words, prolactin *mobilizes* essential fatty acids. Not only does human breast milk contain higher concentrations of fatty acids, essential components for the building of cell membranes, building the myelin sheath, determining fluidity and chemical reactivity of membranes, and increasing oxidation rate, metabolic rate, and energy levels, but one of the hormones involved in breast-milk production helps to ensure that fatty acids are transported efficiently.

Human breast milk contains all the nutrients a baby needs: it is better absorbed than artificial baby milk, resulting in less waste matter; and breast milk comes perfectly packaged, is served at the right temperature, and carries minimal risk of contamination in the process of storage and delivery. Furthermore, the production and content of breast milk is controlled by the *baby* according to its needs. The constituency of breast milk is adapted according to need of the baby from hour to hour and from one day to the next. The content of a mother's milk is different if she is feeding a premature baby or a full-term baby, a healthy baby, or a sick baby. It varies at different times of day and will change and decrease when supplementary feeding is introduced.

Mechanisms of Breast-feeding

Breast milk is produced on a demand-and-supply basis. It is regulated by stimulation to the nipple provided *by the baby*. Regular suckling increases oxidation and metabolic rate, and energy levels, and ensures a continued supply.

Lactation results from the action of a group of reflexes, which stimulate the release of the hormones prolactin and oxytocin. Prolactin initiates and maintains milk supply in response to feeding, while oxytocin, which you will remember from Chapter 4 means, 'to speed up', controls the 'let down' or milk ejection reflex. Milk release is controlled by neuro-endocrine factors which are set in motion by tactile stimulation of the breast. Nuzzling, stroking, and suckling stimulate the production of oxytocin, causing contraction of cells, which propel the milk out in the 'let-down' reflex.

Lactation was suppressed before birth by the action of prolactin-release *inhibiting* hormone. The inhibitory influence of the hormone starts to decrease toward the end of pregnancy, and many women start to produce small quantities of milk several weeks before birth. The inhibitory effect of the hormone is released when oestrogen levels fall, the placenta is delivered, and the prolactin level rises at birth. The level of prolactin is then maintained by the action of the baby feeding at the breast, so it is the baby who 'orders' his next meal by feeding*, and oxytocin delivers it. Suckling sends a message to the mother's brain to produce more breast-feeding hormones, and initially it is suckling that gets the process of breast-feeding started. Once established, a baby's cry, or even thinking about her baby, can activate the let-down reflex. If oxytocin is the hormone of love and attachment, then prolactin is the hormone of mothering.[5]

---

* Demand and stimulation of the breast maintain levels of prolactin

An important difference between breast- and bottle-fed babies is that the breast-fed baby controls the production, quantity, constituency, and, to some degree, timing of feeds. The quality of milk also changes during the course of a feed, beginning with production of 'foremilk'. Foremilk contains lower energy and fat content. It starts the digestive processes working and is followed toward the end of a feed by 'hindmilk'. Hindmilk has a higher fat content and will keep the baby satisfied for longer. This may be one explanation why a breast-feeding mother who is stressed, rushed, or overworked can have a fretful baby who never seems to be satisfied. If feeds are hurried and the baby is taken off the breast before he has finished, he does not get his fill of hindmilk, becomes hungry and fretful sooner, and never seems to be satisfied. The baby, by demanding to be fed more often, tries to increase the supply; but if mother is rushed, stressed, or tired at the end of a long day and has not eaten properly herself, baby is only fed the appetiser at each meal and does not reach the main course. This is sometimes misinterpreted by the mother, who starts to believe that she does not have enough milk to satisfy her baby, or that the quality of her milk is poor. It can be tempting at this point to give up on breast-feeding when the problem could be solved by mother and baby having more relaxed time to devote to each feed. In a social context, this means acknowledging that breast-feeding mothers need physical time, space, and consideration to fulfil a very important job.

In less-developed societies, where the baby is carried by its mother in a sling wherever she goes, after the first few weeks the baby has access to the breast whenever it wants. Feeding sessions tend to be more frequent and of shorter duration as the baby seeks the breast for comfort as well as nutrition. The mother's milk will adjust itself to the demand of the baby, and frequent feeding will ensure an abundant supply.

The Technological Revolution

History books cover the effects of the agricultural and industrial revolutions on society. We are living through a third revolution – the technological revolution – which has had, and is still having, a major impact on our relationship with the natural world and the processes of nature, including our own biology. The modern world seems to have an extraordinary aversion to the three most fundamental processes of life: birth, death, and the natural feeding of our young. We have sanitized and removed these natural events so far from the daily experience of society that each natural event can constitute a major trauma in our lives when we experience it personally for the first time.

In societies where technology has not invaded the way of living, children grow up in direct contact with the birth of siblings, the feeding of babies, and the death of the elderly. Very small children, when not with their mothers, are often left in the care of grandparents or older members of the group, and slightly older children are involved in looking after younger children. They see babies being breast-fed, carried, soothed, and sleeping alongside their mothers on a daily basis, so that when the time comes for them to have their own children, they know what to do. Mothers are not usually isolated from their own mothers or from the help and advice of older more experienced mothers. Experienced mothers help a new mother in the first weeks in adapting to and coping with the demands of motherhood.

Parenting, then, is a skill passed down from mother to daughter, absorbed by imitation and participation over many years, and naturalized through daily experience. This is not to idealize or minimize the very hard work involved in being a mother, but to point out that if we become removed from the *physical* experience of a skill, it is very much harder to learn it at a later age. In technological societies, the instinct to breast-feed our young is no longer a universal instinct. Neither does the technological society help women to regain and practise the most fundamental of human instincts – the instinct to suckle our young; the mammalian instinct.

New mothers often need time, help, and support to get started with breast-feeding. There are many erroneous assumptions about how a baby feeds, and many of the problems encountered in breast-feeding are as much the result of ignorance about how the process works as about physical inability to breast-feed. This is not at all surprising if a new mother has never seen a baby being successfully breast-fed before she has her own. The baby may also have had its natural instinct to suckle suppressed if the mother was given medication close to the time of delivery, or if mother and baby were separated after birth.

You will remember from Chapter 4 that if a full-term baby is placed on its mother's tummy immediately after birth in direct skin-to-skin contact, and the baby is not drowsy from the effects of medication, it will spontaneously work its way up toward the breast and start feeding[6] – it knows exactly what to do. Intervention or the interruption of natural instincts during sensitive periods can make re-establishing the process more difficult later on.

I had three children in less than four years. When my first child was born, I knew I wanted to breast-feed if possible, but I was magnificently unprepared for the process. I would have failed entirely had it not been for the attention of a young midwife on the postnatal ward who spent time with me, trying different feeding positions and teaching me (not the baby) how much of the breast needs to be placed in baby's mouth for the baby to feed successfully and the mother not to become sore. It took a further 2-3 weeks for us to establish a routine, during which time the new mother needs encouragement, rest, and support. Mother and baby need *time* to get to know each other and what works for them as 'a team'. Every baby is different, and even experienced mothers who have successfully breast-fed another baby in the past need some time to get to know the preferences and habits of a new baby.

To breast-feed successfully, the baby needs to take a surprisingly large portion of the breast into its mouth so that the nipple extends back as far as the soft palate. It is this contact which stimulates the sucking reflex. The palate is covered with a set of ridges which help to keep the nipple in place, while the tongue applies rhythmical pulses of compression, stripping milk from the ducts. One of the most common mistakes in first attempts at breast-feeding is to place only a small amount of the nipple into the baby's mouth: milk is not released, the baby becomes distressed, and the mother quickly becomes very sore. This is a frustrating and off-putting process for both, and can easily be avoided with a little help and support.

A variety of different feeding positions can also be tried, from lying and sitting to tucking the baby under one arm with the baby placed face on toward the breast, rather than lying on its side. A baby who seems unable to 'get the hang of' breast-feeding in the traditional position may be an expert when positioned differently. Once again, it takes time, patience, and support to give a first-time mother the confidence to continue experimenting until both members of the partnership are happy.

Benefits of Breast-feeding for the Baby

For the healthy baby, breast-feeding is what it was designed to do. The skin-to skin contact helps the baby to get to know her mother from the outside through a combination of touch, taste, and smell. Feeding distance is also perfectly matched to the baby's immature visual system in the first weeks of life. The newborn is short-sighted for the first weeks of life and can only focus over a distance of up to approximately 17 centimetres – the distance from the breast to her mother's face.

Carl Delacato suggested that the process of breast-feeding helps to develop monocular vision (using one eye at a time),[7] training near-point vision in each eye separately:

> As the infant suckles from the left breast his right eye is occluded by the breast and his right hand is restricted by the breast feeding position. While suckling the left breast he is biased toward left sided function.

This orientation is reversed when suckling from the right breast:

> When we change this natural situation and bottle-feed the child, we invariably see the right handed mother hold the baby in her left arm and hold the bottle in her right hand.

Delacato goes on to suggest that a regular bias to one side when feeding may affect the infant's neurological organization in terms of eye and hand preference. When an infant suckles, the eyes tend to converge, an important mechanism in the development of stereoscopic vision. Until recently there was little research to support Delacato's theory, but in 2007 a study found that young children who had been breast-fed had better stereoscopic vision.[8]

The study carried out at the Institute of Child Health in London set out, first, to test the hypothesis that breast-feeding benefits stereoscopic visual maturation and, secondly, if that benefit was shown, then to ascertain whether it was mediated by the dietary intake of the fatty acid DHA. The study examined 262 children aged between four and six. Some 78 had previously been breast–fed, and 184 had been fed on formula milk. Some of the bottle-fed babies had been given formula milk fortified with the fatty acids DHA and AA. When aspects of vision were tested, the breast-fed children showed superior stereoscopic vision compared to both groups of babies who had been fed formula and formula-fortified milk.

The researchers concluded that factors in breast milk other than increased fatty acid content account for the superior visual skills, but they did not go on to suggest what these factors might be. Delacato's hypothesis, first mooted more than 50 years ago, that the regular training of each eye from different sides during breast-feeding helps the two eyes to work together as a team, seems a plausible explanation.

The *composition* of breast milk is also designer-made not only for this baby but also for how the baby is from one time of day to the next. Mother and baby share the same environment (assuming they are together for most of the day) and are therefore likely to share exposure to the same range of potentially harmful infective agents. Mother's milk contains microphages – cells which gobble up invading bacteria – and immunoglobulins, which have a preventive function by coating the baby's gut with a protective lining, thereby stopping pathogens from getting through. Breast milk also contains immunoproteins which function both to attack disease, and which – remarkably – are also digested as a nutrient protein, serving a dual function as 'natural antibiotics and also a food supplement'.[9] In addition to its anti-bacterial properties, breast milk attacks viruses.

Infant Feeding and Obesity

A study carried out by scientists at Bristol University[10] as part of the Avon Longitudinal Study of Parents and Children examined the feeding habits of 881 babies at four months of age, and compared it to their weight gain in childhood. They found that babies who were fed on formula milk and were weaned on to solid food too early were heavier than expected by 5 years of age, placing them at greater risk of developing obesity.

The differences between breast- and bottle-fed babies only became apparent *after* weaning. Infants given formula milk were less likely to eat vegetables and fruit, and more likely to consume commercial infant drinks, compared with infants who were breast-fed. In breast-fed babies, milk intake was lower when solid foods were introduced, a natural adjustment for the calorific intake provided by an additional food source. In formula-fed babies, milk intake remained the same once solids were introduced.

The study suggests two possible trends. First, children's taste preferences may be affected by being fed on formula instead of breast milk, with that early tasting experience setting up a desire for higher calorie foods in later life. Secondly, it suggests that breast-fed babies self-regulate their milk intake once solid foods have been introduced, whereas formula-fed babies continue to be given, and in most cases take, the same amount. Study nutritionist Dr Pauline Emmett said: 'It seems that breast-fed infants are better able to regulate their energy intake than formula-fed infants',[11] and the results suggest that babies drinking formula rather than breast milk take in more calories, and experience weight gain at a crucial stage of growth. This weight gain, combined with formula feeding, could also lead to a pattern of overeating, which can be difficult to overcome.

The study did not take into account socio-economic status, mother's body mass index (BMI), or eating patterns of the family, all of which could also have a significant impact on subsequent weight gain. However, the difference between breast- and formula-fed babies in volume of milk intake during weaning raises questions about the development of self-regulatory behaviour in regard to hunger, satiety, and taste preference. The natural relationship of demand and supply set up during breast-feeding probably plays an important part in setting patterns of regulation for feeding for later life.

A meta analysis of published research into the relationship between infant feeding and the risk of obesity in later life[12] concluded that 'studies reporting a quantitative estimate provided consistent evidence of a relationship between breastfeeding and reduced risk of obesity'. The association was stronger in small studies but was also observed in larger studies. Moreover, 'The association appeared stronger among prolonged breastfeeders and was unaltered by age at outcome of measurement.'

In their discussion, the authors go on to state:

Several biological mechanisms may explain the association. Breastfeeding affects intake of calories and protein,[13] insulin secretion,[14] and modulation of fat deposition and adipocyte development.[15] If the effects of breastfeeding are sustained through either habituation or more complex programming mechanisms, then the association could persist into adult life, as our results suggest. The consistency of the association with increasing age suggests that the protective effects of early breastfeeding are independent of dietary and physical activity patterns that emerge in later life.

Other long-term health benefits associated with breast-feeding have been identified in relation to adult glucose tolerance, lipid (fats) profile, blood pressure, and obesity.[16] Researchers concluded that although formula-feeding could not be considered the 'common soil' in all disorders connected to insulin resistance syndrome, their findings

supported the hypothesis that the method of infant feeding is an important determinant of health in adult life. Babies who were exclusively breast fed during the first days of their life had favourable outcome with respect to glucose and lipid metabolism, which relates to lower risk of cardiovascular disease.

As we approach the end of the first decade of the twenty-first century, we are seeing in both the United Kingdom and the United States of America an explosive increase in the incidence of obesity amongst all age groups, type 2 diabetes, and cardiovascular heart disease. There are many factors involved in the development and onset of these conditions, and some aspects are directly linked to later feeding habits, exercise, and lifestyle. Future studies are needed to investigate where there is a correlation between the rise in childhood obesity, associated medical problems. and infant feeding.

Trends in obesity, particularly amongst children, raise a number of questions. Are they in part a socially engineered epidemic which has increased as women return to the workplace after having children, with breast-feeding either not taking place or being prematurely curtailed? Added to this are changes in family eating habits, exercise, and the effects of synthetic hormones on metabolism.

Another concern is that nearly half of women are unaware of the benefits of breast-feeding, even for a short time. Formula feeding has become so much a part of the modern way of life that many women do not realise that they are denying themselves and their babies' future health benefits by opting for formula feeding without trying to breast-feed first.

The National Childbirth Trust (NCT)[17] maintains that breast-feeding even for a single day can help improve babies' future well-being, and tries to encourage women to take one day at a time when breast-feeding their child because 'every feed made a positive difference to both mother and baby'. A survey of 500 women for the NCT found that more than half (55 per cent) did not know that the benefits of breast-feeding started from day one.

Its survey also showed that 9 out 10 people (91 per cent) did not know that breast-feeding for just one month had a lasting impact on health during the first 14 years of a child's life.

Almost two-thirds (63 per cent) did not know that mixed feeding – giving both breast milk and artificial milk – still provided some protection from infections for babies under six months of age. In other words, even a minimal amount of breast-feeding complimented with formula can provide a measure of protection.

Almost half of women (49 per cent) did not know that breast-feeding also reduced the risk of osteoporosis and ovarian cancer for *the mother.* This may be because prolactin suppresses ovulation, and the hormonal effects of breast-feeding may help to counteract the potentially carcinogenic properties of oestrogen and progesterone.

Oestrogen stimulates cells lining the womb to grow rapidly and divide. Progesterone puts a brake on oestrogenic activity and urges the cells to produce more starch and protein until the womb is ready to feed a baby. Progesterone levels rise markedly during pregnancy to secure the pregnancy and prevent the mother's immune system from rejecting the embryo as a foreign invading body. One of the functions of progesterone is therefore to suppress immune response to foreign tissue growth and allow the pregnancy to proceed.

The hormones involved in lactation reduce the influence of oestrogen and progesterone for as long as regular breast-feeding continues, and could, in theory, provide natural protection following months of elevated progesterone levels during pregnancy and the fertile environment for cancerous growth provided by oestrogen. When women gave birth to more children, the rates of ovarian and breast cancer were lower. Whilst some of this may be accounted for by earlier death as a result of frequent childbirth, it also raises questions as to whether hormonally induced periods of infertility (oral contraceptive) and drugs given to suppress lactation create a favourable condition for cancerous cells to develop which is different from the temporary infertility induced and mediated by lactation.

Prolactin also increases the rate of conversion of vitamin D into a form which enhances calcium utilization, which may in the long term provide additional protection against osteoporosis by increasing the uptake of calcium from the diet, even though the mother has to source larger amounts to feed herself and her infant.

The aforementioned National Childbirth Trust survey also found that half of women (55 per cent) were aware of the current recommendation for babies to receive only breast-milk for the first six months of life. NCT chief executive Belinda Phipps said the Trust was concerned that many women did not realise that the benefits of breast-feeding started straight away. Even two days is better than none.

Breast-feeding also appears to lend increased resilience against stress in later childhood.[18] In a study which analysed the early feeding practices of nearly 9,000 children who were part of the 1970 British Cohort Study, which monitors a sample of the population from birth onward, teachers were asked to evaluate children's level of anxiety using a 0-50 scoring scale, when they were 10 years of age. Parents were interviewed about major family disruptions including divorce and separation, which had occurred between the ages of 5 and 10 years.

It was no surprise when the findings showed increased tendency of high anxiety among children whose parents were divorced or separated; but what was surprising was that the children who had been breast-fed were significantly less anxious than their peers. Children whose parents were divorced or separated who had been breast-fed were twice as likely to be highly anxious, compared with bottle-fed children, who were nine times more likely to be highly anxious than children whose parents were together.

Whilst this study does not prove that breast-feeding provides a guarantee against future stress, it does suggest that factors involved in breast-feeding provide additional protection. The authors suggest that this may be the result of quality of *physical contact* in the early days of life affecting neural and hormonal pathways involved in the regulation of the stress response. It may also help in early bonding and attachment. Securely attached children tend to be able to become independent at a later age while still remaining connected to sources of love and support than insecurely attached children.

The UK has one of the lowest breast-feeding rates in Europe – almost a third of women in England and Wales never try to breast-feed, compared with just 2 per cent in Sweden.

In 2003 the Government set primary care trusts a target to increase the number of women starting to breast-feed by 2 per cent a year. Surely, with greater awareness, we can do better than that!

Benefits to the Mother

In addition to giving some degree of protection against ovarian and breast cancer and osteoporosis, regular breast-feeding affects maternal hormones involved in the control and return of fertility. Provided the baby is taking a minimum of six feeds (more than 65 minutes in total) in 24 hours, and at least one of those feeds is during the night, ovulation tends to be suppressed for longer.[19] This cannot be taken as a guarantee against becoming pregnant again while breast-feeding, but it does reduce the chances.

In less-developed societies where there is little or no access to contraceptives, prolonged and regular breast-feeding is one of the ways in which a woman can control her fertility once sexual relations are resumed, helping to provide space between pregnancies. This usually occurs toward the end of the second half of the child's first year, and may be nature's way of ensuring that the first child can at least walk before the mother becomes heavily pregnant with a subsequent child. Once complementary or supplementary feeding is introduced, the level of protection afforded by breast-feeding starts to decline as the baby takes less milk from the breast, and intervals between feeds increase.

One of the greatest dangers with formula feeding is the risk of contamination. Milk is a breeding ground for bacteria, particularly milk which needs to be served at body temperature. Breast milk contains anti-infective agents, and the risk of contamination from container to recipient is very small. These same anti-infective agents help to protect the breast from infection.

Formula feeding is reasonably safe provided that sterilizing procedures are scrupulously followed, clean, boiling water is available for making up the feed, and ready supplies of cold water or refrigeration are available to cool the feed. This is one of the reasons why the introduction of formula feed to poor, non-industrialized nations with a hot climate was so disastrous. If women had clean water available, they did not necessarily have a method of cooling it quickly. Harmful bacteria proliferate in a hot climate, providing fertile breeding ground for organisms which cause diarrhoea and gastro-enteritis. These diseases are particularly dangerous for young children because they cause dehydration and, if untreated, death. If the water supply is heavily contaminated with bacteria, or if mothers are unable to read the instructions and follow the proper procedures for making up a feed, formula feeding can result in a very sick baby. Tragically, having opted for the 'modern' way of feeding, mothers in under-developed countries were then unable to help their sick babies by feeding them themselves, because their own supply had dried up.

In the developed world, we do have access to the equipment to provide safe formula feeds but the paraphernalia must accompany the mother wherever she goes. Breast milk is available 'on tap' as long as mother and child are together, and can even be stored in a refrigerator for short periods of time if the mother expresses it in advance. It is delivered at the right temperature without additional cost, and the risks of infection are minimal.

Formula milk also lacks some of the non-essential but beneficial properties of breast milk. Vegetable oils are often added to formula feed after buttermilk has been extracted for commercial purposes. Vegetable oils have a different composition and do not replace the fats present in buttermilk or breast milk. These fats are chemical building-blocks for brain and nervous system development.

Because breast milk provides all the nutrients the baby needs in the right balance, there is very little waste matter, which means nicer nappies!

The skin-to-skin contact that takes place while breast-feeding can be of benefit to mother and baby. Touch results in hormone release of gastrin and insulin, helping to improve the baby's digestion and absorption. A baby usually takes slightly longer to feed from the breast, meaning that there is more time for touching. A mother can also feel from the way her baby sucks what mood her baby is in, and so adjust how she handles him. Touch has been found to confer many health benefits.

Studies carried out on premature babies using tactile-kinesthetic stimulation found that gentle, deep pressure stimulation applied at regular intervals resulted in improved weight gain, increased alertness, more mature habituation, orientation, and motor behaviour, and shorter duration of hospital stay compared to control. Premature babies lack much of the skin-to-skin contact enjoyed by full-term babies, and the combination of maternal deprivation and/or inadequate tactile stimulation may result in impaired metabolic efficiency.[20]

Suckling stimulates the release of oxytocin in the mother – the hormone Michel Odent described as 'the hormone of love' – and a key player in the chemical aspect of the attachment process.

Suckling also stimulates contractions of the uterus, helping the uterus to shrink back to its pre-pregnancy size more quickly. Although some women are afraid that breast-feeding will alter the size and shape of their breasts, in the short term breast-feeding can help a woman to regain her pre-pregnancy flat stomach.

Contra-indications to Breast-feeding

There are a few instances when breast-feeding is contra-indicated. A number of viruses can be transmitted from mother to baby without providing antibody protection for the infant. The HIV virus that causes Aids is one of these, and women who are HIV positive should not breast-feed.

Certain prescription medications are also not compatible with breast-feeding. This can be distressing for the mother who wishes to breast-feed her baby, but who, for her own health reasons, must continue to take medication.

- Bromocriptine (Parlodel) used for the treatment of Parkinson's Disease;
- Most chemotherapy drugs used for the treatment of cancer;
- Ergotamine used for the treatment of migraine headaches;

- Methotrexate for the treatment of arthritis;
- Drugs of abuse such as cocaine and PCP.

Nicotine and excessive use of alcohol should also be avoided.

If either mother or baby is ill following the birth, it can make breast-feeding more difficult to establish. If the baby is too sick to feed naturally, a new mother can express her milk and this can be fed to the baby by artificial means, but this can be difficult to maintain over a long period of time if the baby needs several weeks of special care. Abnormal, damaged, or sore nipples can also mean that breast-feeding is not practical, and a mother should never feel guilty or inadequate if she is unable or advised not to feed her baby herself.

Obstacles to Breast-feeding

The aim of this chapter has been to point out to mothers the benefits associated with breast-feeding so that they can make choices based upon medical, social, and personal needs. Some women are unable to breast-feed for medical reasons; others do not have the luxury of making a choice to stay at home with their baby, but must for financial reasons return to work, and do not see breast-feeding as a practical option. An ample supply of breast milk is dependent on regular demand. Although milk can be expressed in advance, it is more difficult to maintain breast-feeding if separated from your baby for more than four hours of the day.

Some women find the idea of breast-feeding repugnant and others feel that it will have a negative effect on their sexual relationship with their partner. No one should be forced to breast-feed if they have a strong emotional aversion to the process, but better and continued education of the young about the advantages for both mother and child may help to reduce some of the fear and alienation that many modern women feel about a practice they can only experience physically for the first time when they have a baby.

We live in strangely hypocritical times. Breasts are on display in advertisements in public places, newspapers and magazines, television, and films, making women seem more desirable and being offered as objects of pleasure for men. Breasts as sexual objects are no longer shocking, but the idea of a woman breast-feeding in public or at work often is. No one would object to a woman bottle-feeding a hungry baby in a restaurant, but eyebrows are often raised if a woman breast-feeds her child in a restaurant – despite the fact that restaurants are places where people eat and breast milk is gourmet food for babies. These unspoken social taboos can leave women feeling self-conscious about breast-feeding their babies in public, and sitting in a public lavatory to breast-feed your baby is not a pleasant or hygienic alternative.

It is perfectly possible to breast-feed a baby with less of the breast being on display than in many items of daily clothing, but as we have become further and further removed from our natural instincts, some people find the sheer physical nature of a baby feeding at the breast deeply disturbing to observe. The problem is not with breast-feeding per se – it is with the encultured attitude of breasts being primarily sources of sexual arousal and pleasure rather than a natural continuation of the feeding and care that took place in pregnancy. Once again, one of the most natural processes of motherhood has been relegated to second place in favour of financial, social, and adult considerations. If, as a society, we put the needs of children first, there should be no contest.

In a Nutshell...

- Breast milk contains antibodies tailor-made to individual needs of the mother and child to protect against disease and familial allergic reactions; and

- Breast milk is high in fatty acids needed for brain growth and development.

- Breast-feeding supports attachment between mother and baby.

- Breast-feeding may help to develop visual functions.

- Breast-feeding is associated with a lower risk of developing childhood obesity

- Breast-feeding reduces mother's fertility whilst feeding at regular intervals

- Breast-feeding accelerates the return of the uterus to its pre-pregnancy size.

- Breast-feeding reduces the risk of the mother developing cancer of the breast, the ovaries, and osteoporosis.

Endnotes

1 Brown, P., *Eve: Sex, childbirth and motherhood through the ages,* Summersdale Publishers, Chichester, 2004.

2 Blaffer Hardy, S., *Mother Nature,* Chatto and Windus, London, 1999.

3 Finnegan, J., *The vital role of essential fatty acids for pregnant and nursing women,* Celestial Arts, 1993,
http://www.thorne.com/townsend/dec/efas.html

4 Horrobin, D., *The madness of Adam and Eve: How schizophrenia shaped humanity,* Corgi Books, London, 2001.

5 Odent, M., Lecture given to the Society for Effective Affective Learning (SEAL) Conference, University of Derby.

6 Righard, L., *Delivery self-attachment,* DVD, Geddes Production Presents, 1995.

7 Delacato, C., *The diagnosis and treatment of speech and reading problems,* Charles C. Thomas, Springfield, Ill., 1970.

8 Singhal, A. and others, 'Infant nutrition and stereoacuity at age 4-6 years', *American Journal of Clinical Nutrition,* 85/1, 2007: 152-9.

9 Palmer, G., *The politics of breastfeeding,* Pandora Press, London, 1993.

10 Noble, S. and Emmett, P., 'Differences in weaning practice, food and nutrient intake between breast and formula fed 4 month old

infants in England', Journal of Human Nutrition and Dietetics, 19/4, 2006: 303.

[11] Emmett, P., 2006. Noble and Emmett, ibid.

[12] Owen, G.C., Martin, R.M., Whincup, P.H., Davey Smith, G., and Cook, D.G., 'Effect of infant feeding on the risk of obesity across the life course: a quantitative review of published evidence', *Pediatrics,* 115/5, 2005: 1367-77.

[13] Heinig, M.J., Nommsen, L.A., Peerson, J.M., Lonnderdal, B., and Dewey, K.G., 'Energy and protein intakes of breast-fed and formula-fed infants during the first year of life and their association with growth velocity: The DARLING Study', *American Journal of Clinical Nutrition,* 58, 1993: 152-61.

[14] Lucas, A., Sarson, D.L., Blackburn, A.A., and Adrian, T.E., Aynsley-Green, A., and Bloom, S.R., 'Breast vs bottle: endocrine responses are different with formula feeding', *Lancet,* 1, 1980: 1267-9

[15] Von Kries, R., Kolezko, B., Sauerwald, T., and others, 'Breast feeding and obesity: cross sectional study', *British Medical Journal,* 319, 1999: 147-50.

[16] Ravelli, A.C.J., van der Meulen, J.H.P., Osmond, C., Barker, D.J.P., and Bleker, O.P., 'Infant feeding and adult glucose tolerance, lipid profile, blood pressure and obesity', Archives of Disease in Childhood, 82, 2000: 248-52.

[17] Infant Feeding Survey 2005; www.ic.nhs.uk/pubs/breastfeed2005

[18] Montgomery, S.M. and others, 'Breast feeding and resilience against psychosocial stress', *Archives of Disease in Childhood,* 000, 2006: 1-5.

[19] Palmer, G., *The politics of breastfeeding,* Pandora Press, London, 1993.

[20] Field, T., *Touch therapy,* Churchill Livingstone, Edinburgh, 2005.

7.

Movement Instinct

Movement is the first expression of life. At the very beginning of human life, unity of the sperm and the ovum takes place as a result of cellular motility. The beating of the embryo's heart is a form of physiological motility, and the first breath of life taken by the baby moments after birth is the vital movement with which the child embraces life outside of the womb. Words that we associate with living beings such as 'animal' and 'animate' have their origins in the experience and perception of motion. 'Anima' means vital breath; 'animate' is derived from 'æ·nimeit' meaning 'give life to' and also 'stemming from', 'animāre' meaning 'to quicken' or to move; 'anima', meaning air, breath, life, or soul, and 'animus' meaning spirit. The essence of animal life assumes the characteristic of motion.

Movement is also a child's first language. Babies are born with an innate desire to communicate. Communication started in a very physical way before birth when the developing baby was able to sense his mother's emotions through the chemical changes taking place in her body in response to her environment, alterations in the nature and speed of her movements, changes in physiological processes such as her heart rate, as well as subtle variations in the tone, volume, and rhythms of her speech.

Birth changes everything. Not only is there a reversal in the mechanics of breathing and circulation, but the baby must now seek and find fulfilment of her most basic needs herself. Nature has equipped the full-term infant with a remarkable vocabulary of survival instincts to protect it in the first vulnerable weeks of life, but she will still need the constant support and care of her mother for many months. This is because human infants are born at an immature stage in development compared to other land-based mammals, which have the ability to stand and walk within minutes of birth and follow their mothers around. The combination of a large head housing a bigger brain, and an upright posture, has meant that the human baby has to be born before the head is too large to pass safely through the mother's pelvis while the skull is still mould-able, but before the baby is capable in any way of taking care of itself. It is in this context that the first nine months of postnatal life have been described as the second half of gestation – an extra-uterine extension of pregnancy – when growth and brain development occur at a faster rate than they will at any other time in the child's life.

In addition to learning to breathe by herself, the newborn must learn to adapt to the full force of gravity. During life in the womb, floating inside her private ocean of amniotic fluid and supported by the structure of her mother's body, the effects of gravity were reduced. A baby begins life outside the womb with minimal control over its own body, floppy, under-developed muscle tone, and a limited (but highly effective) number of ways of helping herself. Over the course of the first nine months of post-natal life the infant slowly becomes more capable of supporting its own body in small ways, in preparation for standing and walking. Nevertheless, the baby will be dependent on its mother and other adults for many years to come.

Why Does Movement Matter to Your Child?

Movement facilitates integration of sensory experience. As early as the eleventh century, Alhazen,[1] a philosopher, recognized that 'nothing that is seen is understood by the sense of sight alone'. Mature vision is the result of *multi*-sensory experience combined with movement over many months and years, which together build a three-dimensional sense of space. Actions carried out in space help us literally to 'make sense' of what we see. Sight combined with balance, movement, hearing, touch, and proprioception (feedback from the muscles, tendons, and joints, informing the brain about the body's status and actions at any moment in time), help to integrate sensory experience and can only take place as a result of action and practice. Movement is the medium through which this takes place.

Movement in response to sensory stimulation has been observed as early as 5½ weeks after conception. At this time, if the area above the mouth is gently touched with a fine hair, the embryo will shrink away like an amoeba from the stimulus. Over the course of the next few weeks, areas of the body, which become responsive to touch, spread out to include more of the face, the palms of the hands, and the soles of the feet. Eventually the whole body will react to touch, but the embryo's earliest reaction to tactile stimulation is one of withdrawal.

Reflexes – Reflections on the Inner World of the Developing Child

By just nine weeks after conception, the first of a series of *primitive* reflexes begins to emerge. A reflex action is one of the simplest forms of activity of the nervous system. A reflex is a stereotyped response to a specific stimulus – derived from the word *reflectere,* meaning to bend back; a reflex action results from the interaction of a receptor, a conductor, and an effector. Primitive reflexes are special reflexes, which emerge and develop during life in the womb, are present at birth (in a full-term baby), and are active for the first six months of postnatal life. Sometimes described as 'survival' or primary reflexes, primitive reflexes are active while connections to higher centres are still developing, or, in later life, if there is accident or injury to higher brain centres.

A baby's nervous system is immature, and neural connections between different levels in the brain have a lot of developing to do. These pathways mature rapidly in the first six months of life as higher brain centres develop and take more direct control. Increased cortical control facilitates the inhibition of primitive reflexes in the first six months of life. Primitive reflexes are slowly put to sleep or switched off in the brain-stem – the lowest level of the brain – only to be re-awakened if there is accident or injury to higher centres.

Reflex integration takes place as a result of a combination of maturation in the central nervous system *and* physical interaction with the environment. Development of the nervous system depends on the expression of particular genes at particular places and times during development. The factors that control neuronal differentiation before birth originate both from cellular sources within the embryo *and* from the external environment.

Reflexes – Training for Life

Physical experience is rather like loading a software program on to the hard drive of the computer. The hard drive (the nervous system) makes running the software possible, but the software extends the program capability of the whole. If animals are deprived of physical interaction with the environment, their brains show alterations in development. Conversely, an enriched environment has been shown to increase development in specific areas of the brain.[2]

The human brain is particularly vulnerable to sensory deprivation in the early years, when neural connections are being formed. Children raised in the orphanages of Eastern Europe in the last quarter of the twentieth century and who were left alone in their cots for many hours of the day, receiving minimum human contact or space to move and play, continued to showed deficits in cognitive processing and emotional affect many years later. Lacking an adequate diet of sensory motor nutrition, cognitive understanding of spatial relationships, and acknowledgement of their own physical and emotional needs and the needs of others, did not develop at the same rate as their physical growth. These particular skills had to be entrained using specific programmes at a later age, with only limited success.

Reflexes are the primary teachers of basic motor skills. Initially, they provide an innate, unconscious, and therefore unplanned response to specific stimuli, but the movement experience itself starts a process of development and modification of the neural pathways involved. The more a child moves, the better her control of movement becomes. Each time she roots and finds the breast, wiggles and flexes her toes, kicks her legs, or turns her head and stretches her arm, motor cells begin a process of modification, which becomes more definite, permanent, and eventually voluntary, with repetition. These changes, combined with increased muscular strength (also developed through movement), will culminate in stable balance on two feet, and the taking of the child's first steps some time around the end of the infant's first year. Movement helps to map the brain, and reflexes provide a child with some of the earliest pathways.

In order to understand how reflexes play a part in the development of motor skills and the integration of sensory experience in the first years of life, it is necessary to describe some of the reflexes and their function in the first year of life in detail, as well as discussing the longer-term effects on functioning if they are not inhibited at the appointed time.

Rooting and Sucking Reflexes

Rooting reflex.

Searching, sucking, and swallowing movements started to develop in the womb, beginning with pharyngeal swallow from 10-12 weeks after conception. True suckling movements emerge around the 18-24th week using a forward and backward movement of the tongue; but because at this early stage the tongue fills the oral cavity, it limits more advanced oral motor activity.

Frequency of suckling motions can be affected by taste, and the foetus can detect flavours in the surrounding amniotic fluid from as early as seven weeks after conception. By 12 weeks, distinctively mature receptors are present and the foetus will start to recognize flavours ingested by its mother.

The rooting reflex emerges between 24 and 28 weeks after conception and is elicited by light touch of the cheek or area around the outside edge of the mouth. Sometimes referred to as the cardinal points reflex, because the areas of sensitivity form a pattern around the mouth like the points on a cardinal's hat, the reflex signifies the beginning of transformation of the crude withdrawal reaction, which was the embryo's first reaction to touch around the mouth. Ultrasound has shown babies touching the side of their face, opening the mouth, and sucking the thumb while inside the womb.

Self oral-facial stimulation (rooting reflex) usually precedes suckling movements.

> Backward movement appears more pronounced than forward movement. Tongue protrusion does not extend beyond the border of the lips. Serial ultrasound images have shown that suckling motions increase in frequency in the later months of fetal life. By 34 weeks' gestation, a healthy preterm infant likely suckles and swallows well enough to sustain nutrition strictly through oral feedings. So healthy preterm infants may be ready to begin oral feeding by 32 to 33 weeks' gestation and swallowing.[3]

Stimulation of the rooting reflex results in turning of the head and opening of the mouth. After birth, this reflex leads into the sucking reflexes so that the lips are pursed and the touching object is drawn into the mouth. The final part of the feeding reflex trio* is a response to the object touching the roof of the mouth, activating rhythmic sucking movements. The sense of touch, combined with smell and hunger lead into the motor activity of searching, suckling, and swallowing; and it is the motor activity and practice involved in feeding which help to coordinate muscular systems, enhance central nervous system integration, and innervate gastrointestinal functions necessary for digestion. While touch provides the gateway into feeding, motor activity leads into integration with other sensory systems such as vision and hearing.

Peiper[4] observed that:

> when we touch the region of the infant's mouth, reflexes are elicited that turn the head, and move the lips so that the touching object is drawn into the mouth. This life preserving function is innate, but the ability to turn to the nipple or the bottle when it appears in the field of vision is not. This is rapidly learned. From the rooting reflex there develops a conditioned reflex that at the sight of the breast or the bottle turns the head to the correct position in space.

---

*   Trio comprises   • Rooting   • Opening of the mouth
                           • Touching the roof of the mouth

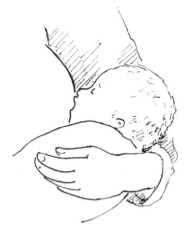

Sucking reflex.

Ashley Montagu[5] described how

> sucking is the major activity of the baby during the first year of life, and its lips presenting the externally furled extension of mucous membrane that lines its mouth, constitute instruments with which he makes his first sensitive contacts, and incorporates so much that is vital to him of the external world. Lips, tongue, the sense of smell, vision and hearing, are all intimately bound up with each other and the experience of sucking.

In the first year of life, a baby uses its mouth to explore the outside world. Beginning with the instinct to feed, the mouth later becomes an important receptor for understanding and testing the world around her – through taste, texture, and later picking up of objects, and placing them in the mouth, learning about size and matching the oral experience of an object (touch) with how it looks (vision).

In embryological development, much of the human head develops from the same original bony structures thought to be a mammalian adaptation of the gill bars of fish. Bainbridge[6] describes how one of these has been re-designed to form two of the three tiny bones in the middle ear – the hammer and anvil; they will transmit sound from the middle ear to the inner ear after birth. One type of jaw muscle will open and close the jaws, the other will pull on the tiny hammer bone to tighten the eardrum and protect the ear from loud noises. Another of the gill bars has been adapted to form the

Eustachian tube – the tube in the middle ear linking the inner ear where the hearing and balance apparatus are housed, to the throat. Other gill bars form structures involved in swallowing and breathing, as well as the hyoid bone – a 'floating' bone – suspended in the throat which pulls the oesophagus up, closing off the larynx and making it possible to swallow food without choking The process of suckling, swallowing, and breathing is highly complex and the pattern of an infant's feeding can affect the functioning of many associated structures.

The action of swallowing is one example. Swallowing alters air pressure inside the Eustachian tube, helping to ventilate the middle ear system and prevent the build-up of fluid in the middle ear – which can result in the development of 'glue ear', a major cause of hearing problems in children. The manner in which an infant sucks can also affect development of the jaw, the ear, and the shape of the mouth.

Suckling leads into social as well as other sensory activities.

> Feeding and swallowing skill development parallels psychosocial milestones of homeostasis, attachment, and separation/ individuation. Infants during the first 2 to 3 months of life strive toward homeostasis with the environment. Goals include sleep regulation, regular feeding schedules, and awake states that are developmentally advantageous in the development of emotional attachment to primary caregivers. Successful pleasurable feeding experiences foster efficient nipple control, reaching, smiling, and social play. Thus, feeding gradually becomes a social event.[7]

The muscular activity, combined with rhythms of feeding and swallowing, also helps to develop muscle control, tongue movements, and swallow patterns necessary for the development of speech and articulation. 'Normal feeding patterns reflect the early developmental pathways that are the basis for later communication skills.'[8]

Babkin and Palmomental Reflexes

Sucking movements are linked to the hands and the feet in the first weeks of life. If deep pressure is applied to the palms of both hands at the same time, it will result in flexion of the head, opening of the mouth, and closing of the eyes (Babkin reflex). This neurological link between the hands and the mouth is sometimes used to stimulate the onset of sucking in a baby who is unwilling to feed. Opening of the mouth allows the breast or bottle to be placed in the baby's mouth. Contact with the roof of the mouth alone is usually sufficient to stimulate sucking, but a similar response can be elicited if the base of the palm of the hand is scratched (palmomental reflex).

The same neurological link works in reverse. Rhythmic movements of suckling are often mirrored in small grasping movements of the hands. Anyone who has tried to hand-rear a young animal, particularly a kitten, will recognize this link: as the kitten sucks, it also kneads with its claws. The Babkin reflex usually declines after the first month of life and is no longer evident after three months. However,

> hands and mouth continue their close relations later in life. Reflex opening or closing of one sensory organ may spread to another sensory organ as a spreading reaction so that the voluntary opening or closing of the mouth or the eyes often spreads during childhood to the hands and, to a lesser degree, to the feet.[9]

In other words, the reflex initially links together in action two different parts of the body, creating a sensory connection which later on should become an independent skill.

> Voluntary closing of the hands may spread to the eyes. Darwin (1872) described how some people continue to move their lower jaws in time with the blades when cutting with scissors and children may occasionally use their tongues in a pattern similar to their fingers.[10]

If this loop is still active in the school-age child, you may see the child's mouth moving as he tries to write or use a pair of scissors; his tongue may protrude as he tries to balance, or there may be a tendency to keep the mouth open, which is associated with persistent dribbling in the older child.

Palmar and Plantar Reflexes

Both Palmar and Plantar reflexes are elicited by touch or by applying pressure to the palm of the hand or just beneath the ball of the foot. Both reflexes result in involuntary gripping – the palmar reflex, by

Example of a continued link between hand and mouth movements
in a school aged child who has retained oral reflexes.

closing the thumb and the fingers over the object, and the plantar
reflex, by gripping with the toes.

Normally inhibited by the developing brain at 7-9 months of
postnatal life, the Plantar reflex can be seen as both a response to
pressure applied to the sole of the foot and also part of a
spontaneous pattern of foot movements exercised repeatedly in the
middle phase of the first year of life. Babies will spend many happy
hours engaged in a game of flexion and extension of the toes,
movements which often precede vocalization, as if the motor pattern
prepares the pathways for the utterance of speech. Continuous
exercise of the toes also exercises some of the longest motor tracts in
the body – those that extend from the motor cortex in the brain all
the way down to the extremities on the opposite side of the body.

Plantar reflex.

The Plantar reflex should be inhibited before a baby learns to stand on its feet and walk so that the foot can be placed on the ground without involuntary gripping of the toes. However, the reflex does remain accessible if upright balance is unsteady when the child may grip with its toes to compensate for temporary loss of control.

Palmar and Plantar reflexes are thought to be a throw back to a time in evolution when we had more body hair and a baby could cling on to its mother's fur. To this day, the reflex is most easily elicited by stroking the palm of the hand with a fine hair.

When an object is placed in the palm of the hand,
the fingers will grasp hold of the object.

Just as the Babkin response can be elicited by sucking movements of the mouth, opening and closing of the hands in a Palmar reflex action can elicit mouth movements linked to sucking.

Asymmetrical Tonic Neck Reflex

Some time around 18 weeks into a pregnancy the mother will become aware of a fluttering sensation originally described as 'quickening'. Before the development of ultrasound, this was the mother's first visible sign of the new life growing inside her, other than the changes that were taking place in her own body. The baby's movements soon become more vigorous and are felt as kicking movements. In fact, her baby has been moving for many weeks before this, but she becomes increasingly aware of the movements as the movements and associated developing reflexes grow stronger.

The reflex most associated with kicking-type movements in the womb is the Asymmetrical Tonic Neck reflex (ATNR). When the baby turns its head to one side, the arm and leg will extend in the same direction as the head movement and the opposite arm will bend. This same movement can be seen in the newborn and for the first 4-6 months of postnatal life.

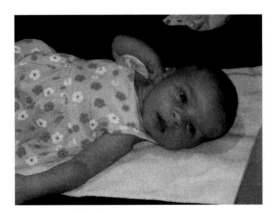

Zoe, practising her ATNR.

Whilst in the womb, the ATNR helps the foetus to move around, to turn, and to adjust its position in response to changes in its mother's posture, to make itself comfortable and explore its tiny world. It also helps to develop independent movements on either side of the body and may help the baby to take an active role in its own birth.

Chapter 4 described how, during a normal vaginal delivery, the baby has to make two turns to pass down the birth canal. Maternal contractions alone are not sufficient to enable the baby to turn, but pressure applied to the baby's head encourages the head to turn, activating the ATNR, which will give some flexibility to the shoulders on either side, helping the baby to manoeuvre into a more favourable position.

After birth, the ATNR should be released when the baby is placed on its tummy, ensuring that the head turns to one side, so that the airway is free and the baby is able to breathe.

Infant under 6 months of age lying in the ATNR position.

Research into the incidence of Sudden Infant Death Syndrome (SIDS) has consistently found the incidence of SIDS is reduced when parents are advised *not* to place their babies to sleep on their tummy. Current advice is that babies should be placed to sleep on their backs to minimize the risk of SIDS, and until research proves otherwise this advice should be followed. However, it does raise a question as to whether babies who succumb to SIDS have an under-developed ATNR at the time when the reflex should be available to fulfil a protective and survival function. We will return later in the book to the implications of the 'back to sleep' campaign for other aspects of development.

In addition to helping to develop differential movement on either side of the body, the ATNR provides an early mechanism for training hand-eye coordination. A baby's visual system is immature at birth, and a newborn baby can only focus at distance of approximately 17 centimetres from its face (the same visual distance needed for most mother-and-baby interactions in the first few weeks of life). Even at this distance, detail is not clear, and the baby sees more of the outline of an object, like her mother's face, than it does the central features. Babies have to learn how to use their vision effectively, and once again movement is an elementary teacher.

In the first weeks of life, a baby is unaware that its own hands are a part of itself. These mobile 'toys' come and go from its field of vision, reappearing as objects to watch and follow. At this time in development, the ATNR ensures that when the head is turned, not only does the arm stretch out on the same side, but also the eyes move in the same direction as the head and with the arm. In this way, baby's focusing distance is extended from near point, when the head is in the middle and the hands are in front of the face, to arm's length, as the head is turned and the eyes follow the direction of the extending arm and hand.

Gabriella, aged 3 weeks. As her head turns, her arm straightens and her eyes try to move from near point convergence to follow her arm.

Demyer[11] wrote, 'since the head and eyes look to the side of the extending hand, we can interpret the ATNR as the forerunner of hand--eye coordination. One's eyes discover one's hand moving in space and learn to grasps visual targets.'

The ATNR probably plays a part in developing both central and peripheral vision. One study videotaped 14 infants seven times within the first 12 weeks of life, to investigate whether the ATNR had a role in placing their hands within their field of vision. They found that when the infants' arms were out of the reflex position, the hands were within the peripheral field of vision, and this situation occurred more often than the arms and hand being in the reflex position or completely out of sight. The amount of time that hands were in a particular visual field varied according to the presence or absence of the reflex, with a higher proportion of reflex observations occurring in the focal or central visual field. When the infants were not in the reflex position, hand observations occurred in the peripheral visual field. More focal field observations occurred in the reflex position for the first six of the seven ages. This study confirmed that when infants are in the asymmetrical tonic neck reflex position, their hands are more likely to be in a position in which they can be visualized or focused on.[12] Activation of the reflex helps the eyes to move from peripheral vision to focal vision, just like Gabriella (see photograph on page 152).

Over the next 2-4 months, the reflex will gradually wane as neck muscles grow stronger, head control improves, and visual abilities become more advanced. Baby's visual focusing distance will extend beyond arm's length as far-distance vision develops. By the time she is four months old a baby can focus at different distances as effectively as an adult. This is remarkable progress from the visual ability of the newborn, whose immature cortex left her unable to voluntarily coordinate the muscles moving her eyes with the image she saw, and who watched any part of an object or movement that caught her eye. For the newborn, 'outlines of things are larger than the elements within and often contrast more against the background, so they catch her attention to the exclusion of all else'.[13] Observation of newborns and one-month-olds watching an assortment of objects showed that most of the time their eyes remain on one spot on the perimeter.

By two months of age, an infant can range broadly with her eyes.[14] By four months of age she can see stereoscopically and her vision is sharper, and by 6-8 months her vision is sharp enough to see texture. While these visual skills result from development of the cortex, movement and sensory experience have been important trainers in the process, providing mechanisms through which motor and visual skills work together in training the brain to 'make sense' of what it sees. Visual understanding of texture has also been fed through a combination of touch and oral experience.

Baby's first arena of discovery is her mouth. Through sucking, chewing, and biting she first learns about texture and shape, and in the second half of the first year of life, any object that is small enough and can be reached tends to be headed for the mouth. An infant starts to place objects in its mouth as the ATNR recedes and the hand can be easily brought to the midline of the body, even when the head is turned. As long as the ATNR is active, the arm wants to stretch out whenever the head is turned to one side, making it difficult to bring the hand to the mouth. This is just one example of how individual reflexes play an important role in supporting the progress of other skills at one stage in development, but interfere with later skills if they are not inhibited at the appropriate time.

Innate Processes and Modern Mothering Practices?

Reflex integration is written into the developmental blueprint of every normal infant. Provided that the baby has space and opportunity to move, to exercise, and to practise movements, the reflexes of infancy should wax and wane in accordance with nature's developmental plan. The human brain is also able to accommodate different styles of parenting and develop in harmony with the physical and cultural needs of the environment, *but* the physical and cultural demands of our modern technological society are changing at a speed which even our adult brains struggle to keep up with. As Sue Palmer wrote in her book *Toxic Childhood*, 'children grow up in physical (biological) time not in electric time'.[15]

Encapsulated within a child's development is the entire evolutionary history of the human species. The movement patterns that an infant passes through in the first year of life provide an eerie reflection of the movement capabilities of lower-order species, starting from the aquatic environment of the womb where the movements of the unborn child are piscean (fish-like) in character. After birth, if an infant is placed on her tummy, she will initially squirm and wriggle like a beached fish or worm, but a few months later she will have gained enough control of her head, trunk, and lower body to creep along the ground on her belly, using a combination of movements similar to a creeping reptile. By approximately eight months of age, she will learn how to defy gravity, pushing herself up off the ground, rocking back and forth on hands and knees until she can hold herself in a crawling position and really start to move.

Crawling on hands and knees is the beginning of independent discovery, as your child demonstrates a will of her own and an ability to move out of sight and parental control at an alarming speed. This motor ability reflects the movement capabilities of many other land-based mammals, and is linked to greater involvement of higher centres in the brain, particularly the midbrain and limbic system, brain centres involved in the physical experience of emotions, emotional memory, and hormonal response to the environment. Your child may then pass briefly through a 'simian' phase, using a combination of crawling on all fours and 'cruising' on her feet, but she still needs to use her hands to hold on to objects to support upright balance.

Finally, when she learns to stand and balance on her feet, leaving her hands free to explore other aspects of the world around her, she has achieved a momentous milestone in human development. Independent standing and walking heralds a departure from the influence of early primitive reflexes and the acquisition of postural reflexes and adaptive mechanisms, which reflect increased control of higher brain centres over lower ones. The ability to stand and walk also releases the hands from involvement in posture and locomotion. Independent use of the hands represents a major departure from the fine motor skills of other species. It has enabled man to use and make tools and to develop other areas of the brain involved in the development of communication and verbal language.

Motor abilities provide a reflection of brain development and integration, but they need *time*, opportunity, and practice to reach optimum performance. This is where modern parenting often seeks to 'accelerate' or 'bypass' phases of natural development to fit in with the demands of the modern age.

In less technologically advanced societies, a child's physical world begins and ends with her mother. In a book *Our babies, ourselves* Meredith Small[16] describes various child-rearing practices of other peoples. A baby born to a !Kung San mother of the Kalahari desert in Botswana and Namibia stays with her mother at all times. She sleeps alongside her mother at night, is carried on her mother's body during the day by means of a sling made from animal skin, the 'kaross', which is hung from her mother's hip so that the baby has both access to the breast and can see everything from her mother's vantage point. From an early age, the baby is able to reach for the breast and feed herself whenever she wants, providing comfort as well as food without necessarily distracting her mother from her tasks.

In other hunter-gatherer societies such as among the Ache of South America who live in the mixed forest region of Paraguay, infants are carried in a sling on the back and also suckle at will. Anthropologists found that during the first year of life, infants spend 93 per cent of their daylight time and 100 per cent of their night time in physical contact with their mothers.[17] Babies are carried in slings for the first 18 months and then learn to ride on the top of carried baskets, later graduating to riding piggyback style with their fathers and other family members, only being forced to walk from about 5 years of age.[18] This makes sense living in an environment where the terrain harbours hazards from insects and other forest dwelling creatures, and children grow up to develop skills appropriate to their environment and their culture. Ache children learn botany from being taught how to forage with the women for fruit and larvae from an early age.

> By eight years of age they can easily read the signs of a trail and can navigate between neighbouring camps on their own. By ten years of age, boys carry their own bows and girls baby-sit and do domestic chores. By the age of thirteen girls gather almost a full adult's load of forest foods. In a sense, children this age are independent of their parents, still tightly connected to the band, but not as physically or nutritionally dependent.[19]

These different styles of parenting lead to the development of different specialist skills. Close physical contact with the mother in the first year of life and access to the breast appears to foster close social bonds, but Ache children are significantly later than American and San children in developing gross motor skills, and they acquire linguistic skills later.

In South Africa, where some children are also carried on their mother's back from the early hours of the morning when she walks to work until she returns home late at the end of the day, their visual skills are affected by the limitations of their visual experiences in the first year of life.[20] Carried on the back, rather than in a sling on the side, the baby's frontal vision is restricted by her mother's body, but there is plenty of time in which to develop peripheral vision. The motion of her mother's body provides comfort and an abundance of stimulation to the balance mechanism, which will support later gross motor skills and visual awareness of the surrounding environment (but which may make it harder to maintain central visual attention necessary in societies where *reading* is a requirement for life).

Nearly all societies in which the baby has almost continuous contact with its mother are close-knit communities in which children are taught life skills through imitation, modelling of behaviour, and apprenticeship from an early age. Mother and baby attachment is simply not in question. The dyad of pregnancy continues as a physical way of life for many months after birth. Whilst some skills do not develop as well as in advanced societies, there are social lessons that the Western world can learn from these societies, who enjoy and foster a simpler and more socially cohesive way of life.

Physical contact with the mother in the first year means that the baby continues to share much of her mother's physical experience of the world. This provides comfort in the transition from the uterine world to beginning to become more physically independent in the outside world (age at learning to walk). The ability to suckle at will enables the baby to regulate her own internal state from an early age, and mother and baby learn to understand the body language of each other. Even in the Western world, up to 90 per cent of effective communication is based on the *non*-verbal aspects of language and the ability to modulate our own response to the needs of others. Physical contact and interaction in the early years seems to nurture the ability to 'read' and respond to the needs of people around us.

However, there is also another side to the argument. Some studies (Xingu Indians) have indicated that children who grow up in societies where free movement is restricted in the first year of life either do not develop a written language or have limited use of written language. Movement opportunity in the first year of life appears to have a profound influence in shaping the possibilities given to us at birth, in developing skills relevant to the environment in which we will be expected to live.

The society of the post-technological revolution demands a different set of skills from those of our grandparents 50 years ago, but we should not forget that even in the modern world, the ability to become technologically literate is still built upon earlier skills of physical and sensory experience, spoken language, reading, and writing.

Written language developed from an oral tradition where wisdom, stories, fable, and belief were handed down from one generation to the next. Spoken language is built upon the language of gesture – the ability to show with our bodies before we can speak. While young children are fascinated by the visual stimuli of a computer game or the fast-moving images on a television, these images excite the visual cortex, but they do not put in place the physical building blocks that support understanding of operations in three-dimensional space, control of the eye movements necessary for reading, and the specific eye-hand coordination skills needed for writing. These skills begin their training when a baby has opportunity for free movement and play in a variety of positions in the first year(s) of life. Early reflex development helps to illustrate this point.

Tummy Time

Time spent playing on the floor is like gymnastics for a baby. In the first weeks of life, the ATNR should protect a baby from suffocating when placed on her tummy by ensuring that the head turns to one side (see illustration on page 151). If the baby wants to shift her head position, she has to learn to *lift it* up. Head control is one of the most important motor skills a child ever develops. Control of balance and coordination *begins* with the head, and gradually works down to the neck and upper torso. At the same time, spontaneous movements of the legs help the baby begin to know where her body begins and ends. As muscular strength and postural tone increase they spread from the head down to the trunk and from the feet upwards.

During the second half of the first year of life, the infant becomes increasingly able to isolate and differentiate movement in separate parts of her body while also starting to make different parts of her body work together in coordinated movement. This occurs as a result of integration of upper and lower body movements through the trunk of the body.

Improved coordination takes place as a result of many processes, but two key factors are increasing maturity in the underlying reflex system, which supports posture; and movement opportunity. Head control, so difficult in the first weeks of life, eventually becomes an automatic function supported by two types of head-righting reflexes:

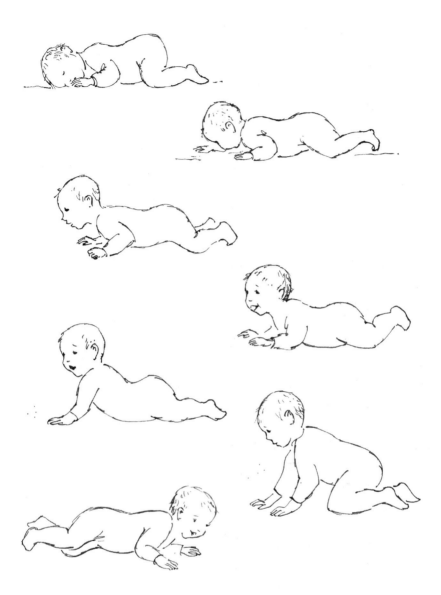

Development of head and body control in the prone
position in the first 9 months of post natal life.

1 Oculo Head-righting reflexes – where head position on the body
   is adjusted in response to visual cues;
2 Labyrinthine Head-righting reflexes – where the balance mechanism
   in the inner ear responds to alteration of head position in the
   absence of visual cues.

Development of differentiated movements
in the second 6 months of post natal life.

The labyrinthine head-righting reflexes respond to the *internal* position of the body, while the oculo head-righting reflexes support posture in response to *external* environmental influences. These reflexes start their development in the first six weeks of life, but will continue to mature and adapt as the child learns new skills in relation to gravity.

Head righting reflexes at work in response to change of body position.

Eventually, wherever the body is in space, the head should automatically adjust its position so that equilibrium can be maintained.

Ray Barsch,[21] author in the 1960s of a number of books on motor perceptual efficiency, described the young child as being as an explorer in space, a 'terranaut' – a space traveller on terra firma – whose first task is to master her relationship with gravity. Head control leads the way to becoming an accomplished explorer in space.

Playtime on the Back

Infant gym.

Time left to play on the back is just as important as tummy time. Before she can learn to sit up, to roll, or to crawl, she must first gain control of head and neck muscles. She must learn how to lift her head, push with one set of muscles, and pull with another. Learning to do this from the floor is far more challenging than from the comfortable support of a baby seat, where a baby is 'placed' in a reclining position with the head already supported.

The ability to control and adjust head position is the beginning of good balance, posture, coordination, control of eye movements, and self-confidence.

Self-confidence begins with being secure in space – knowing your place in space – knowing that you will not fall and that you can adapt to changes in your environment. Only when you know where *you* are, can you effectively find your way. Imagine trying to find your way to a point on a map if you do not know where you are to start with. Even the sense of time develops from the experience of movement through space. How long does it take to reach one point from another? Control of eye movements involved in searching, focusing, and following are all linked to the development of head control and automatic head-righting reflexes, which support visual operations in space. Time spent in space travel in the first years of life provides a foundation for many later life skills.

Ideally, babies need opportunity in a range of positions to work through their reflexes. Modern baby equipment may seem like a godsend to tired and overworked parents, trying to juggle carrying a baby to and from the shops, navigating a busy shopping centre, or simply trying to carry out household chores while knowing that your baby is safe. There is nothing wrong in using baby equipment for short periods of time for convenience and safety, but there is a danger as with all labour-saving devices, that the device takes over the function of the parent. As we see a rising tide of obesity in adults and children, we should remember that if we do not want our children to become couch potatoes, it is important that they do not spend the first nine months of their life as miniature couch potatoes. They also need a range of sensory-motor experiences in different positions, interaction, and *human contact*. In a safe environment, the floor can be baby's first playground. It costs nothing, and the only equipment needed is a clean space, a blanket, your baby, and you.

Knowing your own body and becoming a traveller in space.

Symmetrical Tonic Neck Reflex (STNR)

Some reflexes, like the infant stepping reflex and swimming reflex, are present at birth and disappear soon after birth, only to reappear in a different guise at a later stage. The Symmetrical Tonic Neck reflex (STNR) is one of these reflexes. It has been observed in premature infants born at 30 weeks,[22] is present for a few days at birth, only to recede and then re-emerge at 6-9 months of age, just in time for the infant to learn to how to push herself up off the ground, ready for crawling on hands and knees.

STNR in extension. When the head is lifted up,
the arms straighten and the legs bend.

STNR in flexion. When the head is flexed, the arms bend
and the lower half of the body partially extends.

By six months of age, provided the baby has had plenty of 'tummy time' when awake the baby should be able to support the weight of her upper body with her arms. This means that by the time the STNR reappears, she is ready to defy gravity by getting up on to her hands and knees. However, each time she puts her head up, her arms straighten and her legs bend; if she puts her head down, her arms will bend and her legs straighten. As long as this reaction occurs, she cannot integrate the functioning of her upper and lower body sufficiently to be able to crawl without the bottom dragging along behind.

Infant still under the influence of the STNR in extension. She has control of the upper half of her body, but when her head is up, her bottom still tends to sink back onto her ankles.

Most babies go through a phase of rocking backwards and forwards on hands and knees, sometimes learning to move backwards for a few days before they gain enough control of the STNR and muscle strength in the arms and legs to be able to move forwards without being affected by head position.

Crawling is in itself an integrating function. It provides training for hand and eye coordination at exactly the same visual distance as the child will use some years later when reading and writing. Crawling trains the balance mechanism in a new relationship with gravity. It helps to align the top and sacral sections of the spine in

STNR and ATNR inhibited in the crawling position, enabling Natao to move his head in any direction without affecting upper and lower body control.

preparation for standing and walking, and combines use of left and right sides and upper and lower sections of the body in coordinated movement. Crawling requires the use of all four limbs coordinated with balance and rhythm, reflecting communication between both hemispheres of the brain.

Once mastered in the crawling position, the STNR can still be activated when the baby faces a new postural challenge. In addition to helping the child get up off the ground for crawling, the STNR also helps the infant to pull herself up from the crawling position to

Zoe, using the STNR to pull herself up to a standing position but she still needs to use her hands to support herself, because with her head up her legs want to bend.

standing. As she pulls herself up, her elbows bend, pulling her head forward and making her legs and hips extend, forcing her legs to support her weight in a standing position. This will keep her steady as long as she holds on to something, but if she lets go or looks up, her legs will collapse.[23]

This period of reflex activity corresponds with the 'simian' phase of brain development when a child can stand upright but still needs to use the hands to support her upper body. The STNR remains present in other primates in adult life, but should not be active in humans beyond the first year of life.

Monkeys displaying characteristic STNR postures in walking
(using a primary balance position with arms in the air) and
'cruising' using a combination of hands and feet.

Children who still have traces of an STNR at an older age exhibit simian features in posture under certain testing conditions, particularly sitting posture when the head is bent forward.

When I first started to assess the reflex status of older children in the mid-1980s, amongst the cluster of reflexes tested the STNR would emerge as an 'incidental' factor. As earlier reflexes were corrected using a reflex stimulation and inhibition programme* over a period of 12 months, the STNR was integrated toward the end of the programme. Today, we are seeing a different pattern – a large percentage of the children we see still have a fully retained STNR above 8 years of age as if they were 8-9 month old babies. This has

* Reflex stimulation and inhibition programme. A programme devised by INPP consisting of daily physical exercises based upon infant movement patterns, which would normally be made in the first year of life. These movements are used with older children who have immature reflexes, to give the brain a 'second chance' to inhibit the reflexes of infancy (primitive) and stimulate the development of postural reflexes.

W leg sitting position – often used by children who have a retained STNR in the lower part of the body.

nothing to do with intelligence, but does have a profound effect upon muscle tone, posture, and upper and lower body coordination, making it difficult for them to sit properly at a desk or table. It also has an impact on learning and behaviour because immature posture and control of bodily response results in an unsatisfactory 'match' between perception, motor planning, action, and feedback from the body.

Sitting postures, typical of a child with retained STNR in flexion. When she puts her head forward her arms bend so that when she is writing she is virtually lying on the desk.

The older child who still has an active STNR knows what she wants to do in her head, but her body seems to have a life of its own.

We do not know precisely why the profile of abnormal reflexes that we are seeing in older children seems to be changing, but one explanation might be alterations in child-rearing practices, such as increased time spent in moulded baby seats, children sleeping on their backs, reduced 'tummy time' when awake, and less physical activity in daily life.

How Is This Relevant to Parenting in the First Year of Life?

Vestibular Stimulation

At the core of motor, sensory, and reflex development is the sense of balance. One of the 'hidden' senses, it usually functions below conscious awareness, only surfacing when it is disturbed in some way, such as when we become dizzy, 'lose' our balance, or experience problems which occur as a result of mismatching of messages between the body, balance system, and eyes. Motion sickness and vertigo can be two symptoms of this type of 'mismatch'.

The balance mechanism is located in the inner ear. The inner ear comprises a set of chambers and ducts which house both the hearing mechanism and the balance apparatus. The balance apparatus consists of two types of vestibular organs:*

1 the semicircular canals – three bony tubes which lie perpendicular to each other, and which detect turning movements of the head, and any plane of rotational movement;
2 the otolith organs, which detect linear movements, head tilts, and body position in relation to gravity. One part, the saccule, detects linear movements from side to side and up and down. The second part, the utricle, detects changes in head position in relation to gravity – tilting movements of the head or change of position such as from lying to sitting.

---

* Vestibular – derived from the word 'vestibule' meaning 'entrance hall' or 'court', vestibular organs are the organs of balance housed within the chamber or 'vestibule' of the inner ear.

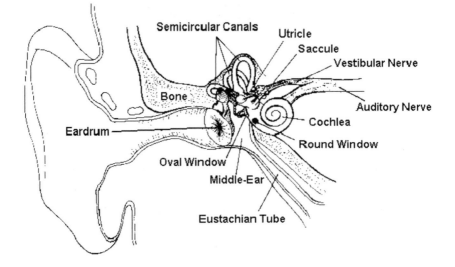

Inner ear showing the vestibular (balance) and hearing apparatus.

Balance and hearing both function by the movement of fluid, which stimulates delicate hair-like receptors in response to movement (balance), or vibration (hearing), which then send an electrical signal to the brain, informing it about the nature of the movement and adjustments that need to be made by other parts of the body.

Several of the foetal and primitive reflexes are a direct reaction to vestibular stimulation; others respond to touch, whilst some are multi-sensory.

Although the sense of touch is the first sensory system to *react* in the womb, the sense of balance is the first system to mature. The balance and hearing organs begin to differentiate at five weeks after conception, and by seven weeks the three semi-circular canals are formed. The pathway linking the vestibular system to the brain stem is in place by 12 weeks, and is the first tract in the brain to mature. It is the only sensory system to be significantly myelinated by the time of birth, although some of its pathways continue to develop up to puberty. Early maturation of the balance mechanism indicates how necessary balance is for the development and integration of other sensory systems and motor control after birth. Balance is the chief sensor of gravity, and a child must learn to function within and against the force of gravity if she is to become confident in space and in control in the use of her body.

Tonic Labyrinthine and Moro Reflexes

When a baby is born, she has only a limited and primitive repertoire of responses to gravity. If her head is not supported, her arms and legs will extend in a reflex action; if her head is flexed forward, she will curl up into a foetal position. This is the *Tonic Labyrinthine reflex (TLR)* at work – a crude reaction to gravity, which comes into play before head-righting reflexes develop. The TLR begins its transformation as the head-righting reflexes begin to emerge at just six weeks of age, first when the baby is able to hold her head up in line with her body when lying on the tummy, but it will take up until 3½ years of age to be completely inhibited. Many other postural skills must be learned before the TLR can be put to sleep. You may well see your toddler accessing part of the reflex when upset or defiant. Toddlers who do not want to be placed in a car seat or high chair will throw their head back in protest, extending their legs and arching the back, making it impossible for the parent to get them into a seated position. This is an example of a reflex being activated when higher control is lost – in this case as a result of strong emotions.

TLR in flexion and extension.

If the head or body position is suddenly changed, the newborn will fling her arms out, extend her legs, gasp, and 'freeze' for a moment, before bringing her arms back across her body in a clasping movement, drawing her legs up and starting to cry. This is the infant *Moro reflex* – an instinctive reaction to sudden vestibular stimulation or unexpected sensory events such as sudden loud noise, change of light, temperature, or touch. Whereas other reflexes respond to specific types of sensory stimulation, the Moro reflex is multi-sensory, although it is most sensitive to vestibular stimulation in the first 2-4 months of life.

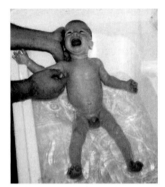

Moro Reflex – a distress reaction response to vestibular
or sudden unexpected sensory stimulation.

The Moro reflex acts as the baby's primitive fight-or-flight reaction, before connections to higher centres in the brain are sufficiently mature to override the reflex. Pathways involved in processing unexpected events mature rapidly in the first months of life, so that by four months of age the Moro reflex should be transformed into a more adult 'startle' response. If something unexpected occurs, the older baby will then react with a short intake of breath, lifting her shoulders, and start to 'search' the environment to seek out the source of danger. She will then decide whether to react to it by crying for help, or ignore it and carry on with what she was doing. The more mature 'startle' reaction reflects the development of higher brain involvement in the processing of sensory stimuli. Cortical involvement is linked to orientation, focused attention, and decision.

Moro, TLR, tonic neck reflexes (ATNR and STNR), and the postural head-righting reflexes are all vestibular reflexes. In other words, they react to stimulation of the balance mechanism and have a direct effect on muscle tone.

Why is the Development of Balance so Important?

Balance supports everything that we do in a world where the force of gravity is experienced by all matter and living things. Balance and proprioception act as our 'internal' senses: they enable us to know where we are in the absence of external cues; and they help two of the external senses (vision and hearing) to process external information needed for orientation and adaptation to the outside world. Touch acts as the barrier and facilitator between the internal and external senses, whilst the sense of smell enables us to detect things that we can neither see nor hear – the chemical sense. Many distinguished scientists and authors have identified cognitive, behavioural. and emotional problems in later life that can be directly linked back to vestibular dysfunction. These include:

Problems Arising from Internal *Security*
- Anticipation of danger
- Increased muscle tension
- Lack of trust
- Negative self-concept
- Frequent accidents
- Fear of heights[27]
- Restlessness (inability to sit still)
- Problems with posture and coordination
- Selective attention
- Awareness of spatial relations
- Delayed development
- Delayed reading and writing[28]
- Fine motor control
- Body image
- Spatial relations and distance
- Head tilting[29]
- Immature postural reflexes
- Poor extra-ocular motor control

- Poor visual orientation to environmental space
- Problems with auditory perception
- Distractibility[30]
- Language impairment[31]

Internal insecurity can then affect how the external senses operate and motor-perceptual efficiency

External Balance-related Problems Affecting Cognition:

- Body schema
- Figure-ground reversal
- Estimation of distance and speed
- Counter-directional and rotated movements
- Symmetry and asymmetry
- Simultaneous and dependent acts
- Chain of action
- Restraints, limits, and minimization (scaling movements down to function in small spaces)
- Predictions of movements[32]

Kohen-Raz[33] stated that all of these physical actions have a corresponding verbal connection. Levinson[34] maintained that immaturity in the functioning of balance and reflex pathways has cognitive and emotional consequences because the reflex, vestibular, and cerebellar systems should act as 'secretary' to the thinking brain. If these lower centres cannot fulfil their functions at a subconscious level, the 'boss' or thinking brain ends up doing much of their work for them.

Infants – Explorers of Space

All cells in the human brain are generated before birth and we only use a fraction of those cells within a lifetime. How brain cells and connections between them are organized is partly influenced by the genes but also by physical experience. Between birth and one year of age the infant brain will double in size. Between one year and six years of age, brain size will double again. If the genes act as the architects of the brain, experience is the builder.

Neurons are born, interact for a while, compete for synaptic connections, then some die off and fewer and more lasting synapses prevail. The infant 'walks' and 'swims' shortly after birth. These primitive reflexes disappear and, years later, walking and swimming appear once again, only this time embedded within the context of different neuronal networks. Neuronal organization produces behaviour. With neuronal reorganization, behaviour disappears. Brain development consists of advance, regression, reorganization, and reappearance.[35]

In the first year of life, the infant brain runs a programme through its own evolutionary past, assembling a jigsaw of pieces through motor and sensory development, which both facilitate and reflect maturity in the functioning of the brain. If as parents we seek to rush through these stages, minimize, or eliminate certain movement experiences in order to fit in more easily with the demands of modern living, we potentially deprive our children of vital building blocks for learning and emotional development. Space, time, opportunity to play, and human interaction are as vital to a baby in the first year of life as food, sleep, and a clean nappy.

Richard Restak[36] described the infant in the first year of life as being

the quintessential existentialist. Future and past – mere conceptualisations born of the ruminations of the present – have no existence to this creature who has yet to learn language. With language, a new brain organisation will emerge; life will no longer be defined in terms of 'reach out and pick it up'.

When the fundamentals of movement have been mastered, the infant is ready to set out on the journey of language.

In a Nutshell…

• Movement is a child's first language.

• Movement enables information received by the senses to be integrated.

• Early-childhood reflexes provide reflections of the functioning of the nervous system. They begin as primary teachers of basic motor skills, but should be inhibited and transformed to sub-serve higher centres in the brain as the nervous system matures.

• Reflex integration takes place as a result of maturation and physical interaction with the environment. Movement is the medium through which the processes of maturation in the motor system are entrained.

• Children need plenty of opportunity for free movement and exploration in the early years.

• The first sensory system to mature is the balance system. Balance is trained through movement experience. Balance supports many functions in addition to posture and motor skills. It supports centres involved in the control of eye movements, spatial awareness, and the executive sense of time, as well as being physiologically linked to biochemical pathways involved in anxiety.

• Space, time, opportunity to play, and human interaction are vital to a baby's healthy development.

Endnotes

1 Alhazen, cited in Arnheim, R., *Visual thinking*, University of California Press, Berkeley, Calif., 1969.

2 Diamond, M.C., *Enriching heredity*, The Free Press, New York, 1988.

3 Arvedson, J.C., 'Swallowing and feeding in infants and young children', *GI Motility online*, 2006, www.doi:10.1038/gimo17.

4 Peiper, A., *Cerebral function in infancy and childhood*, International Behavioral Science Series, Consultants Bureau, New York, 1963.

5 Montagu, A., *Touching: The human significance of skin*, Columbia University Press, New York, 1971.

6 Bainbridge, D., *A visitor within: The science of pregnancy*, Orion, London, 2000.

7 Arvedson, 'Swallowing and feeding in infants and young children'.

8 Ibid.

9 Peiper, *Cerebral function in infancy and childhood*.

10 Ibid.

11 Demyer, W., *Technique of the neurological examination*, McGraw-Hill, New York, 1980.

12 Coryell, J. and Henderson, A., 'Role of the asymmetrical tonic neck reflex in hand visualization in normal infants', *American Journal of Occupational Therapy*, 33/4, 1979: 255-60.

13 Maurer, D. and Maurer, C., *The world of the newborn*, Viking Penguin, New York, 1989.

14 Aslin, R.N., 'Oculo-motor measures of visual development', in G. Gottlieb and N. Krasnegor (Eds), *Measurement of audition and vision during the first year of life: a methodological overview*, Norwood, NJ, 1985, pp. 391-417. Maurer, D., 'The scanning of compound figures by young infants', Journal of Experimental Child Psychology, 35, 1983: 437- 48.

15 Palmer, S., *Toxic childhood*, Orion Books. London, 2006.

16 Small, M.F., *Our babies ourselves: How biology and culture shape the way we parent*, Anchor Books, New York, 1999.

17 Kaplan, H. and Dove, H., 'Infant development among the Ache of Paraguay', *Developmental Psychology*, 23, 1987: 19-198. Hill, K. and Hurtado, A.M., Ache life history: The ecology and demography of a foraging people, Aldine de Gruyter, New York, 1996.

18 Small, *Our babies ourselves.*

19 Ibid.

20 Naude, D., 'Cognitive visual therapy and creative learning', paper presented at Vision, Basic Skills Development and Bridging the 'Skills Gap' Conference, London, November 2006.

21 Barsch, R.H., *Achieving perceptual-motor efficiency: A self-oriented approach to learning, Volume 1 of a perceptual-motor curriculum,* Special Child Publications, Seattle, 1968.

22 Capute, A.J. and Accardo, P.J., *Developmental disabilities in infancy and childhood,* Paul Brookes Publishing Co., Baltimore, 1991.

23 Bender, M.L., *The Bender-Purdue Reflex Test and training manual,* Academic Therapy Publications, San Rafael, Calif., 1976.

24 Prechtl, H.F.R., *Klin. Wschr.,* 1956: 281.

25 Dickson, V., personal communication, 1989.

26 Butler Hall, B., 'Discovering the hidden treasures in the ear', paper presented at the 10th European Conference of Neuro-Developmental Delay in Children with Specific Learning Difficulties, Chester, UK, 1998.

27 Cleeland, L., 'Vestibular disorders – learning problems and dyslexia', *Hearing Instruments,* 35/8, 1984.

28 de Quirós, J.B. and Schrager, O.L., *Neuropsychological fundamentals in learning disabilities,* Academic Publications, Novato, Calif., 1979.

29 McHugh, G.E., 'Auditory and vestibular problems in children', *The Laryngoscope,* 1966.

30 Ayres, A.J., 'Learning disabilities and the vestibular system', *Journal of Learning Disabilities,* 11, 1978: 18-29.

31 Schrager, O.L., 'Postural adaptive reactions in one-leg position depending upon normal and abnormal vestibular-proprioceptive-oculomotor-visual integration', unpublished manuscript, 1983.

32 Kohen-Raz R, *Learning disabilities and postural control,* Freund Publishing House, London, 1986.

33 Kohen-Raz, R., 'Posturographic correlates of learning disabilities and communication disorder', European Conference of Neuro-Developmental Delay in Children with Specific Learning Difficulties, 2004.

34 Levinson, H.L., *Smart but feeling dumb,* Warner Books, New York, 1984.

35 Restak, R., *The infant brain,* Doubleday, New York, 1986.

36 Ibid.

8.

Language Instinct

Babies are born with an innate desire to communicate. This communication began before birth when the baby was able to feel his mother's emotions through the chemical changes that took place in her body in response to her environment, alterations in the nature and speed of her movements, and the tone, volume, and rhythms of her speech.

In the first months of postnatal life, babies have a special language more akin to music and mime than to the speech of the adult world. I was surprised when I learned that up to 90 per cent of effective adult communication is based on the non-verbal aspects of language – posture, gesture, eye contact, facial expression, tone of voice, speed, rhythm, and cadence – to name but a few. Babies are able to detect, and increasingly to use, these powerful components of universal language in the first year of life, and in this sense the first language of life is one of touch, music, and movement.

Babies are born mimics. In the 1970s and 1980s, Melzoff, Moore, and co-workers[1, 2] carried out a series of studies in which they observed mother-infant interaction. They noticed that babies will imitate adult gestures like sticking out the tongue only a short time after birth. They surmised that humans are born with the same capacity to assimilate movements, feelings, and gestures through simple imitation, and that this early language becomes part of the vocabulary of a mirror neuron system, which is able to sense and recognize the needs and feelings of others – the origins of sympathy.

Mirror neurons are brain cells in the pre-motor cortex. They were first identified in macaque monkeys in the early 1990s[3] and they fire both when a monkey performs an action itself and when it observes another living creature perform that same action.

It has not been possible to observe the action of mirror neurons directly in humans, but brain imaging and evidence obtained from EEGs have confirmed that the same mechanisms are at work in humans. The human mirror-neuron system is thought to be involved not only in the execution and observation of movement but also in other aspects of non-verbal language, such as being able to imitate and learn from the actions of others, decode the intentions of others (derive meaning from actions), and sympathetic understanding of the feelings and intentions of others.

The repertoire of gestures available to the baby increases and becomes more refined as motor skills develop, but imitation of expressive movements has been observed within an hour of birth.[4] In the first hour after birth, the newborn responds to being held in its mother's arms, to gentle stroking, and to the dulcet sounds of his mother's voice. The language of a new mother toward her baby is also special. New mothers instinctively talk to their babies softly, using short repetitive rhythms, a type of speech that has been termed 'motherese', and is particularly attuned to mother-infant conversation. Motherese characteristically comprises 'short, evenly spaced utterances with gently "breathy" voicing and undulating frequency in a moderately high pitched range'.[5, 6]

The newborn is not able to see his mother's face clearly for some time. A special part of the eye, the fovea, which sharpens focus on to a central point, is not yet fully developed, and the vision of the newborn is drawn to peripheral visual information, such as the outline of her face and her hairline. It is through a combination of touch, smell, and voice that a baby first learns visually to recognize his mother. The timbre, cadences, and rhythms of her speech will already be familiar to him, from his last months in the womb, but the pitch of her voice and the sharpness of sounds will be quite different once he has made the transition from the inner world of the womb, surrounded by water, to the world outside, where sounds are transmitted through the air.

Being held close to her body will make her voice sound more familiar because he will be able to hear her voice through a combination of vibration and bone conduction, closer to how he sensed the sound of her voice in the womb. It will take several days for fluid to clear from his ear canals and he can awaken to the full range of human hearing.

Colwyn Trevarthen[7] described the progress of early dialogue between mother and child as 'having orientated towards one another, mother and child go through a process of reciprocal mirroring, each moving to reflect the form, to synchronize with the timing and to balance the intensity of the other's expression'. This same mirroring of one another continues to take place in effective conversation in adult life – an 'attuning' to the language and mood of the other.

Trevarthen and Reddy[8] have carried out studies in which they observed mother-baby interaction in the first weeks of life. They discovered a dialogue taking place between the two, with mother uttering short phrases to her baby in a sing-song voice. If she stopped and waited for a few seconds, the baby sang an answering phrase in return. Researchers[9] put examples of the dialogue through a spectograph – a piece of equipment, which analyses the sound frequencies. When printed out, this early conversation showed all the features of a musical composition – timing, melody, and phrasing, one member repeating and answering the musical phrase of the other, suggesting that in the words of a song by ABBA, 'we learn to sing long before we can talk'.

Music as the basis for language has been the focus of research, and the writing of musical programmes for mother and child by Russian paediatrician Michael Lazarev.[10] It is his belief that sound – both music and the sounds of the mother's speech before birth – prime the human brain, making it ready not only for language but also for the underlying rhythms of the physiology of the developing child. His theory is based on seven premises:

1. Human evolution occurs when there are changes in how the potential inherent in the millions of neurons available in the prenatal brain are stimulated, connected, and used.
2. Neuronal potential means that every child is a prenatal genius waiting for the right circuits to be formed.
3. During pregnancy, it is the mother's voice as the primary source of sound stimulation, which optimizes the neuro-generative processes involved in the development of language in the prenatal brain.
4. Prenatal sensory-motor stimulation builds the basis for the formation of intellectual development.
5. In the prenatal period and early childhood, the identity of the

child is strongly influenced by the emergence and development of its motor analyzer.

6. The intonation and motor speech of the foetus provides the background for the growth and development of prenatal neuronal potential.

7. Prenatal education of the child should be taken into account and provide the foundation for all future education of the child.

Lazarev goes on to say that the mother's voice is the most powerful acoustic stimulation for the developing child before birth, providing a vibrational pattern of both the uterine and the external environment. He uses the word 'mummibaby' to describe the unity of this shared vibrational environment. It is his belief that the mother's voice provides the pattern not only for speech and language but also for the underlying structure and functioning of the developing cardio-vascular, respiratory, biorhythmic, motor, tactile, and light-image reflexes. During the postpartum period, neuro-reflectory patterns primed during life in the womb provide the basis for the formation and consolidation of new patterns. His programme of prenatal sound and movement exercises used by the mother before birth is performed again after child-birth and repeated with increasingly active particip-ation of the child over the next 5-7 years. Lazarev has used his method of pre- and postnatal music and voice stimulation with more than 14,000 children in Kazakhstan and Estonia. Results have shown not only advanced motor and language skills, but also a reduction in bronchial asthma and Sudden Infant Death Syndrome amongst families who have integrated his method into their daily lives.

Lazarev's work provides one example of how babies are wired for sound from before birth and awareness of vibratory patterns begins during life in the womb. The hearing system becomes differentiated from the vestibular system at 7½ weeks gestation, but you will remember from earlier chapters that both are involved in the detection of movement and spatial awareness, becoming more specialized with maturity. Paul Madaule[11] maintains that the vestibular system remains involved in the perception of the timing of movement, particularly rhythm, while the cochlea is the specialist for detecting pitch. He describes the vestibular system as being 'the ear of the body' – the part of the ear involved in the motor and rhythmical aspects of sound – while the cochlea is the ear for tone. Foetal response to sound has been observed from 22-23 weeks gestation when the foetus shows signs of 'attending' to his mother's speech by slowing of the heart rate. DeMause,[12] in his description of foetal activity in the second trimester, described how the foetus becomes excited by loud noises. Hepper[13] found evidence of foetal learning in response to sound by studying babies' reactions to theme tunes from television programmes routinely watched by the mother during pregnancy.[14, 15] At just 2-4 days of age, babies of mothers who had watched the Australian soap opera 'Neighbours' regularly during their pregnancy became alert, stopped moving, and their heart rate decreased (a physiological response to orienting) when they heard the theme tune, but they did not react in the same way to theme tunes of programmes not watched by their mothers during pregnancy.

The 'sound' environment of the foetus prepares the baby for the universal aspects of language – the music of language – as well as the more specific sounds and patterns of the mother tongue. Due to the vast number of brain cells and 'open' range of hearing available to a baby at birth, a baby also has the ability to learn any language under the sun if he is surrounded by the sounds of another language (or other languages) on a daily basis, and continues to use the language into later childhood. This is because it is during the first three years of life that the infant's wide range of hearing is 'tuned in' to the sounds of surrounding language(s) at the same time as connections between brain cells are rapidly increasing.

Connectivity and selectivity between brain cells is a life-long process, being strengthened and made more efficient through use, or falling into redundancy and eventually dying off if they fall into disuse. The combination of selective tuning, combined with the developmental period for making and strengthening new connections within the nervous system, makes the first three years of life the sensitive period or window of opportunity for learning to understand and use the sounds of language.

This capacity not only to store the sounds of language but also to use them selectively in the appropriate context can be seen in children growing up in bilingual families. Spanish friends of ours moved to Italy shortly before the birth of their first child. Mama speaks to him in Spanish, his mother tongue; Papa, who is also fluent in English, speaks to him in English and reads English stories to him; while everyone else speaks to him in Italian. At three years of age, Leo is able to adapt his limited vocabulary to the language that is spoken to him, although he will sometimes insist on his father speaking to him in the same language as he speaks to his mother – Spanish! If Leo grows up in Italy and his father continues to speak to him in English, he will retain an oral understanding for both languages. If, however, regular contact with either language ceases before he has developed cortical knowledge of that language, the ability to use it will start to decline in favour of the mother tongue.

The nervous system goes through several periods of increased myelination when pathways that are routinely used become stronger and more differentiated (one of the effects of increased myelination is reduced interference or 'cross chatter' from neighbouring pathways). At the same time the nervous system carries out a spring-cleaning exercise. Pathways that have been allowed to fall into disuse die off in a neural pruning exercise that is designed to facilitate greater efficiency of functioning. Major periods of neural 'housekeeping' take place at 2-3 years of age, at 6-7 years, and again at puberty, enabling increased specialization of function, but at the cost of reduced generalization. This is one of the reasons why establishing the basis for language in the first three years of life is so important. The brain's ability to 'hear' becomes less sensitive and less flexible with time.

Each of the many languages in the world includes its own set of rules for phonology (phonemes or speech sounds), morphology (word formation), syntax (sentence formation), semantics (word and sentence meaning), prosody (intonation and rhythm of speech), and pragmatics (effective use of language). Every language also has its own range of sound frequencies, which are isolated, combined, and blended in different ways.

Only a few days after birth, a baby's ears open up to a wide range of sound frequencies, somewhere in the range of 20-20,000 hertz. Babies listen to the sounds of speech around them, picking up sound patterns and frequencies that are unique to their mother tongue. As they learn to tune into the specific sounds of the language(s) spoken around them, so the developing brain also gradually loses some of the ability to detect the fine-tuning differences between sounds that are *not* used on a regular basis – one of the reasons why the older we are, the harder it is to learn an entirely new language and to speak it without a trace of accent.

Most spoken languages use sounds in a relatively narrow range, from circa 125-8,000 hertz, with the greatest concentration of sounds being between 2,000 and 4,000 hertz – the same range of frequencies carried within most musical instruments and within the foetal hearing range, particularly that of his mother's voice before birth. Hence, training of the ear and of the brain to detect, separate, and combine the sounds of speech began before birth, are carried within the sounds of music, and are given meaning through the words, the stresses placed on syllables, and the grammatical rules of each language. Children learn language by hearing, seeing, and doing, but they cannot learn it alone.

Mimetic Aspects of Language

Children communicate with their bodies before they learn to use words and string them together. They register attention to sounds with temporary stilling of movements; excitement with increased motor activity, especially movements of their toes and their legs. You will remember from Chapter 7 that the Babinski and Plantar movements of the feet often precede vocalization, as if thought must be translated into action before it can be uttered as sound. Reflexes can be used to facilitate communication in positive and negative ways. Use of the TLR in extension was one example of using body language to register protest. Mouth movements not directly involved in speech production can signal interest or desire; and the opposite can also be true.

Neurological investigation of individuals with communication disorders often reveals a connection between speech and motor skills, particularly those of the hand. When carrying out neurological assessments of children with reading and writing problems, I have yet to come across a child who demonstrates difficulty with articulation of fine finger movements (dysdiadochokinesia) who does not also have a history of speech problems. It would appear that motor areas within the brain involved in the development of hand and finger movements are intimately connected to speech production. Other clinicians have noted links between loss of limb movements and impairment in verbal communication. Similarly, patients with aphasia (inability to speak or to understand speech) often make limited use of gesture in communication, and children with motor coordination problems, such as Dyspraxia, have difficulty in reading the body language of others and modulating their responses to the demands of the environment. Consequently, they appear to be clumsy not only in terms of physical coordination but also in social interaction. The body speaks in many ways.

The body is a superb instrument of expression. So used are we to reading body language that we forget how much it plays a part in our understanding of the needs of others, or how much it reveals! Simple gestures, such as turning the head away, signal dislike or rejection; reaching for something (and reaching can be done with eyes and the mouth, not just with the hand) suggests wanting to know more. Opening of the arms suggests a willingness to receive information, whilst placing our hands between ourselves and the other person(s) indicates the need to create a barrier between the communicator and the listener (watch ex-Prime Minister Tony Blair delivering a speech). We learn how to use as well as read non-verbal language, not just by watching others, but also by having our own attempts at communication reflected back. This is where *interaction* is a vital part of every child's language development.

The Importance of Interaction

Children learn by experimenting, waiting for a response, *reflecting*, and trying again. As adults we do much the same when trying to learn a foreign language. First attempts at pronunciation sound atrocious, but the more we listen, the more often we try; and if we can *watch* as well as listen to a native speaker *and* repeat the sounds after them, pronunciation begins to improve quite quickly. This involves not only listening but 'feeling' the sounds with different parts of the mouth, and then comparing the sound uttered to the sound of the native speaker. It is very difficult to learn to speak a foreign language well without using it (motor experience) and receiving feedback.

A child learning its first language also needs time to listen, to practise, and to hear again. This means time spent with parents, being willing to talk to their child, *wait* while the child processes the information, listen to the response, and then be willing to reflect back. This is a uniquely human skill, and cannot be substituted with electronic media. Television doles out a surfeit of speech, but does not *listen* to what the child has to say back. It is a passive process. It omits the motor-sensory integration stage of the child responding to what is on the screen. It provides stimulation and arousal but no physical outlet for that arousal.

When words and gestures are paired, it is possible to start to understand the general *meaning* of words. This is another example of why physical interaction, tone of voice, and facial expression are so important in helping a child to grasp the meaning of language and having a desire to communicate. Babies are fascinated by faces and by movement. Faces that move (during conversation) attract and hold their attention, hence that wonderful moment when a baby returns your smile and will do it again – if you do the same. Facial motion is also helpful in recognizing familiar faces.[16] A face in motion carries a personal 'signature', similar to the individual range, rhythms, and timbre of speech, making it easier to recognize. Actors and mimics utilize these individual characteristics when preparing to play a part.

Sound is transitory, passing within a moment, leaving nothing of itself behind except a brief echo and fainting memory traces. In order to understand speech, a child needs to be able to hear and discriminate between rapidly changing sounds, remember individual sounds and sequences of sound, and recall them. Speech requires the ability to reproduce sounds in cooperation with the motor system and breathing. The ability to recall sounds becomes easier if it is associated in some way with something else, such as a visual image or gesture. This is where written language has provided a system of visual symbols, which represent sounds in time and space. Writing systems transform passing aural events into permanent visual ones, but before a child can rely on the 'back up' of a visual representation of language, he must first learn to hear and remember the sounds of language.

The evanescent nature of sound means that it has to be remembered to be of use. One way of storing sounds is to repeat them. When the voice is activated the body acts as a resonator, making it easier to hear. In young babies, where the head is small and the ears are closer together, vocalization helps to train the ear, while the ear refines what the voice can do. In the hearing impaired, it has been found they respond to much quieter sounds than would be expected if they make the sound themselves, because use of the voice provides vibration through bone conduction, which by-passes the middle ear, while giving voice to sounds helps to improve the efficiency of pitch learning and threshold of discrimination. Use of the child's own voice is rather like a gymnastic session for the ear.

Babies also use visual cues to separate where one word begins and another ends – something we often find difficult to detect when we hear someone else speaking a foreign language at speed. Research, which investigated the effects of visual cues on children's language confirmed how important it is to be able to see the face of a person while being spoken to.[17] The research showed that young children are easily distracted by background noise, particularly when the noise is at the same volume or louder than the person talking. Researchers found that the ability of infants aged 7½ months to separate words in a stream of speech was reduced when there was background noise and the baby could not see the face of the speaker. The researchers concluded that 'children learn best when they are gathering information with their eyes and ears'. Additional experiments showed that

> a second source of sound can interfere and now we know being able to see something along with the audio in a noisy situation plays an important part in infants' language development.... Unlike the printed word, speech doesn't use commas, spaces or periods to separate words and concepts. If there is more than one source of speech, it's especially hard for the infant to know when one word ends and another begins. That is why infants need *to match what they hear with the movements of the speaker's face.*[18]

Another reminder of the importance of undisturbed time spent in adult-baby interaction.

The research carried out on the effect of background noise on an infant's ability to separate sounds within a stream of language has implications for the modern world, in which increasingly quietness is a rare phenomenon. Why has the modern world become so afraid of silence?

The Nature of Sound

Musician and sound researcher Ingo Steinbach said that 'sound is not sound'. Sound is the result of specialized receptors in the ear, skin, bones, and brain which are able to detect vibrations travelling within a specific range of frequencies. All forms of life share the characteristic of motion, and we detect different speeds of motion through our different sensory systems. A world in which we can sense neither sound nor movement is a world lacking in familiar physical energy – a world in which we cannot 'make sense' of what is happening around us. Silence then becomes a source of anxiety.

Occasionally, in a life-time we may for a few fleeting moments experience partial loss of these spatial sources of energy. When there is a total eclipse of the sun, the birds stop singing; unable to use the source of light to orientate in space, we become more dependent on gravity to 'ground' us, until the source of light returns and the birds resume their singing. Hearing assists balance in making possible the ability to orientate oneself within the immediate environment. Gravity tells us where we are, while sound and visual cues inform us about the things around us. When there is only one major source of sound it is easy to attend to it. If there are many sources of sound, it becomes difficult to locate individual sources of sound and to distinguish one source from another.

The Significance of Background Noise

The modern home is awash not only with the sounds of nature but with the sounds of technology: the radio, television, computer waking up, going to sleep, and letting us know that a message has arrived; the mobile 'phone, washing machine, tumble dryer, vacuum cleaner, taps being turned on and off, heating and air conditioning systems, traffic, and the noises of neighbours. As I walked through one of the main shopping streets in Chester in the week before Christmas, I picked up the sounds of different music blaring from four separate shops, all competing with each other, as well as of a busker and a violinist outside, for the attention of the weary passer-by. All of these sounds must be occluded for a child to concentrate and hear the sounds of speech. Is it then surprising that a recent report on children's language in the UK found that in one area of social disadvantage in the UK, the proportion of children starting school with impoverished language was as high as 84 per cent in some areas?[19] The report went on to say that in addition to the 6 per cent of children who have specific speech and language impairments and others who have communication difficulties as part of other conditions,

> there is also a significant group of children who start school with impoverished levels of language which may be transient. A city-wide survey of children's language skills on school entry in Stoke on Trent showed this to be as high as 84% in some areas. Studies in other areas of social disadvantage paint an equally concerning picture. Over half of nursery children are assessed as having language delay,[20] information which confirms Foundational Stage Profile assessment results. These statistics identify communication, language and literacy as the lowest scoring skills areas for children in the early years, well below that considered to be a 'good level of development'.[21]

A Basic Skills Agency survey showed that these startling results are mirrored in the concerns of school staff who believe that around 50 per cent of children UK-wide start school lacking the skills that are vital to an effective start to learning.[22]

Background noise is only one factor that can affect children's language development, and not just because it makes it difficult to hear the sounds of speech. Children who are accustomed to incessant background noise learn to 'switch off' from unwanted sound at an early age. Children who do not receive the stimulation of regular 1:1 conversation may also fail to develop language skills commensurate with their age, and in a growing multi-cultural society, with children growing up in families where English is a second language not spoken at home, these children enter the school system at a linguistic disadvantage. Good childcare and nursery education can provide many benefits, but they do not provide the same amount of 1:1 conversation that can take place between a stay-at-home parent or regular caregiver within the home. When it comes to language development, quantity of time engaged in spoken language is as important as quality of time. These are just some of the social factors, which may be contributing to the picture of impoverished language development in our young.

Adding to this the findings from the INPP assessments carried out in over 20 schools across the UK, that more than a third of primary school children have poor control of balance and immature motor skills, it would appear that something in childhood is changing. Many children are no longer developmentally ready for school.

One study examined the balance and motor skills of more than 600 children in mainstream schools in Northern Ireland. The findings revealed that 48 per cent of children in the sample age 5-6 years and 35 per cent of 7-9 year olds still had traces of primitive reflexes which should not be active beyond the first year of life, together with immature balance and motor skills.[23] Immature motor skills can affect many aspects of language, from non-verbal components involved in social interaction to the fine muscle coordination needed for clear speech and articulation, control of the hand when writing, and the eye *movements* needed for reading.

Behaviour is also a form of language. If a child does not have the verbal language with which to express him- or herself adequately, he or she will revert to 'acting out' what he or she needs to say and will be less responsive to the adult voice of reason.

Early communication and interaction are vital building blocks for later language. Children need to be able to hear nuances of tone, speed, and volume because these provide additional meaning to words. Your baby quickly starts to learn when you are annoyed or upset by sensing subtle changes in the tone of your voice and movements, as well as your posture. Paired with alterations in facial expression, body language and words combine to convey meaning, feeling, and intent to verbal language. When all these aspects of language are congruent it is easier for your baby to grasp the meaning of words. Sometimes there can be conflict between what is said and the language of the body, leaving behind feelings of confusion about the true intentions behind the words. We will return to this theme in Chapter 9 when we explore the importance of consistency in developing emotional security.

First Sounds

Babies' first sounds are cooing sounds using open vowels such as 'ooo, oo oooo', then consonants 'm', 'b', 'g', followed by syllables, naming words, and doing words.

Research carried out by Dr Peter F. MacNeilage, a professor of psychology, and Dr Barbara L. Davis, an associate professor of communication sciences and disorders, published in the 21 April 2000 issue of *Science* magazine, showed that there are four patterns (consonant-vowel combinations) common to babies' babbling and first words in several languages. These include:

- lip consonant-central vowels (mama);
- tongue front consonants-front vowels (dada);
- tongue back consonants-back vowels (gogo); and
- a preference for starting words with a lip consonant-vowel – tongue-front consonant sequence (i.e. 'mad', which has a lip consonant, followed by a vowel, then a tongue-front consonant).

'These patterns, created by basic open and close movements of the mouth and jaw during speech, indicate that purely physical effects may be more important to the creation of conceptual language than previously thought', wrote MacNeilage and Davis.[24]

Matching Sounds to Gestures

'Before man could speak he could mimic; before he could mimic he could pantomime; before he could pantomime he could gesture.'[25] Timing in the use of gesture also undergoes change with development. During the babbling stage up to 9-12 months of age, while they are still partly under the influence of the primitive Palmar reflex, babies reach out with all of the fingers of an open hand to convey that they want something. At about 10-11 months in girls and a little later in boys, babies begin to point with one finger. At this stage, pointing and verbalization start to become more synchronized. By 14 months, more precise finger pointing is used, but the spoken word still lags behind.[26] As adults, we still tend to 'search' for words using motor movements. We also use timing and gesture to add emphasis or alter the meaning of what is being said.

Gesture has an advantage over speech in so far as it is universally understood. Although there are cultural differences in the meaning of gestures, others transcend language. In primitive life, for example, it was a symbol of peace to drop the weapon and extend the hand unarmed, and from this crude beginning, the modern hand-shake probably developed.

Different cultures *use* gesture in slightly different ways. Speakers of Romantic languages such as Spanish or Italian tend to use gestures to accompany the action part of a sentence – the verb; users of Teutonic languages such as German, English, or Dutch tend to use gesture to add emphasis to describe the nature of the action – *how* something was done. Apparently, body language changes as well as the words, according to the language that is being used, lending subtle alteration to the precise meaning and emphasis of the message. One of the signs that a person is beginning to become fluent in another language is when their body language also changes. This may be one of several reasons why it is so difficult to make an exact translation from one language to another in writing. In addition to grammatical differences, the accompanying gestural features cannot easily be translated into the written form.

The importance of congruence in body and verbal language was brought home to me a number of years ago when I was having dinner with an American friend who had escaped from Germany to the United States just before the Second World War. She was 15 years old when she left Germany, and had learned to use American English like a native speaker. At one point in the conversation, she started to imitate something her German grandmother had said. Everything about her changed – her posture, her vocal range, facial expression, and 'attitude' (originally from the French – meaning 'the manner in which the body is held'). The transformation was more than a simple imitation of someone else's manner of speaking. When she changed her language, *she* changed with it. When I remarked on the change, she said that I was not the first person who had noticed the difference. This story has many implications, but in terms of infant language development, it is a reminder of how important it is for children to have, observe, and practise the physical aspects of language in addition to simply hearing what people say.

Communication of Affect

The body also finds it very difficult to lie. Psychologist Paul Ekman has spent more than 40 years studying human facial expressions and the feelings that lie behind them. Ekman's meticulous observations suggest that there is indeed a universal repertoire of facial expressions which help to convey the emotional content of language. He found that basic human emotions, such as happiness and sadness, fear and anger, surprise and disgust have a universal biological basis irrespective of cultural traditions. He and his colleague Wallace Freisen[27] were able to identify 43 specific facial expressions which could then be re-arranged into more than 10,000 possible combinations – an expressive vocabulary quite independent of verbal language, and part of the basis of affect.

Ekman found that facial expression not only revealed feelings but also affected them. After spending a day in his laboratory trying to develop a sad look he found that he felt depressed; if he then spent time mimicking the movements of smiling, his mood started to improve.[28] These observations suggest that in addition to being a vehicle of expression, the body can also be used to change mood or affect. The concept that laughter is the best medicine does not tend to be taught to students of psychiatry!

Mary Bellis Waller also found that physical expression could be used to improve the ability to read the emotions of others.[29] She worked with youngsters whose mothers had been addicted to crack-cocaine during pregnancy. As a result of maternal addiction, part of the frontal lobes of the brain normally involved in the ability to recognize the feelings of others and respond sympathetically, had not developed, resulting in impaired capacity to register and understand the feelings of other people or the effect of their behaviour upon them. She found that if she showed them a picture or a scene of an emotionally charged event and then physically altered their facial expressions to match the emotional content of the event, they gradually began to develop a better understanding of the basic range of human emotions, such as happiness, sadness, surprise, disgust, fear, or relief. As they developed a physical vocabulary with which to acknowledge and describe emotions, their ability to sympathize with others and modify their behaviour also underwent change.

There are several neural connections between the muscles of the face and the limbic system. EEG analysis has shown that mood and facial expression appear to have reciprocal effects on brain functioning:

> Several laboratories have now demonstrated that happy feelings, even sustaining a voluntary but sincere smile, will induce arousal (alpha blocking) in left frontal areas of the brain,[30] while unhappy feelings, including disgust, will evoke larger arousal in right frontal areas.[31] Individuals who are prone to depression tend to exhibit more right frontal arousal than those who are not.[32]

So in addition to the sounds of speech, posture, and gesture, facial expression is an important aspect of language, and can even alter feelings and the geography of brain arousal. Physical expression goes beyond the boundaries of words and individual language, enabling us to understand the emotions of the people around us and respond to them.

Factors which Can Affect Mother-Child Interaction

The importance of early interaction raises questions about the effects of maternal depression on the mother-child relationship. One study investigated an index group of 49 mothers who had had depressive disorders in the postnatal year, and 49 control mothers who had been free from any psychiatric disorder since delivery. Nineteen months after child-birth, the interaction between mother and child was assessed by blind assessors using defined observational methods. Compared with controls, index mother-child pairs showed a reduced quality of interaction (e.g. mothers showed less facilitation of their children, and children showed less affective sharing and less initial sociability with a stranger). Similar but reduced effects were seen in a subgroup of index mothers and children where the mother had recovered from depression by 19 months. Social and marital difficulties were associated with reduced quality of mother-child interaction.[33]

Within the 'medical model' understanding of depression, it is not something people choose to have. On this view there are two main categories of depression: *exogenous,* meaning that depression develops as a result of external stressors, such as loss of a loved one, overwork, change of life circumstances etc.; and *endogenous,* meaning that internal factors affecting brain chemistry have resulted in the onset of depression in the absence of obvious external stressors. Postnatal depression is different in that it can arise from either exogenous or endogenous factors, or a combination of the two.

Hormones exert a chemical action on the brain and the nervous system, and investigations into the effects of hormones on the brain have shown that periods of emotional vulnerability tend to be linked to times of rapid hormonal change. It is not only the action of individual hormones that affects mood but the rate of rise and fall in hormone levels over a short period of time. Some women experience these sudden shifts in hormone levels as pre-menstrual tension. Birth is also associated with rapid hormonal changes, particularly a sharp drop in progesterone, one of the hormones responsible for the 'bloom' and feeling of well-being that many women experience in the second half of pregnancy. Coupled with loss of progesterone at birth are the circulating hormones and stress of labour, lactation, or artificial suppression of lactation. If there have been complications during the birth, the mother may also have received a cocktail of drugs to stimulate labour, and opiates for pain relief. These drugs suppress the body's own production of hormones such as oxytocin, and endorphins, which can affect mood and behaviour.

Many women feel weepy 2-3 days after giving birth, and may feel tired and have feelings of inadequacy about their ability to cope with a new baby, particularly if they are first-time mothers. This is perfectly normal, and quite different from the dragging sense of fatigue, futility, disaffection, and misplaced guilt felt by the mother who develops postnatal depression. If one adds to these endogenous factors affecting the chemistry of the body the demands of a new baby and change of role for the mother, then the combination of changes over a very short period of time can tip the balance of body chemistry to affect the mind. Postnatal depression is nothing to be ashamed of, although many women do feel ashamed of their disinterest in the baby and the loss of love for themselves. Postnatal depression can be understood as a medical condition. It should be diagnosed and treated as soon as possible so that mother, baby, and the rest of the family do not suffer. What happens to mothers, matters to everyone.

Stages of Language Development

The development of language begins in the womb with the experience of sound. Sounds in the womb come from both the internal environment of the womb – the sounds of the mother's body at work, heart beat, digestive system etc. – and sounds that can be perceived from outside the womb. The foetus's experience of sound is multi-sensory and is transmitted to the developing ear and brain as a result of a combination of bone, fluid, and touch receptor conduction. The foetus is particularly responsive to the sounds and patterns of his mother's voice in the final trimester of pregnancy, these patterns forming an acoustic bond between mother and child before birth, and being the sounds most easily recognized by the baby after birth. Preference for the sound of the mother's voice in the first weeks of life is not indiscriminate favouritism, but born of physical familiarity.

By one month of age (usually within the first week) the baby will show signs of response to sound using a motor response such as blinking, moving, rate of breathing, or heart rate, or if the sound is sudden, loud, or unexpected, a Moro reflex response. Social as opposed to reflex smiling emerges at about six weeks of age, and is an example of the baby using a *motor* reaction to signal social communication. Cooing using long extended vowel sounds appears at about three months, and by four months the baby will turn his head toward the source of sound (orientation and location).

Actions which accompany words, such as waving 'bye bye' or pointing toward a desired object, appear at about nine months. Naming sounds for important people, such as 'Da da' and 'Ma ma' emerges between 10 and 11 months, with the word for 'Da da' often preceding 'Ma ma' in English-speaking children. This is not necessarily indicative of a shift in preference for one parent over the other, but connected to the motor aspects of sound production – the tongue movement for 'Da' is usually slightly in advance of the closed lip movement needed for 'Ma'. At 12 months, a baby can follow a simple one-step command accompanied by gesture, and can do the same without a gesture cue at 15 months. At 15 months, a child usually has a single word vocabulary comprising 4-6 words, but may also 'chatter' using the general inflection, cadence, and

Stages of language development pre-birth to 5 years

Age	Type of Response	Understanding	No. of words	Type of sounds	Average length of sentence
6 months in utero					
Birth	Ears may still contain fluid for first few days. Open to 0–20,000 htz. Hears echo and vibration.	Hears sounds as echoes reverberating many times. Head reflexively turns toward the source of sound.	None		
3 months	Acoustic orienting reflex inhibited – *voluntary* head turn toward source of sound not yet developed.	Soothed by sounds, but frightened by sudden loud noises	None	Cooing (open vowel sounds) and gurgling.	Melody, short musical phrases.
6 months	Orientates to sound. Able to ignore reflections and echoes. Can perceive a single sound. Treble tones.	Responds to voice tones.	None	Babbling, repetition of consonant sounds. Babbles or coos to music.	Syllables
1 year	First words appear (talking and walking emerge, at the same time – cerebellum	Responds to own name and a few others. Understanding ahead of speech.	(Single naming words)	Use of single nouns.	1 word

	involved in both). Naming words.				
18 months	Doing words (verbs). Understanding is far ahead of speech.	Understands simple commands.	6-20	Nouns	1 word
2 years		Understands much more than can say.	50+	Verbs, nouns and introducing pronouns. Pronouns: I, me, you. Questions: What? Where?	1-2 word phrases
2½ years		Enjoys simple stories, songs and rhymes, particularly if familiar.	200+	Plurals. Verbs in present tense. Questions: Who?	2-3 word phrases
3 years		Will follow complex commands.	500-1,000	Verbs in past tense. Questions: Why? Where? How?	3-4 word phrases.
4 years		Listens to long stories.	1,000-1,500	Complex sentences using adult forms of grammar.	4-5 word sentences.
5 years		Developing the ability to reason using language.	1,500-2,000		

sounds of a sentence, without using intelligible words. Once again, the baby practises the music of language before words are available.

At 18 months, vocabulary increases to 7-20 words, with continued nonsense chatter, sometimes referred to as 'jargoning'. By 18 months he can recognize one body part, three parts by 21 months, and five parts by 23 months. Two word phrases appear at about 21 months, and speech development accelerates apace from this point onward, *provided* that the child has good hearing, motor development is normal, and he hears and receives verbal response to his speech efforts.

Auditory and linguistic milestones chronicled by Capute and others,[34] demonstrate how the orienting, motor, and musical aspects of universal language precede the more specific sounds of speech.

Pre-linguistic milestones (based upon Capute et al.)

Milestone	Mean age in months	Standard deviation
Receptive		
Alerting	1.15*	1.54*
Orienting (voice)	3.64	1.20
Orienting (bell)	6.08	1.84
One step command + gesture	11.41	1.78
One step command – gesture	13.82	2.36
	*weeks	
Expressive		
Social smile	4.90*	1.90*
Cooing	6.14*	2.33*
Ah-goo	3.29	1.29
Razzing	4.21	1.58
Babbling	5.83	1.54
Gesture	8.45	1.39
Dada/Mama not applied to appropriate person	8.72	1.77
Dada appropriately used	11.09	2.98
Mama appropriately used	11.33	2.76
One word	11.15	2.41

What are the Implications of These Pre-language Milestones for Parent-Child Interaction?

At all stages in development, music, particularly song, can be used to set the scene for the next episode in language development. Song is important because it is a special type of speech: it alters the length of the sounds used in speech, particularly vowel sounds, the earliest conversational sounds that a baby makes, and some of the hardest to detect when speech is translated into written form some years later when formal education begins. When we sing lullabies or nursery rhymes, we educate the earliest of the senses: the vestibular system through gentle rocking rhythms; the tactile system through the effect of gentle vibration on the hair receptors of the skin; and hearing through tone, timbre, repetition of similar sounds, and the *prolongation* of certain speech sounds.

'Lu-lly , lu-lla-, thou li-ttle tiny chi-ld. Lu-lly, lu-lla- lu—llay'

Singing uses vowels for long open tones. Consonants stop or close the open tones, making it easier to detect where one word ends and the next one begins. In 1872, Charles Darwin wrote, 'I have been led to infer that the progenitors of man probably uttered musical tones before they had acquired the powers of articulate speech'.[35] Darwin's observations have been confirmed by scientists at St Andrew's University who found that gibbons, already known to 'sing' to attract mates, also use a type of song to utter warning cries when under threat. They found that animals signal threats using songs made up of seven different notes, and that the frequency and order of the notes change according to the circumstances and nature of the danger.[36]

We live in an age when the visual image reigns supreme, often forgetting that written language developed from an oral culture where knowledge was passed from one generation to the next through the *spoken* word – through stories, songs and ballads that were repeated from memory. The sounds of the stories were familiar long before a child understood the subtleties and message of the story. In this tradition, it was the *voice* that was the medium of learning.

Paradoxically, cultures that preserve an oral tradition often retain a more extended knowledge of history than cultures that have recorded details of their history through documentation. The Aborigines, for example, tell of a time in the Northern Territory when continuous rain resulted in the gradually submergence of the land under a rising sea. All that remained was a mountain top to which all men of the bird totem* retreated, building a dam of stones around their island to keep the rising waters at bay and feeding on animals that managed to swim to safety. When the waters started to retreat, the head man ordered bird-men to fly out over the ocean to see if new land was showing. Eventually they returned with a branch of leaves in their beak, and the survivors were able to travel to new lands over the stretches of land that rose out of the seas.[37] The story bears remarkable similarities to the story of Noah and the Ark, but nowhere was the Aboriginal story recorded in writing. It was passed down from one generation to the next through the telling of stories. Similarly, the Eskimos talk of a time when the earth tilted and the climate changed. Both cultures from opposite ends of the earth appear to refer to an earlier period of global warming when the weather changed and the seas rose.

When children first develop speech, they practise sounds for many months before the sounds convey verbal meaning. The sensitive parent can understand his/her child's language through a subtle combination of pitch, tone, rhythm, cadence, phrasing, and body posture before the infant's babbling makes sense to anyone else. These are the musical and postural aspects of speech, which *præcede* both spoken and written language.

Music, Reading, and Writing

Paul Madaule, Director of the Listening Centre in Toronto, explains how these early skills will be combined later on when learning to read and write. Reading and writing involve instantaneous translation of visual to auditory symbols in both directions. Reading, for example, requires the translation of a visual symbol on the page to an internal 'heard' image inside the head. Creative writing is the opposite process: a thought or 'internal auditory image' must be transformed into a sequence of meaningful visual symbols on the page. The child's own

---

*   **Totem** – a natural object, usually an animal considered to have a close connection with a family or tribal group, which acts as a symbol and talisman for the group.

voice is the medium through which visual-audio-visual information is practised and exchanged – a medium Madaule describes as an 'audio-vocal feedback loop'. Madaule maintains that any break in the functioning of the audio-vocal feedback loop can result in specific language or literacy problems.[38]

In his book *Music and the mind* Anthony Storr[39] describes how good readers carry an internal voice inside their heads when reading silently, as if they were reading aloud. Poor readers do not seem to have developed the capacity to 'hear' this internal voice.

The internal voice is developed through listening and vocalizing in the early years. In the last few months of pregnancy, the unborn child can detect many of the sounds that fall within the range of speech, which correspond with the span of octaves on the piano and the range of the human singing voice. In addition to pitch, the foetus has been exposed to the sounds of the mother's heartbeat (pulse), the rhythms of her breathing, and her movements – but most important of all, the overriding melody and phrasing of her speech. Although the individual sounds and high frequencies are muffled by amniotic fluid and surrounding absorbent tissue, the tones, timing, and inflection of her speech will be familiar before birth. Young babies pay more attention to the sounds of stories and music that they heard before being born, and these same sounds have a soothing effect on the infant in the first year of life.

Most children pass through a phase between about 3 and 4 years of age when they engage in private speech. Pretend play involves imaginary conversations between 'players' in their private world, and if there is sufficient opportunity for vocalization, this *ex*ternal voice can eventually become *in*ternalized and recruited into higher aspects of learning. Private speech can be meaningful, as in play, or simply involve copying the inflections and rhythms of adult speech. Time spent in 'practising' the sounds of speech and regular opportunity to read *aloud* are important stages in developing the 'inner' voice for silent reading and problem solving later on. The modern child is often not given enough time to work through the vocalization and 'sounding out' stages when learning to read in order to internalize the self-voice, which is so important for reading comprehension and spelling at school. Singing is another way of training awareness of the inner voice.

Studies carried out at the universities of Rutgers and Yale by Paula Tallal[40] and Sally Shayvitz[41] showed that children with dyslexia process the sounds of speech more slowly than good readers. As a result of these findings, Tallal devised a special computer program that slows down the sounds of speech, allowing the child more time to 'hear' all the sounds within a word. As the child's discrimination improves, the rate of language sounds used in the programme is gradually increased. A similar effect can be achieved simply by getting children to sing.

When children first learn to read and write, it is developmentally normal to miss out some of the sounds when writing, particularly the vowel sounds, so that children in reception class may write 'cat' as 'ct', or 'Mummy' as 'Mmy'. These are the very sounds that tend to be muffled or glossed over in colloquial speech, but which are sounded out when singing or chanting because a musical time value is assigned to each syllable, and in singing the vowels provide the open sounds while the consonants start and stop musical tones. An example of this can be seen in a simple sentence. 'The cat sat on the mat' can be said quickly, but when the words are put to music, the vowel sounds can be assigned several notes so that the time value of the sentence is extended.

'the ca–t sat o–n the ma–t'.

Singing also has a tactile dimension, because all sound is vibration and any form of vocalization sets up a column of vibration within the vocal tract, which provides tactile feedback to the body, helping to complete the 'audio-vocal loop'. Just as in learning to speak a foreign language we need to practise the sounds of the new language by producing the sounds from a different part of the mouth, so children need the opportunity to 'feel' the sounds of their own language and match those sounds to the visual symbol on the page. In children who become cathedral choristers and learn to sing in several languages from an early age, such as Latin, French, and German, this sounding-out process is often far in advance of their actual understanding or reading ability. At this stage, understanding the words is not of prime importance – it is the ability to pitch a note and articulate and inflect the word with the appropriate meaning which prepares the voice and the mind for more advanced reading later on.

Musical *meaning* is achieved without words, and tends to create visual images in the mind of the listener – a right-brain function – illustrated by the description of certain styles of orchestration as 'mood painting'. The process of sounding out *individual* sounds and syllables involves the left brain, whilst music helps to build a general storehouse of vocabulary (right brain), which can be called upon at any time. In other words, music helps to train *both* sides of the brain.

Language also involves both sides of the brain. The right side is more involved with the non-verbal and emotional aspects of language (body language, intuition, intonation, and the meaning behind the words), but the purely verbal aspects of language are predominantly a left-brain function for up to 96 per cent of the general population.* The articulate brain is the product of many earlier stages of motor, sensory, and emotional language, which are integrated into higher aspects of cognition and language. These are all stepping-stones on the road to verbal fluency.

Visualization and the Emotional Aspects of Language

When we learn to speak we start to lose conscious memory of much of the motor, sensory, and emotional language which preceded spoken language – as if the 'higher' system of communication has imposed a memory wash on the feelings we had before we had the words to describe them. If, however, we do not have words to describe emotion, then we regress back to the earlier language of *behaviour* to express what we want to say. You will see this when your child is very upset – too much emotion, overrides the ability to communicate using speech, and your child may revert to tantrums or inappropriate behaviour.

The same is true in degenerative brain disorders. At the end of her life my mother developed secondary cancers that travelled up her spine to attack her brain. In her last few weeks of life she developed what I can only describe as 'picture language' using picture symbols to replace the words she could no longer find. To an outsider, her words were so unrelated to anything in the immediate environment

---

* A small percentage of the population has their main language centre located in the right hemisphere. This is more common amongst left-handers but can occasionally occur in people who are right-handed..

that they appeared to be nonsense, but combined with gesture and context they did make a kind of sense. Because she was paralysed from the waist downward, she needed a pillow to be placed between her legs before going to sleep at night to prevent the weight of one leg cutting off the circulation of the other. Each night she would try to remind us to place the pillow before tucking her in for the night. She would ask for her 'foghorn', something the relief nurses could not understand, but the 'image' did make sense. A ship's foghorn is a warning system, a buffer between safety and danger.

Reading Aloud

The music of the voice seems to have a powerful effect at all stages in life. In the United States, Snowden[42]carried out a study into the incidence of Alzheimer's Disease in the aging population. In order to eliminate the effects of different lifestyle on his sample he selected a community of nuns as his subjects, and analysed the biographies they had written about their lives prior to entering the convent many years before. The researchers found that those nuns who had had the most advanced vocabulary at the time of entering the convent were the ones who retained their mental agility for longer into old age, some of them into their late 90s and beyond. When questioned further about their early lives, it emerged that as young children, *all had been extensively read to by the adults around them.* When one of the researchers was asked what she thought was one of the secrets of cognitive health in old age, she said, 'when your child is young, *read* to your child, *read* to your child and when you have finished, *read* to your child again'.

This message is apparently in danger of being forgotten. A survey carried out for Granada Television in 2006 revealed that 40 per cent of parents admitted that they had *never* read to their child. These children are missing out not only the development of vocabulary but also on developing the ability to listen, to remember, to sequence the elements of a story, pick up the subtleties of characterization, and perhaps most important of all, how to *imagine.*

Some years ago, I remember hearing a story of two people discussing the relative benefits of radio and television. The man in favour of radio said,

How much would it cost you as a TV producer to cover the sky with missiles filled with maraschino cherries and drop them on Chicago until it was submerged? On radio or in a book, I can create that image in 30 seconds, awaken your taste buds, and make your mouth water!

It would cost the TV or film producer considerably more to show the image visually. The same is true with hearing or reading the written word. The written word encourages the reader to develop his or her own ideas of the scenery, characters, and events as they unfold, which are then pictured in the mind's eye: the entire sensual tableau can be created and manipulated in the mind of the reader, and the imagination is stirred so that each person's experience of the story is entirely their own. Television, film, and DVD provide wonderful entertainment, and the ability to create scenes and illusions is awesome, but the images and interpretation are largely done for us. This is one of the reasons why seeing a film production of a much-loved novel can be disappointing. The film does not always match our vision of how the story or the characters should look.

Putting the Pieces Together

Because the acoustic aspects of speech pass at speed, they must be detected and remembered if the brain is to 'make sense' of what it has heard. Children need repetition and practice to develop a lexicon of sounds. Expressive language involves the translation of thoughts, feelings, impressions, and images into verbal form, which must then be articulated through the motor apparatus. The process of translating thoughts and feelings into words has to pass through the same processes as when carrying out a motor action: visualization, ideation (translation of visual image into motor planning), and execution. In order to put thoughts and feelings into words, those thoughts must be condensed down from multi-sensory experiences into the modalities of bytes and patterns of sound combined with motor coordination for speech. These complex skills begin their training when adults talk to babies and babies talk back.

Look Who Is Talking

How can some of these general concepts be used to help children learn language?

- Listen to music, sing, and talk to your baby before he is born. Watch to see whether certain types of music cause his movement to still, or whether he seems to wake up. Do not use loud music or over-stimulate. Chronic noise can also be associated with birth defects.[43]

- Talk to your baby right from birth. Choose times when your baby is awake and receptive – you can combine 'conversation' times with normal activities, such as when changing, bathing, or out walking with your baby.

- Sing to your baby. It doesn't matter if you do not think you can sing very well – your baby thinks you have the most beautiful voice of all, and it is always easier to perform to a receptive audience!

- Narrate your daily activities to your baby; talk about what you are doing while you are doing it – 'Now we're putting your hat on and your shoes. It's cold outside.' This is then a good time to play games with your baby's feet such as, 'This little piggy went to market' and finish with 'and now all the little piggies are going to sleep', as you put his socks on.

- Have conversations with your baby. If your baby coos, coo back. Be prepared to *wait*. Adults tend to want to hurry on to the next piece of conversation and 'interrupt' before baby has had a chance to reply. If he smiles, smile back.

- Read aloud. This can be a variety of material, from nursery rhymes to stories and poetry. Make your voice lively; act out the characters in the story.

- Play with your baby.

Music Is More than a Pretty Tune

Finally, a reminder that music can enhance many aspects of learning as well as mood and behaviour, and music has the power to civilize or disorganize.

My children all spent a number of years as cathedral choristers. When my eldest son was admitted to the choir, the Master of

Choristers mentioned that the reading age of all of his boys improved by 12 months within six months of joining the choir, irrespective of whether they were good or poor readers at the time of admission. Some of the reasons for this were discussed in an earlier book *The well balanced child*,[44] but in addition to the specific effects of singing on reading, the ethos of a cathedral choir encourages a healthy degree of competition amongst choristers, and sets goals for performance which are far beyond the average school child's experience.

Every chorister succeeds within a very short period of time in attaining standards of musical performance that are equal to the adult members of the choir. Much of this expertise is learned directly through the experience of singing alongside adults with a high standard of musicianship almost every day, as well as the daily discipline of choir practice, and the support and training of highly skilled organists and choir trainers. It is expected that a chorister will rise to and meet the demands of new and different music every week. Within a few months of being choir members, very few children doubt their ability to learn, to adapt, and to perform.

The effect of this type of music goes beyond the singers themselves. Some years later, one of my sons was singing as a bass lay clerk at Liverpool Cathedral. In addition to the regular singing of services in the cathedral, cathedral choirs also go out into the diocese to sing at parish churches. One Christmas, they went to sing carols at a church in Speke, an area near the airport, which at that time was in need of urban regeneration. The doors of the church were open, and by the end of the service, a crowd of local youths had gathered near the door. As the choir processed out of the church they wondered if they would be taunted, but the group stepped back in awed silence to let the choir pass and one was heard to whisper to the other, 'I didn't know anything could sound like that. It's the most f--- lovely thing I have ever heard'. The tragedy is, it may be many years before he ever has the chance to hear anything like it again.

A similar effect was seen when the BBC commissioned a professional choirmaster to start a school singing group from scratch at a comprehensive school in Northolt, west London. The aim was to take a group of children with no previous classical music training and to prepare them to compete in the Choir Olympics in China in the space of a few months. The project was greeted with a degree of cynicism by many of the children at the outset, but a number were willing to audition and did join the rehearsals. Musically, it was an enormous challenge for the choirmaster, as none of the children could read music, or had ever learned to sing using their 'head' rather than their 'chest' voices. Added to this was the problem of newly broken tenor and bass voices with poor range and control, trying to sing the most difficult parts. The fact that they reached a sufficient standard to be included in the competition was an achievement in itself, but the change that took place in the children during the course of the project was the most striking of all.

A rabble of youngsters gradually became a cohesive group with a sense of pride, purpose, and ambition. They designed their own choir uniform; they started to support each other and to criticize those who did not pull their weight, beginning to take on responsibility for the group's success. They became passionate in their desire, first to be allowed to go to China, then to perform to the best of their ability. When they did not get through to the second round, although disappointed, they all agreed that the experience itself had been the best thing they had done in their lives. Through music, teamwork, and competition, they had started to 'grow up'.

Classical music was used in a different way in a school in South Wales. A science teacher with a background in physiology and biochemistry was struggling to motivate a disinterested group of children with special needs in a comprehensive school. Based on information that the behaviour of children with special needs may partly result from frustration arising from poor physical coordination, and resulting inability to perform manual tasks, she set about trying to find a way of improving the coordination centres in the brain by using frequency specific stimulation. During the 1990s there was an explosion of interest and enthusiasm for the music of Mozart and the benefits believed to be derived from 'the Mozart effect'.

Mozart's music uses a wide range of sound frequencies, and is particularly rich in high frequencies (thought to be partly the result of Mozart's young age when he started to compose). Savan[45] decided to introduce Mozart into the classroom to see whether there would be any effect on the behaviour of the pupils. She also carried out physiological measures of blood pressure, pulse rate, and temperature to see whether Mozart affected physiology and behaviour.

In the sessions where music was introduced, there was significant improvement in behaviour and reductions in all physiological measures – a sign of lowered hyper-arousal. These physiological changes did not take place when background music was not being played, and during these sessions body temperature also rose. She concluded that 'certain kinds of background music can lead to an improvement in behaviour of children with emotional and behavioural difficulties'. Certain frequencies and certain rhythms are known to have an organizing effect upon the brain and to stimulate cognitive processes.

Not everyone can tolerate background music. Some people find it helps them to concentrate, others do not, and the type of music is also subject to individual taste, so caution should be exercised in applying these findings to different situations and problems. Nevertheless, these previous three examples provide illustrations to support the theory that music has many functions. Lazarev maintains that it stimulates pathways involved in communication, motor control, physiological rhythms, and affect prenatally; Darwin believed that music was a precursor to language; Trevarthen and others have shown how early language is music, and music education later on influences learning, states of arousal, and behaviour. Mother, movement, and music are 'the 3 Ms' of pre-school education.

In a Nutshell…

- Babies have an innate desire to communicate.

- Early expressive language in the first year of life is more akin to music and mime than to adult speech.

- The mother's voice in the last few months before birth as well as after birth is a powerful instrument of communication.

- Movement through gesture, and song through cooing and the use of answering phrases precede verbal expressive language in infancy.

- Babies respond best when adults take time to listen and respond to the infant's attempts at communication.

- Non-verbal language accounts for up to 90% of effective communication.

- The body has a language of its own. Body postures, gestures and expression not only reflect mood but can also influence emotional state.

- Interaction and social engagement with primary care-givers are essential ingredients of language development.

- Written language evolved from oral tradition.

- Use of the child's own voice is the primary medium through which a child learns to match speech sounds to written language.

- Background noise tends to reduce listening ability.

Endnotes

1 Meltzoff, A.N. and Moore, M.K., 'Imitation of facial and manual gestures by human neonates', *Science*, 198, 1977: 75-8.

2 Meltzoff, A.N. and Moore, M.K., 'Newborn infants imitate adult facial gestures', *Child Development*, 54, 1983: 702-9.

3 Gallese, V., Fadiga, I., and Rizzolatti, G., 'Action recognition in the pre-motor cortex', *Brain*, 119, 1996: 593-609.

4 Kugiumutzakis, J.E., 'The origins of development and function of early infant imitation', Uppsala University Ph.D. thesis, *Acta Universitatis Uppsaliensis*, 35, 1985.

5 Fernald, A., 'The perceptual and affective salience of mother's speech to infants', in L. Feagans, C. Garvey, R. Golinkoff, and others (Eds), *The origins and growth of communication*, Ablex, Norwood, NJ, 1984.

6 Fernald, A. and Simon, T., 'Expanded intonation contours in mothers' speech to newborns', *Develop. Psychol.*, 20, 1984: 104-13.

7 Trevarthen, C., 'Development of early social interactions and the affective regulation of brain growth', in G. Von Euler, H. Forssberg, and H. H. Lagercrantz, (Eds), *Neurobiology of early infant behaviour*, Wenner-Gren Center International Symposium Series. 55; Macmillan Press, London, 1989, pp. 191-216.

8 Trevarthen, C. and Reddy, V., 'Consciousness in infants', in M. Velmer and S. Schneider (Eds), *A companion to consciousness*, Blackwells, Oxford, 2006.

9 Trevarthen, C., 'Pleasure from others' movements. How body massage and music speak with one voice to infants and give meaning to life', paper presented at the GICM Professional Conference, Coventry, 7 October 2006.

10 Lazarev, M., 'Foetal neurogymnastics', paper presented at the 16th European Conference of Neuro-Developmental Delay in Children with Specific Learning Difficulties, Chester, March 2004.

11 Madaule, P., *When listening comes alive*, Moulin Publishing, Box 560, Ontario, 1993.

12 deMause, L., *Foundations of psychohistory*, Creative Roots, New York, 1982.

13 Hepper, P.G., 'Fetal memory: does it exist? What does it do?', *Acta Paediatrica*, Supplement 416, 1996: 16-20.

14 Hepper, P.G., 'Foetal "soap" addiction', *The Lancet,* 11 June 1988: 1347-8.

15 Hepper, P.G., 'An examination of fetal learning before and after birth', *Irish Journal of Psychology,* 12, 1991: 95-107,

16 Barrett, S.E., Spence, M.J., Abdi, H., and O'Toole, A.J., 'Psychological and neural perspectives on the role of motion in face recognition', *Behavioural and Cognitive Neuro-science Reviews,* 2/1, 2003: 5-46.

17 Hollich, G., Rochelle, S., Newman, R.S., and Jusczyk, P.W., 'Infants' use of synchronized visual information to separate streams of speech', *Child Development,* 76 (3), 2005: 598-613.

18 Hollich, G., cited in A. Patterson- Nueubert, 'Research: Noise, visual cues affect infants' language development', *Purdue University News,* 15 June 2005, italics added.

19 **www.stokespeaksout.co.uk**

20 Locke, A., Ginsborg, J., and Peers, I., 'Development and dis-advantage: implications for early years', IJCLD, 27/1, 2002.

21 Department for Education and Skills, Foundation Stage Profile 2005. National Results (Provisional), National Statistics Office, 2006.

22 Basic Skills Agency, *Summary report of survey into young children's skills on entry to education,* 2002.

23 Goddard Blythe, S.A., 'Releasing educational potential through movement', *Child Care in Practice,* 11/4, 2005: 415-32.

24 MacNeilage, P.F. and Davis, B.L., 'On the origin of internal structure of word form', Science magazine, 21 April 2000: 527-31.

25 Eichler, L., *The customs of mankind,* Heinemann, London, 1924.

26 Wachsmith, I., 'Gestures offer insight', *Scientific American,* Oct/ Nov. 2006.

27 Ekman, P. and Friesen, W.V., *Manual for the Facial Action Coding System,* Consulting Psychologists Press, Palo Alto, 1977.

28 Ekman, P., *Emotions revealed: Recognizing faces and feelings to improve communication and emotional life,* Times Books, New York, 2003.

29 Bellis Waller, M., personal communication, 2003.

30 Ekman, P., Davidson, R.J., and Friesen, W.V., 'The Duchenne smile: emotional expression and brain physiology II', *J. Person. Soc. Psych.,* 58, 1990: 342-53.

31 Davidson, R.J., 'Anterior cerebral asymmetry and the nature of emotion', *Brain Cog.,* 20, 1992: 125-51.

32 Panksepp, J., *Affective neuroscience: The foundations of human and animal emotions,* Oxford University Press, Oxford, 1998.

33 Stein, A., Gath, D.H., Bucher, J., Bond, A., Day, A., and Cooper, P.J., 'The relationship between post-natal depression and mother-child interaction', *British Journal of Psychiatry,* 158, 1991: 46-52.

34 Capute, A.J., Pasquale, J., and Accardo, P.J., 'Linguistic and auditory milestones during the first two years of life: a language inventory for the practitioner', *Clinical Pediatrics,* 17/11, 1978: 847-53.

35 Darwin, C., *The expression of the emotions in man and animals,* New York, 1872.

36 Clarke, E., Reichard, U.H., and Zuberbühler, K, 'The syntax and meaning of wild gibbon songs', *PLoS One,* 1(1), 2006: e73.

37 Robinson, R., *Aboriginal myths and legends,* Sun Books, 1966; cited in James G. Cowan, The Aborigine tradition, Element Books, Shaftesbury,1997.

38 Madaule, P., Workshop on the Audio-Vocal Feedback Loop, delivered to the Institute for Neuro-Physiological Psychology, Chester, November 2001.

39 Storr, A., *Music and the mind,* Harper Collins, London, 1993.

40 Tallal, P. and Piercy, M, 'Developmental aphasia: rate of auditory processing and selective impairment of consonantal perception, Neuropsychologia, 12, 1974: 82-93.

41 Shayvitz, S., 'Dyslexia', *Scientific American,* 11, 1996: 77-83.

42 Snowden, D., *Ageing with grace,* Fourth Estate, London, 2001.

43 Szmeja, Z., Slomko, Z., Sikorski, K., and Sowinski, H., 'The risk of hearing impairment in children from mothers exposed to noise during pregnancy', *International Journal of Pediatric Otorhino-laryngology,*1, 1979: 221-9.

44 Goddard Blythe, S.A., *The Well Balanced Child,* Hawthorn Press, Stroud, 2003.

45 Savan, A., 'A study of the effect of background music on the behaviour and physiological responses of children with special educational needs', research in progress, 1997.

9.

Building on the First Year: The Neuroscience behind Regulation of Emotions

Emotional Development

Michel Odent[1] described the first years of life as being the primal period. 'This is the time when a human being is completely dependent on its mother. It includes foetal life, the time of childbirth and the period of breastfeeding. It is the time when the primal adaptive system reaches its maturity.' The primal adaptive system describes the ancient brain stem (from where the primitive reflexes are mediated), up to and including the limbic system. Because these areas mature rapidly during foetal life, birth, and infancy, the 'primal period' is crucial in affecting the course of stages of its development and future regulation.

Daniel Siegal[2] explained how environmental factors in the first years of life

> play a crucial role in the establishment of synaptic connections after birth.... Caregivers are the architects of the way in which experience influences the unfolding of genetically pre-programmed but experience dependent development.... The release of stress hormones (at key stages in early development) leads to excessive death of neurons in the crucial pathways involving the neocortex and limbic system – the areas responsible for emotional regulation.

He goes on to say that

> for the growing brain of the young child, the social world supplies

the most important experiences influencing the expression of genes, which determines how neurons connect to one another in creating the neuronal pathways, which give rise to mental activity.

The roots of emotional development begin with attachment. *Attachment* describes how infants use adults to teach them how to survive and supplement their functioning until they can do it for themselves. Children need nurturing, protection, and regulation in order to feel safe and able to grow and take care of themselves. A child's attachment to others provides a set of expectations derived from those around him. How does the child expect to be treated by others?

When an infant's needs are met in a consistent manner, he or she will develop trust in others. That trust ultimately results in the child's attachment to the caring adult. For a young child to succeed in life, becoming securely attached to a caring adult is of overriding importance. The attention to needs and attachment produce the roots of trust. Without attention and secure attachment in the early months and years of life, the child will have difficulty developing trust.

Initially, an intrinsic attachment system motivates an infant to seek closeness to parents and other primary caregivers and to communicate with them. Attachment has a primitive survival function as the human infant cannot survive alone; but in terms of emotional development, attachment uses close personal relationships to help the immature brain to use the mature functions of the mother's brain to organize its own emotional regulation.[3]

Hofer[4] described the mother's role as being that of the

infant's auxiliary cortex which serves as an external regulator of the neurochemistry of the infant's maturing brain. Severance of this relationship, neglect or abuse at any stage during the primal period theoretically has the potential to arrest development of those pathways that were particularly active at the time of separation, so that associated emotions or experience in the future re-activate old patterns of behaviour.

We have seen how events during pregnancy, birth, feeding practices, and lifestyle can all affect the process of bonding and attachment. Separation at the time of delivery can interrupt the 'sensitive period' and alter maternal behaviour. Kenell and others[5] found that mothers who had one hour of close physical contact with their nude full-term infants within the first two hours after delivery and who had 15 hours of contact in the first three days behaved significantly differently during a physical examination of the infant at one month and at one year, and in their speech to their infants at two years, compared with a control group of mothers who had only routine contact.

A study carried out in Canada[6] found that increased parental carrying in the first three months of life was associated with a substantial reduction in crying and fussing behaviour in first-borns, particularly at times usually noted for increased fretfulness – circa six weeks of age and in the later afternoon and evening in the first three months. In other words, physical contact fosters increased contentment in the infant and more positive infant-caregiver experience. The researcher suggested a number of reasons as to why this takes place. Babies who were carried through the day were not only more alert and content, but the mothers were more in tune with their infant's demands, responding to them sooner.

When an infant's crying becomes excessive it can arouse negative emotions in the mother and reduce her coping skills. Not only does the baby become more demanding and more difficult to soothe, but the mother's confidence in her ability to comfort him also starts to be eroded. The child also learns that he must cry for longer and more vigorously for his needs to be met.

Paradoxically, securely attached children who have a close and positive relationship with the primary care-giver tend to be willing to explore, tackle new situations with confidence, seek help when they need it, have a positive view of themselves, and express emotions freely. Having received positive and consistent responses to their needs in the early months, they are better able to regulate their emotions later on and 'take care' of themselves.

Every child is different and the time at which an individual child is ready to cope with short periods of separation from the primary source of care varies considerably depending on age, temperament, life experience, and the circumstances of separation. In general terms, the younger the child is, the less it is able to understand that separation is temporary, or to understand the concept of time, and is therefore more likely to experience distress.

The history of childhood shows a disturbing picture of cruelty, neglect, abuse, and exploitation in different sections of society and in attitudes toward children at different stages in history. The wealthy were not necessarily better than the poor, tending to view women as breeders rather than mothers in the nurturing sense and handing child care over to servants, tutors and schoolmasters. The good news is that despite harsh conditions, many children did survive, and the social reforms of the last two centuries have improved the lot of children and what society considers acceptable in the treatment of children. However, as medicine and science have found ways to replace the need for mothers to be physically present at all times, society has forgotten that children still need mothers. As governments make it increasingly necessary for parents to return to the workplace for the financial security of the family, and lure women back to work with the promise of childcare from a younger and younger age, the emotional needs of young children are at risk of being neglected.

We know that babies evolved to be cared for by their mothers for a long time after they are born. We also know that they were meant to develop in a relationship of human tenderness. Babies and children who successfully elicit a tender response from their mothers on a consistent basis grow up to be very different from those who do not. They learn that they and the world are good.[7]

In the eyes of a baby, every mother is a good mother. She has been his world since the moment he was conceived and she is his mirror on the world outside. He has no way of knowing or judging her style of parenting – simply that she is his passport to life. What he does not understand is how difficult the role of mother can be.

Social Factors Affecting Motherhood

Modern society has tended to place new mothers in a state of relative social isolation. Despite government initiatives to increase paternity leave, many mothers in the UK are left on their own with the baby within a week or two of giving birth. This is very different from less complex societies where older women and the community are on hand to help for many months after delivery. Becoming a mother is a matter of biology. Being a mother has to be learned.

Nothing in formal education prepares a woman in the modern world for the arrival of a baby. Babies do not understand logic, reason, or explanation. And having gone on to higher education does not necessarily make it any easier to adapt to the sheer physical nature of a baby's needs. Well-meaning advice on childcare can sometimes separate a woman even further from her natural maternal instincts to respond in a physical way to the physical needs of her baby.

New mothers are often encouraged to establish sleeping and feeding routines, only to find their baby has no idea what routine is. Experienced mothers tend to behave more like mothers in less-advanced societies, throwing the rule book out of the window, following the rhythms of their baby's feeding and sleeping patterns, and gradually easing them into a schedule which fits with the rest of the family. Although the advice given to mothers at the time of writing is that co-sleeping is *not* recommended because research in the West has linked co-sleeping to a higher incidence of Sudden Infant Death Syndrome (SIDS) in the first four months of life, many babies sleep better if they can sleep within sight and sound of their mother in the first few months (a cradle alongside the parental bed is a good compromise). Every baby is different and it can take some time before a mother 'tunes in' to her baby's needs and rhythms and is able to listen to her maternal instincts.

Labour-saving devices such as washing machines, dryers, microwaves, and so on have all helped to make the physical work involved in motherhood easier, but none of them can do what another pair of hands can do. They cannot get up in the night to soothe a baby who will not settle; they cannot replace the mother when she has 'flu and needs to take three days' rest in bed to recover; and they cannot baby-sit for half an hour on a sunny morning when she wants to walk to the top of a hill where there is no track suitable for a buggy. Nor do they provide adult conversation and company. For mothers used to the predictable world and camaraderie of the workplace, the new role of motherhood can seem a very lonely one. Why are we then surprised that many women, who do not financially *need* to return to work in the first year, *choose* to do so, while an increasing number of women do not have a choice for financial reasons? In the current fiscal climate of borrowing, relatively few families can afford the luxury of one wage earner whilst maintaining mortgage payments and regular household bills. The economy exerts a powerful influence on *how* women decide to parent in the first years of their child's life.

The role of motherhood also has a very poor rating in terms of social status. When my children were younger I used to dread certain social events, where inevitably at some stage in conversation I would be asked the question, 'What do you do?'. I soon came to expect the glazed look of fading interest that would pass across the questioner's face when I replied, 'I have three small children'. It was as if I had just issued them with a certificate which confirmed my intellectual level was the same age as that of my youngest child. I remember thinking at the time, and have seen little in the last 25 years to change my opinion, that there is something fundamentally wrong with a society which regards motherhood as a temporary mental aberration which will only be restored to normalcy when she returns to the world beyond children. This is in stark contrast to other societies where the role of motherhood is revered and a girl is not regarded as an adult until she gives birth to her first child.

Allan Schore[8] suggested that in the first year(s) of life, mother acts as the auxiliary cortex to her child's developing brain in the ways in which she responds to his needs and demands. The pattern of external regulation she provides forms the basis for the child's ability to regulate his own emotional state in later life. The primacy of mother as the main regulator gradually alters over time so that father has an increasing share during the second year of life. If this view is correct, then parents and parenting play a crucial part in setting the scene for later emotional regulation and behaviour. The lifelong process of parent*ing* as opposed to simply becoming a parent is of prime importance to society, but society barely gives recognition to the fact that of all the many roles we play and jobs we do in life, parenting has the greatest impact on the future of society.

Choices about Child Care

Much will depend on family circumstances: finances; whether there are two parents involved in the child's upbringing; number and age of siblings; and whether grandparents or other family members are available to assist in child-care. It is not the purpose of this book to make value judgements about what parents should and should not do, merely to point out factors that can affect children's development in different ways so that informed parents can make choices based on the circumstances in which they find themselves. We live in an imperfect world, and it is not always feasible to follow the 'ideal' path.

The Nursery and Child-care Debate

Government-funded studies indicate that children whose experience of education begins as young as two are likely to have a head start of several months in reading, writing, and arithmetic over those who are exclusively cared for at home. However, their findings also pointed to a slightly higher risk that children who had attended pre-school education would develop social and behaviour problems.

In 1997, the then Department for Education and Skills commissioned a study to look into the benefits of pre-school education – the Effective Provision of Pre-school Education (EPPE) study.[9] This study has followed 3,000 children from the age of three to the end of Key Stage 2. So far, the study has demonstrated that there are benefits of pre-school education for attainment and social and emotional development in Key Stage 1. Other findings include that children with experience of pre-school education demonstrate significantly higher attainment in Key Stage 1 national assessments in mathematics and English compared with children who have no experience of pre-school education. This study also found that the children of those parents who actively engaged in activities such as teaching songs and nursery rhymes and reading to the child did better at the end of Key Stage 1 compared to children whose parents did not engage in such activities. The EPPE study will continue to follow children's development to the end of Key Stage 2.

The conclusions about behavioural and social consequences of early child-care have been less clear. Children with 1-2 years pre-school experience were *least* likely to behave anti-socially on arrival at primary school, but for children who had three years of pre-school experience, the incidence of anti-social behaviour at school was *higher* than for children who had been cared for at home or those who had had only two years of pre-school education. The researchers concluded that, 'although moderate levels of childminder care were not associated with increased anti-social behaviour, extremely high levels were'. When the care was provided by a relative such as the grandmother, the children's behaviour was more cooperative.

The Department has also commissioned the University of Bristol to look at the impact of different types of childcare (including informal care, for instance with relatives) on children's behavioural and cognitive outcomes at ages five and seven, using data from the Avon longitudinal study of parents and children.

One interpretation of the findings* is that social integration is one of the earliest developmental skills, which begins within the warm and caring environment of close and familiar relationships nurtured within a family environment provided in a consistent manner by a small number of familiar care-givers. This hypothesis has been given substance by a number of studies carried out around the world, which indicate that larger group-based care can have damaging effects on some aspects of emotional and social development for children under two.

The situation reverses between two and three years, when group-based care appears to benefit all aspects of the child's development. A study carried out by the National Institute of Child Health and Human Development in the United States found that 'the more time children spend in childcare from birth to age four and a half, the more adults tended to rate them as less likely to get along with others, as more assertive, as disobedient and as aggressive'.[10] This is the opposite of what many people expect, as it is often assumed that being with other children and a range of adults will improve children's social skills. Caution should be exercised in interpreting results, because the emotional and social effects appear to be closely linked to the age at which a child is placed in child care, as well as quality and quantity of time spent away from the primary care-giver.

A meta-analysis[11] of the 101 childcare outcome studies from many countries published in peer-reviewed journals between 1957 and 1995 found robust evidence of adverse outcomes associated with non-maternal care in the areas of children's infant-mother attachment security, their socio-emotional development (including increased anger, anxiety, and hostility in boys, and over-dependency, anxiety, and depression in girls), and in their behaviour (including hyperactivity, aggression, and non-compliance). They found no support for the belief that high quality day care is an acceptable substitute for parental care.[12]

---

* This is the author's personal interpretation having reviewed the literature

In the UK, a government-funded study carried out by the University of London Institute of Education concluded that, 'high levels of group care before the age of three *(and particularly before the age of two)* were associated with higher levels of antisocial behaviour at age three'. This study suggested that higher quality care could reduce anti-social/worried behaviour, but did not eliminate it.

Cortisol is a hormone that is released under stress. Level of cortisol can therefore be used as a physiological indicator of stress. Sims and others[13] carried out a study in which they used samples of saliva to measure the cortisol level of children aged 3-5 years attending full day-care centres in Perth, Western Australia. The quality of the day-care programmes was also assessed using a standardized system of evaluation. The findings showed that children who attended day care demonstrated higher levels of cortisol than children in their homes. Children who attended high-quality programmes showed a decline across the school day, whereas children who attended programmes rated as unsatisfactory demonstrated an increase in cortisol level across the day.

Young animals and young children exhibit stress in the form of anxiety when separated from the primary source of love and care. In animals, separation from the parent can act as a trigger to a fear paralysis response, a primitive, withdrawal reaction which temporarily inhibits action by setting in motion a 'freeze' response, accompanied by slowing down of vital physiological processes, such as heart rate, breathing, and blood pressure.[14] An example of the Fear Paralysis Response can be seen in rabbits caught unexpectedly by the head-lights of a car at night. Instead of continuing to run away from the approaching vehicle, the 'petrified' rabbit is frozen to the spot, gripped by a primitive startle reaction, unable to either flee or fight.

Some children are easily overloaded by multiple or novel sensory stimuli. Although the ability to cope with multiple stimuli and new environments improves with age as sensory perception and processing become more mature, very young children can become easily stressed by busy environments from which they have no escape. If this occurs at an age before they have acquired the language to describe their discomfort, they will respond by 'acting out' their distress through behaviour. The key to providing safe and positive child-care seems to be to ensure that the child is mature enough to cope with the environment, and the quality of the environment meets the needs of your child. Constant over-arousal can be as damaging in different ways as an impoverished environment.

Similar results to the Australian study were found at the Institute of Child Development of the University of Minnesota where researchers also examined the effects of day care, and found that in children younger than three, levels of cortisol rose in the afternoon during full days, but fell when they went home and when they were at home for the day. *Quantity* of time spent away from home, as well as age of the child, appear to be mediating factors.

In the Minnesota study, children whose cortisol levels increased were also children that were described by their caregivers, teachers, and parents as being shyer and quieter. Shy children tend to feel overwhelmed by group settings or outside of the home, making it more of a struggle to integrate into a day-care environment. However, several of the studies point to there being a crucial difference in effect on behaviour, depending on the age of the children involved. Once again, the results indicate that before the age of two, children feel more secure if child-care is provided within the home and by a close family member. By three years of age, when language skills are beginning to take off, children seem to benefit in educational *and* emotional ways from some time spent in day care. Maturity is probably a key factor in the degree of stress experienced and subsequent behavioural outcomes.

This raises questions about present government policy in pushing for more day-care provision to the exclusion of other types of child-care. While educational skills such as reading, writing, and arithmetic can be caught up with later on (in other European countries children do not *begin* their formal education until 7 years of age, and at 6 years in the USA), the developmental period for establishing emotional security is harder to put right at a later age. It is my belief that we should be planning for greater flexibility in the time that mothers can return to work, enabling them to spend at least the first year and preferably the first two years at home, before being eased back into part-time work until the child is of school age. Although this view flies in the face of political correctness and what many people would like to hear, the purpose of this book is to write about what *children* need, not what adults would like to do.

Lieselotte Ahnert and Michael Lamb suggest that 'maladaptive behaviour on the part of children who spend many hours in child care may reflect not the direct effects of nonparental care but the inability of parents to buffer the enhanced levels of stress experienced in child care'.[15] In other words, parents by their very presence act as external regulators of the child's internal state, just as Allan Schore suggested.

Child care from the age of three seems to be a positive force for educational and emotional development. Before the age of three, the child benefits educationally but may pay a price in social development. The degree to which social and emotional factors will come into play depend on the age of the child, quantity of time spent in care related to age, quality of care, and the personality traits of the individual child.

Neurological Effects of Early Separation, Neglect, or Abuse

Lack of integration between affect and cognition can emerge in the absence of major trauma or neglect. Michael Commons and Patrice Miller,[16] based at Harvard Medical School's Department of Psychiatry, examined child-rearing practices in the United States compared to other cultures. Technology-driven societies such as the United States and United Kingdom tend to try to foster independence in their children from an early age. There is a fear that giving a child too much attention will result in the child becoming spoiled and over-dependent. Commons and Miller suggest that the opposite is true, and that children who are left to cry for long periods of time and who sleep in separate rooms from an early age may be more likely to develop stress and panic disorders as they reach adult life:

> Early stress resulting from separation causes changes in infant brains that makes future adults more susceptible to stress in their lives. Having their babies cry unnecessarily changes the nervous system so they're overly sensitive to future trauma. The way we are brought up colours our entire society.[17]

They go on to point out that America is a nation characterized by violence and loose, non-physical relationships.

Stress can affect the brain in a number of ways. Much of the research on the effects of stress on the brain has focused attention on the limbic system, functional symmetry of the frontal lobes, and the neuro-chemistry involved. It is also probable that prolonged or repeated stress experienced during times of rapid brain development can affect the *hierarchical* organization of the functioning of the brain in later life, so that repetition of events similar to unhappy, anxiety–provoking, or stressful events in the past activate less mature centres in the brain involved in handling stress in later life. In order to understand how this could take place, it is necessary to describe some of the systems within the brain involved in the stress response.

The Limbic System

The Limbic System (derived from the Latin word *limbus* meaning border) describes a group of interconnected structures that lie deep within the brain, close to its core, and linking lower-brain centres from the top of the brain stem to the higher reasoning centres of the cerebral cortex. The limbic system, sometimes referred to as the 'mammalian' brain,[18] is involved in instincts, drives, and automatic regulation of body processes, whereas the newer and higher, uniquely human brain areas, which are associated with the cerebral cortex, enable advanced reasoning and planning.

The limbic system controls our internal environment, how we feel about things, and how our body reacts. The limbic system can function independently of cortical control, at times allowing feelings to override logic. The limbic system comprises the thalamus, hypothalamus, amygdala, hippocampus, cingulate gyrus, and orbito-frontal cortex, which is important for decision making. Additional structures involved in the limbic system are the mammillary body, important for the formation of memory; and the nucleus accumbens, involved in reward, pleasure, and addiction.

The thalamus acts as a station for the communication of information from the senses to the cortex. It receives incoming information from the senses, and determines the source and evaluates its importance before passing the information on to the cortex. The only sense not to reach the limbic system directly without first being filtered through the thalamus is the sense of smell. The olfactory sense plays a stronger part in animals than in humans, but even in humans, smell is the

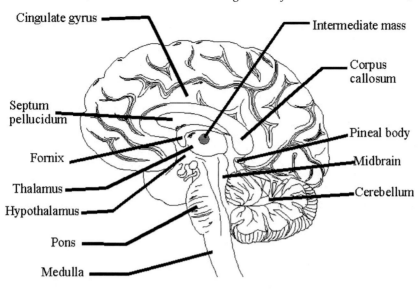

Limbic system – hierarchical organization of sub-cortical structures involved in emotional response.

most powerfully evocative of the senses, triggering memories, emotional responses, and hormonal changes as a result of direct limbic stimulation. It is also very important in young babies, who use the sense of smell to recognize their mother and find breast milk.

The hypothalamus (hypo meaning 'below') has been described as 'the head ganglion of the sympathetic nervous system'.[19]

The sympathetic nervous system is one of two divisions of the autonomic nervous system that controls activities such as hormone secretion and heart rate. The sympathetic division is controlled by two chains of nerves passing from the spinal cord throughout the body, which release the hormones epinepherine and norepinepherine into associated organs and structures. Activity of the sympathetic nervous system is increased under stress and during the fight or flight response, increasing heart rate, dilating the airways and blood vessels for increased energy output, and constricting those of the skin and abdominal muscles to increase blood flow to the muscles, decreasing salivation and activity of the digestive system. It also dilates the pupil of the eye, helping it to focus on distant objects, presumably an evolutionary adaptation to seek and locate the source of danger in the wild.

The *parasympathetic* division is responsible for slowing and steadying the body's internal activities such as heart and breathing rate. It exerts its influence by secreting a different hormone, acetylcholine, which has an opposite effect to the sympathetic nervous system, slowing down heart and breathing rate, increasing salivation, the release of digestive juices, and stimulation of the intestinal wall to promote the movement of food through the digestive systems. Fibres of the parasympathetic nervous system also contract the pupil, allowing the eye to focus on close objects. Both divisions of the autonomic nervous system work together to maintain homeostasis. Fear, stress, or strong emotions can trigger one system into increased action, affecting the biochemistry of the body and the brain. The brain triggers the release of hormones into the body, which responds with changes to physiological processes, that in turn affect the neurochemistry of the brain.

We have all experienced the feelings of discomfort that arise when one or other of these systems is stimulated into over-activity. Extreme anticipatory fear over which we must exert cortical control, such as the prospect of having to give a public speech, can be sufficient to innervate the parasympathetic nervous system in some people, causing them to need to run to the bathroom several times before standing up to speak. Long-term stress can cause over-activity of the digestive system, leading to over-production of stomach acid and the eventual development of stomach ulcers. Others respond with increased sympathetic activity. When they stand up to speak, their mouth is dry, they cannot ignore the rapid beating of their heart, and they have difficulty focusing their eyes on the script in front of them. On rare occasions, severe shock or emotional stress can stimulate both systems into over-activity – the neurological equivalent of applying the brake of the car and the accelerator at the same time: the cortex is confused (like the driver during a skid), and the limbic system runs amok until cortical control is re-established. This can happen at times of extreme fear, anger, or grief, when we are said to be 'beside ourselves' or to have 'lost it'.

In young children, the balance between these systems is delicate, due to the immaturity of the cortex and the greater activity of lower brain centres. Experience during the primal period helps to 'set the clock' for the regulation and control of these centres in early life, so that in later life similar experiences can trigger a 'set' limbic reaction. The limbic system responds before the cortex has had a chance to direct a more appropriate response – the neuro-hormonal basis for impulsive behaviour.

The hypothalamus controls the sympathetic nervous system, comprising nerve cells that are sensitive to temperature, glucose levels in the blood, water levels, the need for sleep, and sexual appetite. The hypothalamus has connections to the pituitary gland, the gland which produces many hormones as well as endorphins (opiate-like chemicals which render a feeling of well-being). The hypothalamus stimulates the pituitary gland to secrete hormones that control the secretion of other endocrine glands such as the sex organs, the adrenal cortex, and the thyroid gland and growth hormone. In this way the hypothalamus affects the functioning of many systems and functions, including blood pressure, menstrual cycle, and immune responses, as well as temperature regulation, hunger and satiety, sexual drive, and activity, mood, and emotions. Abnormal activity in the hypothalamus has been implicated in eating disorders.

Another component of the limbic system is the *cingulate gyrus*. This is involved in the control of certain autonomic functions such as the regulation of heart rate and blood pressure as well as cognitive and attentional processing.

Sensory information from certain cortical areas enters the limbic system directly through the *amygdala*. This almond-shaped structure is responsible for bringing emotional content to memory. While it does not directly process memory, it is thought to harbour the emotional content of memory and therefore give emotional meaning to memory, and switch on emotional response to emotionally loaded information. Perceptual information appears to be matched to information about its biological significance in the amygdala. It is sometimes referred to as the aggression centre, as direct stimulation of the amygdala can elicit angry emotions.

The consolidation of information for storage in other brain areas is thought to be carried out in the *hippocampus*. The hippocampus, named after its shape, which reminded scientists of a sea horse, is one of the earliest structures of the brain, and links nerve fibres involved in touch, vision, sound, and smell with other parts of the limbic system. It responds to repetitive stimulation by synapatic modification according to previous experience, enabling us to learn from new experience by storing new information in short-term memory. It is also important in converting new sensory information into a form that can be preserved elsewhere in the brain, and seems to play a part in deciding whether information is worth remembering.

The *cerebellum** is also linked to the functioning of the limbic system. Primarily concerned with balance and the fine tuning of motor output, the cerebellum links primitive parts of the brain to the higher brain through the limbic region, which combines the cerebellum's unconscious directions with the cerebrum's conscious instructions (motor planning) on how and where to move body parts. The cellular structure and function of the cerebellum is different from any other part of the brain. It comprises the only group of cells within the central nervous system whose function is

> to inhibit rather than to excite, to restrain rather than to act. And it is the restraining action of the cerebellum that organizes the flow of movements initiated by the cerebral cortex and ensures that they proceed in an orderly and effective way.[20]

The role of the cerebellum is not confined only to the regulation of motor output. Investigations using functional imagery have shown that the cerebellum 'contributes to mental and language functions and may serve as an adaptive mechanism whose signals enable the frontal cortex** to execute learned procedures optimally'.[21] If there is a failure in cerebellar functioning, the restraining influence of the cerebellum on associated structures may be impaired, resulting in loss of control. It has been suggested that this may play a part in limbic rage – when cortical control is lost – and we are said to be 'beside ourselves' with rage.

This theory involving the cerebellar-limbic-frontal lobe complex proposed that the cerebellum has a major role in the regulation of sensory-limbic*** activity, which should integrate the activity of the cerebellum with higher brain processes. Prescott[22] suggested that lack of mother love results in

> developmental brain dysfunction and damage which underlies the depression, stereotypical movement disorders (e.g. rocking behaviours

---

*   Cerebellum means 'little brain'
**   frontal cortex (executive part of the brain)
*** sensory-limbic (emotional)

and self-mutilation), hyper-reactivity to sensory stimulation, particularly touch with, paradoxically, impaired pain perception; social alienation, rage and pathological violence against other animals that have been commonly described in isolation reared monkeys and in other isolation reared animals.

He goes on to say that the study of other scientists[23] demonstrated that isolation or lack of movement experience in infancy and early childhood amongst monkeys was associated with abnormal cerebellar functioning linked to rage, fear, anger, hyperactivity, and autistic behaviour.[24] These findings 'opened the "vestibular-cerebellar" gate to brain structures and processes not previously implicated in emotional and social disorders'. In other words, the cerebellum, traditionally regarded as a motor organizer also plays a part in ordering emotional regulation and restraint.

This may be particularly relevant to early child-rearing practices because the cerebellum undergoes its greatest period of rapid growth and development between birth and three years of age, the same time as early motor patterns are developing, the transition from primitive to postural reflex takes place, and the critical period for establishing secure attachments. The cerebellum is an outgrowth of the vestibular system, and insufficient social-emotional or physical stimulation would also result in insufficient vestibular activation. These processes take place as a result of maturation *entrained* through physical interaction with the environment.

The cerebellum also plays a crucial role in integrating sensory experience through motor action, thereby providing a stable platform for perception. Various studies have found that the vermis of the cerebellum is smaller in children diagnosed with autism. This may play a part in the inability of children with autism to integrate sensory perceptions and go some way to explaining some of the *symptoms* of autism – fragmented sensory perception – and difficulty connecting emotionally to the outside world.

Cerebral Cortex

In the 1960s Roger Sperry carried out a series of operations on patients with severe epilepsy which involved surgically severing the connections between the two sides of the cortex. The two hemispheres of the cerebral cortex are connected by millions of nerve fibres which facilitate transfer of information between the two sides of the cortex. This bridge of nerve tissue, the *corpus callosum,* has both facilitatory and an inhibitory function in either the transfer or screening of information from one side to the other. The latter function allows greater specialization of functioning, protecting one side of the brain from 'interference' from the other for specific tasks. As a result of surgical severance of the corpus callosum, the two sides were separated from each other and it was possible to gain greater insight into the specialized functions of each hemisphere.

Almost all mental processes involve both hemispheres, but Sperry, Gazzaniga, and colleagues' work revealed differences in the way in which each hemisphere handles different types of information. Table 9.1 lists some of the specialized functions of each side.

Left and right brain

Left Brain	Right brain
Logical	Holistic
Analytical	Visio-spatial skills
Attention to detail	Intuition
Phonological decoding	Music (untrained)
Speech – comprehension and expression	Recognition of facial expression/paralanguage
Word recognition	Unconscious mental processing (thoughts without words)
Grammar	Abstract mathematics
Sequential processing*	Rhythm
Conscious mental processing	Spatial orientation
Executive sense of time	Abstract aspects of maths
Orbito-frontal inhibition, link to emotion	Orbito-frontal inhibition, link to emotion

---

* The cerebellum is also involved in sequential processing

Subsequently, techniques using functional imagery have shown that stressed and depressed individuals show increased activity in the right hemisphere compared to non-depressed individuals. This is relevant because the right hemisphere of the cortex has more neurological connections in a downward direction to the limbic system and primitive brain centres than its left-hemisphere partner. It would appear that when we are in our 'right mind' we *feel* more. This is important because the right brain is associated with increased negative emotional affect and feelings of pessimism, whereas the left brain is more positive and registers happy feelings. The British comedian Ken Dodd says that we all have a 'chuckle muscle' somewhere. Initiated in early life by simple physical experiences such as being tickled, rough and tumble play, or surprise, this chuckle muscle is linked cognitively in later life to the left brain or the ability of the two sides of the brain to perceive something in exactly the same way at the same moment – synchronicity of functioning or 'double intent'.

The right brain also feels emotions in an abstract sense, but cannot explain them through verbal language: the language of the right brain is sensory-emotional, similar to the language of a young child before it develops fluent speech. The ability to verbalize feelings is important in acknowledging feelings, categorizing them, and being able to decide on a course of action. These are precursors to effective emotional release or 'letting go' of negative emotions. This is primarily a left-hemisphere function and may be one reason why 'talking' therapies are helpful in some cases. Putting feelings into words opens a window on right-brain affect, making it possible to realise cognitively the source(s) of negative emotions, let go of some feelings and act on others. This may also be important because the right brain is more associated with a tendency to withdraw from difficult situations, while the left hemisphere is involved in approach. These different types of response probably underpin individual tendencies toward introversion or extroversion. Observations of patients following a stroke (cardio-vascular accident) have found that when the left brain is intact, patients have more positive emotions and optimism. If the left brain is damaged and the right brain remains untouched, patients are more prone to depression and pessimism.

Adverse life events at any age can contribute to the development of mood and anxiety disorders, but the system is particularly vulnerable at times of rapid development when the architecture of the brain is being built. What affects us emotionally becomes part of the physiology of the body – a type of cellular memory. The good news is that as with all architectural designs, they are open to modification even after they have been built. The nervous system undergoes change throughout life. Genes and early development will play a major part in shaping the structure but experience can still mould the structure and open up or close off new pathways all through the life span.

Severe neglect or a history of physical or sexual abuse during childhood increases the probability of developing major depression or committing suicide by as much as four times.[25] Affective disorders are closely linked to early parental loss and non-specific life stressors. Parental separation through divorce or abandonment resulting in impairment of the child-parent relationship with one or both parents, and conflict of loyalties, is more strongly associated with later depression than death of a parent, where the parent-child relationship had been strong.[26] A number of studies have shown that cold and distant parent-child relationships predispose not only to depression but also to Type II diabetes and heart disease.[27]

Franklyn Sills[28] described the neurological effects of severe neglect or abuse as a form of 'primal wounding'. He suggested that a single traumatic event, a series of shocks, or long-term neglect inflicted on a child *before* the child has the neurological or emotional resources to deal with it affects the neurobiology of the individual, leading to neurological imprinting, which alters the neuro-hormonal response to stress in the future. The child attempts to defend itself from the unpleasant event by 'shutting down' and closing off access to pathways, which if activated again, could result in the re-experiencing of pain, the emotional equivalent of a self-administered local anaesthetic. This primitive defence mechanism can also prevent the child from receiving *positive* as well as negative experiences in the future, effectively isolating one part of the emotional psyche.

We see this mechanism at work in children suffering from attachment disorder and individuals suffering from various anxiety and stress-related disorders. Cognition and emotionally loaded aspects of affect become divorced from each other. This can occur as a result of alterations in the development of lateral processing – the right brain feels, the left brain interprets, but they do not hear each other speak – or immature hierarchical organization resulting in primitive defence mechanisms being triggered into action *before* the cortex, the executive part of the brain, has had time to direct a more appropriate response.

Hierarchy of mechanisms Involved in the Stress Response

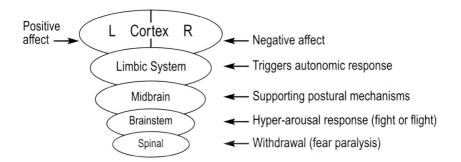

Model to illustrate hierarchy of mechanisms involved in the stress response

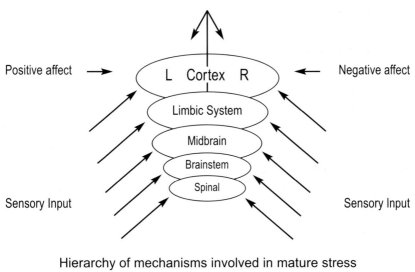

Hierarchy of mechanisms involved in mature stress response, with cortex involved in overall control.

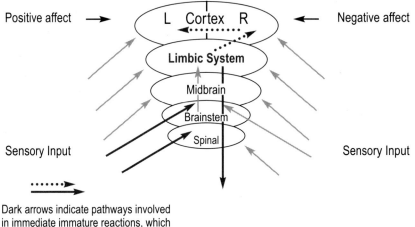

Dark arrows indicate pathways involved
in immediate immature reactions, which
respond *before* the cortex has had time
to process the information and direct a
more mature response.

Immature stress response.

Sensory stimuli are processed at the level of the brain stem (hyper-arousal) or spinal (withdrawal), stimulating structures within the limbic system, which react *before* information is received by the cortex. Reaction first, thought afterwards.

Innervation of limbic structures by lower brain centres (more active in young children) stimulates the autonomic nervous system to respond. Physiological sensations associated with the response are received by the cortex only *during or after* the reaction has taken place. The cortex then interprets the event as being unpleasant. Similar events in the future are sensed by the cortex as anxiety provoking, resulting in a conditioned response instead of an adaptive response. In this way, exposure to noxious events in early development can pre-dispose the child to react in negative ways* when confronted with similar situations in the future.

---

* The reflexive basis for this sequence of behaviour was first mooted in a paper, 'The fear paralysis response and its interaction with the primitive reflexes', 1989, Goddard, S.A., INPP Monograph Series and explored further in the book *Reflexes, learning and behaviour*, 2001. Goddard, S.A., Fern Ridge Press, Eugene, Ore.

Self-regulation is a cornerstone of early childhood development,[29] describing a child's ability to gain control of bodily functions, manage powerful emotions, and maintain focus and attention. Parenting provides the basis for self-regulation by helping the child learn how to meet his own needs using consistent routines and helping the child know what to expect. When a child anticipates his needs being met, levels of anxiety and stress fall. If a child does not know when, how, or if his distress will be answered, anxiety and stress levels rise together with anticipatory anxiety in the future. The same is true for adults placed in dependent situations such as hospitalized patients or elderly people in care. When care is reliable, consistent, and effective, patients tend to recover faster and have a more positive outlook.

Affection, the **b**iochemistry of bonding, **c**ommunication, **d**evelopmental opportunity and **e**nvironmental interaction – these are the primary teachers who shape the emotional structure of the young child's brain – the A, B, C, of emotional development. Parents cannot control everything. Their own lives are also subject to the sea of life. However, there are many factors that parents *can* influence, and these are the focus of the next chapter.

Tips for Daily Living

- Make eye contact
- Smile and talk to your child
- Express warmth and touch
- Be sensitive and responsive
- Get in tune with your child
- Follow your child's lead in play
- Sing and dance together
- Read together
- Spend time together
- You are the most important thing in your child's world – enjoy and share this unconditional love
- Avoid overstimulation

In a Nutshell...

- The environment influences the architecture and the neuro-chemistry of the brain.

- The emotional brain is 'primed' during the early years of life.

- A child's natural home is anywhere in close proximity to its mother in the first weeks and months of life.

- Early separation, neglect, or abuse can affect attachment, stress responses, relationships, and cognitive functioning later on.

Endnotes

1   Odent, M., *Primal health*, Century Hutchinson, London, 1986.

2   Siegal, D.J., *The developing mind: Toward a neurobiology of interpersonal experience*, The Guildford Press, New York, 1999.

3   Brotherson, S., 'Keys to building attachment with young children', **www.ag.ndsu.edu**, 2006.

4   Hofer, M.A., 'Relationships as regulators: a psychobiologic perspective on bereavement', *Psychosomatic Medicine*, 46, 1984: 183-97.

5   Kennell, J., Trause, M.A., and Klaus, M.H., 'Evidence of a sensitive period in the human mother', *Ciba Foundation Symposium*, 33, 1975: 87-101.

6   Urs, A., Hunziker, M.D., and Barr, R.G., 'Increased carrying reduces infant crying: a randomised controlled trial', *Pediatrics*, 77, 1986: 641-8.

7   Kimmel, J., 'Are mothers necessary?', The Natural Child Project, **www.naturalchild,com**, 2005.

8   Schore, A.N., *Affect regulation and the origin of the self*, Laurence Erlbaum Associates, Hove, 1994.

9   EPPE Study, **www.dfes.gov.uk/research**

10 National Institute of Child Health and Human Development, *Early child care and cognitive outcomes associated with early child care: results of the NICHD study up to 36 months,* NICHD, Bethesda, Maryland, April 1997, Research Network.

11 Violato, C. and Russell, C., 'A meta-analysis of the published research on the effects of non-maternal care on child development', in: C. Violato, M. Genuis, and E. Paolucci (Eds), *The changing family and child development,* Ashgate, London, in press.

12 Cook, P.S., 'Rethinking the early childcare agenda. Who should be caring for very young children?', *Medical Journal of Australia,* 170, 1999: 29-31.

13 Sims, M., Guilfoyle, A., and Parry, T.S., 'Children's cortisol levels and quality of care provision', Child; Care, Health and Development, 32/4, 2006: 453.

14 Kaada, B., *Sudden infant death syndrome,* Oslo University Press, 1986.

15 Ahnert, L. and Lamb, M.E., 'Shared care: establishing a balance between home and child care settings', *Child Development,* 74/4, 2003: 1044.

16 Commons, M.L. and Miller, P.M., 'Emotional learning in infants: a cross-cultural examination', paper presented at the American Association for the Advancement of Science, Philadelphia, Pa., February 1998.

17 Cited in Powell, A., 'Children need touching and attention, Harvard researchers say', *The Harvard University Gazette,* April 1998.

18 MacLean, P., *A mind of three minds: educating the triune brain,* The National Society for the Study of Education, Chicago, 1978.

19 Pliszka, S.R., *Neuroscience for the mental health clinician,* Guildford Press, New York, 2003.

20 Binney, R. and Janson, M. (Eds), *The atlas of the body and mind,* Mitchell Beazley Publishers, London, 1976.

21 Leiner, H.C., Leiner, A.L., and Dow, R.S., 'Cerebro-cerebellar learning loops in apes and humans', *Ital. J. Neurol. Sci.,* 8, 1987: 425-36.

22 Prescott, J.W., 'The origins of human love and violence', *Pre- and Perinatal Psychology Journal,* 10/ 3, 1996: 143-88.

23 Mason, W.A. and Berkson, G., 'Effects of maternal mobility on the development of rocking and other behaviours in the rhesus monkey: a study with artificial mothers', *Developmental Psychobiology*, 8/3, 1975: 197-211.

24 Harlow, H.F., 'Prolonged and progressive effect of partial isolation on the behaviour of macaque monkeys', *J. Exp. Res. Pers.*, 1, 1965: 39-49.

25 Agid, O., Kon, Y., and Lerer, B., 'Environmental stress and psychiatric illness', *Biomedicine and Pharmacotherapy*, 54, 2000: 135-41

26 Ibid.

27 Pliszka, S.R., *Neuroscience for the mental health clinician*, Guildford Press, New York, 2003.

28 Sills, F., 'Pre and perinatal psychology', draft extract from a paper on clinical issues related to pre and perinatal wounding, Karuna Institute, Widecombe in the Moor, 2004.

29 Shonkoff, J. and Phillips, D. (Eds), *From neurons to neighborhoods: The science of early childhood development*, A report of the National Research Council. National Academies Press, Washington, D.C., 2000.

10.

Factors Parents Can Control

The Role of Discipline in Establishing Self-regulation

The word 'discipline' is derived from 'disciple' or 'pupil', meaning one who is taught. The original meaning of discipline is therefore associated with teaching rather than chastisement, although teaching often needs to be carried out within a controlled environment to be effective. Parents act as sounding boards for negative emotions and bad behaviour. Attending to children's needs does not mean giving in to them on every occasion. Discipline provides a safe framework within which to operate, with boundaries that should not be crossed and can be enforced if required. Disciplinary boundaries help children to learn where behaviour is acceptable and when it needs to be changed. They help children to feel safe. A child whose behaviour is out of control is rarely a happy child. The goal of discipline is to help children be responsible, to help them realise that they are accountable for the consequences of their behaviour, and to teach them how to modify their behaviour within developmentally appropriate parameters. This can be taught in a number of different ways.

There are several styles of parental discipline, and parents do not necessarily fit neatly into one category or employ one system throughout a child's upbringing. They may also vary their parenting style according to the temperament of the child. This is one reason why one can never assume that just because children come from the same family, their experience of family life will be the same. Every child has a unique relationship with its parents, and siblings who have grown up in the same household will often have a very different view of childhood, and how their parents treated them.

Parenting Styles

1. Authoritarian Control

Authoritarian control tries to shape and control children's behaviour by enforcing a rigid set of standards and behaviour. Obedience is required, and punishment is used to enforce proper behaviour.

2. Authoritative Control

Authoritative parenting attempts to direct children's behaviour using a combination of firm (but not necessarily punitive) control, using verbal give-and-take and, when possible, giving reasons why discipline is being imposed.

3. Permissive Control

Permissive parenting is usually non-punitive. Parents react in an accepting and affirmative manner to their child's behaviour, and the child is consulted about policy decisions and given explanations for family rules.

Of the three styles, authoritarian and permissive parenting are generally the least effective. Authoritarian parents tend to be domineering, requiring submissiveness and conformity from their children, which tends to breed resentment, rebellion, and aggressiveness later on. Children brought up under a primarily authoritarian regime often have difficulty solving problems for themselves when they leave the parental nest, because initiative has not been encouraged.

Permissive parents who do not provide clear guidelines and boundaries tend to foster selfish and immature behaviour, with little thought for the needs of others.[1] The most favourable outcome results from the *authoritative* method where an environment using assertive (rather than bullying) tactics and consistent standards within the home fosters independence, self-confidence and a tendency to be more cooperative and sensitive to the needs of others. Good behaviour receives positive feedback, bad behaviour is not accepted and children are encouraged to understand the wider consequences of inappropriate behaviour. Specific techniques that are successful at one age and with one child need to be adapted as the child grows and develops. Parenting like childhood is a continuous process of development.

Being a Consistent Parent

Whether we are talking about discipline, affection, or teaching methods, adults who behave in a consistent manner are more likely to be perceived as reliable and secure. When behaviour and reaction are predictable, it is easier to 'fit in' with what is required. Parents who threaten their child with sanctions and then do not follow through, or who laugh at their child's inappropriate behaviour and then become angry when it goes out of control, create feelings of confusion and insecurity, which often have the effect of exacerbating unwanted behaviour as the child tries out various possibilities to find out which one works best.

The same is true for daily routines such as regular bedtime and mealtimes. Bedtime can be a time of the day for your child to look forward to, if there is a regular sequence of events, culminating in a bedtime story and finite 'good night' routine.

In large families, it can be difficult for each child to have time with one or both parents as an individual. I am constantly reminded of this when we give children physical exercises to carry out at home on a daily basis under parental supervision. The INPP exercise programme only takes between five and eight minutes a day, but the exercises must be performed accurately, and it requires a parent to be involved. Many parents say that although the exercises are boring, the process of having to do them together brings about a new relationship between parent and child. Often, the 5-8 minutes exercise time each day is the *only* time that the child has the parent to himself. Bedtime routine can be an opportunity for parent and child to have a few minutes of 1:1 time every day.

Mealtimes Matter

Regular mealtimes are also an important part of family life. Physiologically, regularly spaced meals help to maintain stable blood glucose levels through the day. Unstable blood-sugar levels are associated with reduced concentration and hyperactivity (when high), and poor impulse control, loss of concentration, and aggression when low.

Family mealtimes provide an opportunity to introduce your child to a range of different foods, and to set an example for healthy eating habits. Your child can be encouraged to help in simple aspects of meal preparation such as preparing vegetables, measuring ingredients, and laying the table. These sound like minor tasks, but by being actively involved in the preparation of meals, mealtimes become more interesting. It is often tempting for a busy mother, when time is at a premium, to do all the work herself because it is quicker and less messy, but spending a little extra time involving your child in what you are doing usually pays off later.

Family mealtimes are also important for developing social and conversational skills. The age at which you decide to include your child in grown-up meals will vary from family to family, but a child should have regular experience of sitting down to a meal table with other age groups well before starting formal school. This is when table manners (etymologically – the way that something is handled) are learned: learning to handle a knife and fork, sitting up straight, eating with the mouth closed, waiting for others and learning how to take turns and listen, and the art of conversational give and take. These skills learned at the meal table are transferable to many other social situations.

I see an increasingly large number of children in my practice who only sit down to a meal with their parents when they are on holiday or when they eat out. The first clue I have that this is probably the case is that these are the children who constantly interrupt and cannot wait for a pause in the conversation without demanding attention. When parents start to include them regularly in adult mealtimes, the behaviour improves markedly within a couple of months.

Establishing family mealtimes can be difficult if both parents are working, and especially if parents work different hours to run 'shifts' to cover child-care, the school run, and so on. Some couples long for a short time each day when *they* can be grown-ups together. In this situation it can be very tempting to feed the children first and delay the adults' meal until after the children have gone to bed. This is fine, provided there are also regular days in the week when the children do eat with you.

Formal mealtimes tend to take longer than food eaten in front of the TV or 'on the hoof'. The amount of time taken over a meal may be one factor in helping to prevent the development of obesity. This is because it takes up to 20 minutes for the hypothalamus (the satiety centre in the brain) to register when the body has eaten enough. If food is gobbled, there tends to be a continued desire for more, because the brain hasn't had time to register when enough is enough. When groups sit down together at a table, conversation tends to make the meal take longer, and the second course is not usually served until everyone has finished their first course. This allows time for the stomach and the brain to get to work and decide how much more is actually needed. Fast-food eateries and cafeteria-style feeding encourage people to select everything in advance, whether they are going to need it or not. However tedious the preparation and process might be, the manner and manners of mealtimes matter.

Modelling

Children learn as much from example and modelling of behaviour as they do from direct teaching. As parents, you are the model, which your child will imitate or reject, as well as the yardstick by which your child measures, judges, and tries to make sense of the greater world. The small things you do on a daily basis are absorbed and reproduced, sometimes years later and in a different context. This was brought home to me when my children invited their much younger half-sister to come and stay with us for a few days one summer. At that time, my daughter had not taken a great interest in cooking at home, but when I came home the first evening, I found her busy in the kitchen with her little sister baking together and preparing a dish I had only taught her how to make a couple of weeks earlier. As I watched her chattering away, and showing her sister how to do things, I heard parts of myself – the only difference was that Gabriella was making a much better job of it than I would have done!

Just as young children will pick up bad language or snippets of adult conversation and reiterate them in the most embarrassing and inappropriate of situations, so what you do on a daily basis is also absorbed. Although growing children can be incredibly self-absorbed and selfish in their behaviour in the second decade of life, they can also be extraordinarily kind and considerate if called upon in a crisis. These are the times when you will see the results of years of apparently unobserved habits being remodelled for another generation.

Reciprocal Emotion

Children discovered abandoned in the orphanages of Romania in the 1990s were later found to suffer the effects not only of physical neglect but also corresponding cognitive impairment. Although many of them flourished when placed in an enriched environment, specific aspects of cognitive functioning were under-developed.

One girl whom we shall call Sarah was adopted at the age of four by an English couple. She had spent the first 3½ years of her life in a cot, with food handed to her through the bars. The only time she was picked up was when she or her bedding needed to be changed. It took only a few weeks for her well-intentioned new parents to discover that a child who has been neglected in the early years behaves very differently from a child who has grown up expecting to be well cared for. Having never had children of their own, they felt unable to cope with Sarah's needs, and she was placed in foster care within six months of being brought to the United Kingdom. Her foster mother brought her to see me when she was nine years old. Sarah was extremely pretty, well dressed, polite, and tidy. She had developed a good grasp of English, smiled at everything that was said to her, and appeared to be much like any other nine year old girl.

Her foster mother had brought her to see me because she had problems with attachment, which showed up as 'living like a lodger in the family house'. In other words, she neither showed nor appeared to need reciprocal emotional connection to the family around her. The ability to live in emotional isolation was reflected in her physical awareness. If she fell over and grazed her knee, she would never cry; if she had a high temperature she would still get dressed and ready to go to school. Because her physical and emotional needs had not been attended to during crucial formative years, she did not acknowledge them later on, either in herself or in the people around her.

As part of the INPP assessment, she was asked to draw a picture of a human figure. Her picture was of a person with a head, face, arms, upper body, a space, and then feet. When I remarked on the lack of legs, her foster mother said she always drew people without legs, even though the missing parts had been pointed out to her on many occasions. It occurred to me that she would have had very little opportunity to make leg movements or experience the proprio-ceptive feedback of standing and walking when she had been confined to the cot during the first 3½ years of her life. We gave her a series of physical leg exercises to carry out each day with her eyes closed. Two months later, her drawings of people had acquired legs.

During the assessment I also carried out a number of tests for balance. On one test it was very difficult to assess how much effort she used in compensation when trying to maintain her balance. Foolishly, I asked her, 'If you had a scale of 0 to 10 and 0 meant that you were as steady as a rock – nothing could make you fall over – and 10 meant that you felt you could fall over at any moment, where would you put yourself on that scale?'. Sarah looked at me as if she didn't understand a word I had said. Her foster mother explained that this was exactly the kind of problem she had at school, particularly with maths. She could not understand abstract concepts and could not visualize what I was talking about.

The ability to visualize is a non-verbal, right-hemispheric ability, which is fed in the early years through sensory-motor experience. Sarah was not an unintelligent girl, but because the part of her brain involved in visualization and imagination (making images in the head) had not been stimulated in the early years, higher cognitive processes that depend on visualization to solve problems were still undeveloped.

Problem solving involves communication between the cerebral hemispheres in both directions. If one side does not provide the information the other side needs, the child hits a mental brick wall in being able to solve the puzzle. This inability to imagine probably also played a part in her lack of reciprocal emotional affect by forcing her to be over-dependent on left-hemispheric verbal communication – very correct, precise, and literal – but disconnected from emotional content.

Sarah's case provides a reminder of how essential sensory-motor experience and reciprocal affect are in the early years. *Under-*stimulation and neglect have far reaching consequences. When I last saw her, some 10 years ago, Sarah had started to make progress using a combination of a sensory-motor programme and play therapy. The first sign of change was when she started to become rebellious, angry, and naughty, something her foster family had never seen before but was happy to accept because as she began to display negative feelings for the first time, so she also started to need them.

The Changing Face of Child's Play

Play is child's work. Play is the process through which children explore, gather information, and learn about the world around them. Play can be informal or free, social, or purely imaginative. Activities provided by parents for older children such as riding, sports, and music are part play and partly a process of training. Just as important as guided play is the process of *free* play, periods of time when children are left to entertain themselves. Both physical and mental space is necessary for a child to engage in free play.

Play in the early months of life begins with the body, with the experience of movement and exercising the senses. Early communication between mother and baby is through play, and all forms of play help children to learn about themselves and the world around them, gradually extending the scope of their play to a wider circle. Children can play alone as well as with others. Short periods of time where no activities are provided by other sources can be times of invention and creativity. Boredom is only a negative process if a child does not have the resources from past experience to amuse him- or herself.

Between three and seven years of age, millions of neural connections are formed between lower centres in the brain concerned with sensory-motor functions and higher centres involved in cognitive processes. Until approximately seven years of age, the right hemisphere is slightly ahead of the left in its development. Through physical experience, the right hemisphere develops cognitive understanding of space, of visualization and imagination, and as yet unopposed by life experience or the literal logic of the left hemisphere, young children believe that anything is possible. This is one of the reasons why young children can believe in imaginary lands, castles, and people, fairies at the bottom of the garden, pictures in the clouds, and Santa Claus. For the fertile right brain, anything is possible if it has not been tempered by fact. Many great inventors and creators continue to harbour this aspect of the childish mind throughout life. Education and enculturation may restrain it, but the magical thinking of the right brain is what allows us to see beyond what is, and create a better world. Imagination is the mother of creativity.

In the post-technological revolution we have become a generation who seem to have an insatiable appetite for gadgets – toys for grown-ups – which do much of our imaginative work for us. No longer do we have to visualize the person at the other end of the mobile phone, we can see them. I am continuously surprised by how children who have grown up with play stations and other sophisticated gadgets will occupy themselves in my office for as much as 40 minutes while I talk to their parents, provided only with a box of soldiers from the market and a wooden train set.* They will set up elaborate battlefields, plans of campaign, and small towns around the railway station. Many will ask their parents if they can go to the toyshop afterwards to buy a set of their own. In other words, it is sometimes more fun to create a world from simple toys than have one created for you.

As a child, my mother gave me a book called *A little house of your own*. It showed how, within your own home, there were lots of other little houses that you could create for yourself: under the kitchen table with a big table cloth on it, behind a chair, inside a cardboard box, or under a shrub in the garden. My father once created a ship with a look-out post for us simply by nailing a few planks of wood between two branches of a tree in the garden so that we had a makeshift ladder and a crow's nest. We had hours of fun and adventures, travelling to all sorts of distant parts of the world with mutinous crews, weathering devastating storms, and picking up booty from wrecked pirate ships, all in the space of a morning without ever leaving the garden.

Many of the great architects, sculptures, composers, and writers of previous centuries created exquisite works of art from a very young age, producing their finest works in their twenties and thirties. Were people more intelligent and creative with the limited technologies that had existed in previous generations, or have the comforts of the modern age made us indolent with our brains as well as our bodies? Why, in an age where education is accessible to all, do we seem to be *less* able to produce things of beauty and enduring craftsmanship than our forbears?

---

* For those parents who do not agree with giving boys soldiers to play with, children who are allowed to play at being soldiers often work through their aggression in play and are less aggressive later on.

Impact of the Electronic Media

Before the invention of radio or television, for those who had the luxury of leisure time, they had to occupy the mind in other ways: outdoor pursuits, reading, drawing, music-making, socializing, and discussion. The negative side of leisure technology is not in what it does provide for us – there are many benefits; it is what it does *not* provide, or what it prevents us from doing.

On average, American children spend four hours a day in front of the television, and British children are not far behind. This accounts for more time in a single activity than anything else we do except work and sleep. Based on these figures, by the age of six, a child has already spent a whole year of his life watching television.

Hours spent in front of the television, computer. or play station are sedentary hours. They arouse the brain to various states but they do not exercise the body. There is no physical experience or social interaction. The television is not interested in what a child thinks or what he, or she has to say.

The way in which television programmes are produced has also changed over the last 50 years. No longer do TV dramas and stories require sustained attention for the duration of the programme to follow a story line from beginning to end. Scenes are presented in bytes of up to 40 seconds juxtaposing different elements of the narrative, scenery, and characters so that several parts of the story must be held in the memory at one time. Whilst this may be good for multi-tasking, it also encourages rapid shifts of attention and discourages sustained attention on a theme, necessary for sequencing information in an orderly and chronological fashion. While rapid shifts of attention are useful in primitive environments where danger could come from any source, they are not good for processing individual elements of a narrative or remembering detail, as many of us will know if we have had too many interruptions when trying to complete a task at work. Frequent shifts in attention give an overall impression but do not improve recall.

Interviewers and presenters of children's programmes do not help. While the former frequently interrupt their interviewees or are forced to cut them short to fit into the time constraints of programming, the latter tend to shout, despite the fact that children's hearing is more acute than adults'. Is it surprising that children find it difficult to wait their turn and continue to follow a conversation that lasts for more than a few seconds?

Jane Healy, an educational psychologist and author of two books, *Endangered minds: Why children don't think and what we can do about it* and *Your child's growing mind: A guide to learning and brain development from birth to adolescence,* said that over-use of television, particularly at a very young age when a child should be actively engaged in language development and manipulative play, can affect development in a number of ways:

> Higher levels of television viewing correlate with lowered academic performance, especially reading scores. This may be because television substitutes for reading practice, partially because the compellingly visual nature of the stimulus blocks development of left-hemisphere language circuitry. A young brain manipulated by jazzy visual effects cannot divide attention to listen carefully to language. Moreover, the 'two-minute mind' easily becomes impatient with any material requiring depth of processing.[2]

A longitudinal study investigated whether early television exposure (ages 1-3) was associated with attentional problems at age 7.[3] Using data from 1,278 children aged one and 1,345 aged three years, 10 per cent had attentional problems at age seven. In a logistic regression model, hours of television viewed per day at both ages one and three was associated with attentional problems at age seven: 'For every hour of television watched daily, toddlers face a 10% increased risk of having attention problems by the age of seven.' Dimitri Christakis, author of the report, argued that

> the newborn brain develops very rapidly during the first two to three years of life. It's really being wired. We know from studies of newborn rats that if you expose them to different levels of visual stimuli, the architecture of the brain looks very different.... the truth is, there are lots of reasons not to watch television.[4]

There is also a danger that without the sensory experiences that accompany real-life events, and exercising the judgements that need to be made in the context of real life, children become inured to violence and the effects of violence on other people. Bullying and violence have always been a part of society and childhood, as has the grisly spectacle of watching violent acts for entertainment. Citizens of the Roman Empire would watch gladiators being mauled to death, and in the sixteenth and seventeenth century public executions were a spectacle for all. While children are able to separate the fantasy elements of a television programme from reality, continuous exposure to acts of violence without direct experience of the *consequences* of those acts may, over a long period, have a desensitizing effect on the individual sense of responsibility and understanding of the social consequences of violent behaviour.

> The brain's executive control system, or pre-frontal cortex, is responsible for planning, organizing and sequencing behavior for self-control, moral judgment and attention. These centers develop throughout childhood and adolescence, but some research has suggested that 'mindless' television or video games may idle this particular part of the brain and impoverish its development. Until we know more about the interaction of environmental stimulation and the stages of pre-frontal development, it seems a grave error to expose children to a stimulus that may short-change this critical system.[5]

Herbert Krugman[6] discovered that TV dampens the activity of the critical left brain within 30 seconds of starting to view. Brain-wave activity switches from an alert waking state, associated with increased beta activity to predominant alpha waves, indicating an unfocused, dream-like state. 'The right brain then becomes highly receptive to images and feelings. Both advertisers and politicians intuitively know how powerful the TV/Brain effect is', wrote Martin Large in an article entitled 'Toxic TV? How the TV medium affects children's learning': 'They both aim to get positive images across whilst knowing that rational arguments are secondary. But from this research, children need help switching off as TV undermines the decision-making area of the brain.'[7]

The brain constantly generates electrical activity in both sleep and waking states. Electrical activity of the brain can be recorded using an electroencephalograph or EEG machine. German psychiatrist Hans Berger (1873-1941) was the first to record brain waves from the scalp and discover that there was a change in activity when subjects became drowsy or fell asleep. Other scientists subsequently confirmed Berger's observations, and the technology for detecting and analyzing brain waves states has advanced considerably. The two fundamental aspects of brain activity measured using an EEG are *frequency* and *amplitude* of the waves.

Frequency of human brain waves and associated states of arousal

Type	Frequency	Associated State
Beta	13-30 hz	Cognitive and emotional activation. Shifting of attention to specific stimulus or task.
Alpha	8-12 hz	Relaxed waking state.
Theta	4-7 hz	Meditative states. Unconscious processing. Information processed in the hippocampus. Rapid Eye Movement (REM) Sleep (Dreaming)
Delta	0.5-3 hz	Deep dreamless sleep

Research carried out at the Australian National University in Canberra found that television viewing reduced the quantity of the highest-frequency brain waves involved in alert attention and decision making and increased *theta* activity. Whereas alpha activity is associated with relaxed waking states, theta is associated with drowsiness and a generalized dampening down of the brain's ability to send or receive information by decreasing vigilance, and is linked to states of passive inattention. Merrelyn Emery, one of the researchers in the Australian study, concluded that the abundant constant theta activity, which approaches a drowsy or hypnogogic pattern when watching TV, affects the way that knowledge is processed and acquired: 'We can confidently predict that as theta activity increases during viewing, there will be at the ontogenetic level, a corresponding increase only in "knowing of" and not "knowing"' (observational rather than experiential knowing). Theta activity is also associated with a different kind of perception: 'An increase in theta represents a breakdown between person and environment in the sense that environmental vigilance is neglected.'[8] The comment of a number of spouses that 'if they could have cited the TV as co-respondent in their divorce...' has a basis in neuro-physiology!

While recent research findings[9] do not appear to find a direct correlation between television and poorer *learning* outcomes, other research into the effects of brain functioning suggest that increased regular exposure to TV may affect aspects of social development by dampening activity involved in vigilance, arousal to attention, sustained attention, and environmental neglect. To return to Emery's concept of 'knowing of' versus 'knowing', 'knowing of' is information gleaned second hand and is not integrated in the same way as information learned from direct experience, which roots knowledge into the self. Krugman described this type of knowledge as being, 'recognition without recall, exposure without perception'.[10]

In the same article Martin Large goes on to write:

> TV viewing is highly addictive, a plug in drug.[11] People spend long hours watching, say they cannot switch off, the longer they watch the less they can turn it off, sacrifice many important social activities, and report withdrawal symptoms. Recently, researchers have found that TV is not just habit forming, but that dopamine, strongly connected with a number of addictions, is implicated. Dopamine rewards our brains for paying attention, especially to stimulating, fast paced images. So Aric Sigman[12] concludes that, 'We are being chemically rewarded for looking at a screen full of changing images and becoming neuro-chemically dependent.'

Dopamine is a neurotransmitter* involved in pleasure and reward systems in the brain, as well as in the inhibition of involuntary movement when at rest. It is one of three neurotransmitters collectively known as monoamines, of which the other two are norepinepherine

---

* **Neurotransmitter** – a chemical substance made, stored, and released by neurons. Neurotransmitters are chemical messengers between neurons at synapses.
Neuron – An individual nerve cell.
Synapse – functional junction between neurons. Can be either electrical or chemical in nature. Neurotransmitters act as chemical messengers across these junctions.

(noradrenaline) and seratonin. Norepinepherine acts as a key chemical in mediating the physical changes involved in arousal, and it is important in the regulation of hunger and alertness. Seratonin is important in the regulation of sleep, particularly the onset of sleep. Anti-depressant medications such as Prozac act by blocking the uptake of seratonin at the synapse, increasing the availability of seratonin in the brain. Certain carbohydrates, particularly potatoes, are converted into seratonin when eaten, a chemical connection which goes some way to explaining why depressed individuals sometimes find that increasing their consumption of carbohydrates makes them feel better in the short term. This may be the body's natural attempt to restore the balance of the brain.

All of the monoamines are closely linked to mood states and emotional disorders. Dopamine *deficiency* is implicated in a disease affecting the basal ganglia – Parkinson's disease – characterized by a progressive loss of fine motor control, muscle rigidity, tremor at rest, and difficulty in the initiation and execution of movement. *Excess* dopamine has been implicated as a factor in the chemical basis for schizophrenia, while stimulant drugs, such as cocaine and amphetamines, increase dopaminergic activity of the brain.

Studies carried out on rats in the 1950s[13] discovered that when electrodes were implanted in specific brain areas, particularly the medial forebrain bundle, rats could be trained to press a lever to electrically stimulate themselves. This area of the brain comprises a group of neurons which travel directly to the lateral part of the hypothalamus, the part of the brain involved in the regulation of hunger and satiety, arousal, sexual appetite, and temperature control. When rats had been trained how to self-stimulate this area, the positive reinforcement led to compulsive self-stimulation, leading Olds to refer to it as the 'pleasure and reward center' of the brain. Although this interpretation is still controversial, the original observation is important because it helps to explain why certain drugs, and activities that mimic the effects of drugs, are rewarding and therefore potentially addictive. The dopamine pathway is one of the major neurotransmitter pathways associated with the medial forebrain bundle.

Dr Amen in his book *Healing ADD: The breakthrough Program that allows you to see and heal the 6 types of ADD*, writes that children with Attention Deficit Hyperactive Disorder (ADHD) are particularly susceptible to the addictive properties of electronic games. A study published in the journal *Nature* carried out PET scans on subjects playing action video games. They discovered that the basal ganglia, where dopamine is produced, were more active when playing the game than at rest. Amen goes on to write, 'both cocaine and Ritalin (a stimulant drug used to treat the symptoms of ADHD) work in this part of the brain as well'. One of the properties of Ritalin is to make more dopamine available to the brain: 'Video games bring pleasure and focus by increasing dopamine release. The problem with them is that the more dopamine is released, the less neurotransmitter is available later to do schoolwork, homework, chores and so on.'[14] While the brainwave theory partly explains the dulling effect of television on the brain, the neuro-chemical theory explains some of its addictive properties with the let-down or withdrawal symptoms that follow.

As adults we tend to use television as a way of 'switching off' at the end of the day, a way of relaxing while still occupying the idle brain. It has enabled us to see images of events in far-flung parts of the world as they are happening; to be more aware of world events and to see the wonders of the natural world from the comfort of an armchair. It has widened our scope of general knowledge, provides the illusion of company when we are alone, and entertains. It has given us much, and as with all luxuries, once we have had it, we are reluctant to let it go. Children also derive some of the same benefits as adults, but children's brains are different. The brain-wave activity of children and elderly persons is different from that of adults, leaving them more susceptible to conditioning if exposed to brain-wave modifying technology for long periods of time each day.

The young child's brain is still developing in terms of the connections that are being formed, and information without physical integration is a poor substitute for experiential learning. Television as limited entertainment is probably here to stay, but it should never replace the simpler pleasure of play or social interaction, or become the surrogate babysitter.

Over-use of computers and computer games may also affect the developing visual skills of the young child. Whereas *early* reading*

---

* There is a school of thought that says that reading *readiness* does not occur until a child starts to shed his/her first milk teeth, usually around 6 years of age. Children who are encouraged to read from a very early age may learn to accommodate at near distance, to the detriment of far-distance vision.

has been associated with visual near-point stress,[15] possibly leading to the development of non-hereditary short sight, computer use requires intensive periods of focus at extended near distance – a focusing distance just beyond the ideal reading distance – with a tendency to develop convergence and focusing problems at reading distance. While many hand-held computer games help to train accommodation between field vision and central vision, they do not train the eye tracking skills needed for reading. Children become good at rapid shifts of visual attention within their field of vision, but hand-held computer games do not develop the smooth sequential eye movements needed to follow a line of print without the eyes jumping further along the line, to the line above or the line below. Children become good at rapidly decoding individual symbols, shapes, or 'pictures' on a screen, but are not as good at following a series of symbols from left to right and decoding them in an accurate sequence. This is also important for spelling.

The effects of electronic devices are not confined directly to their effect on children. When I was lecturing to a group of schools in the North of England, one head teacher described how, as a school in a deprived area with a high proportion of very young parents, they had started to offer parenting classes on a weekly basis. She described how many of the young parents would attend the classes with expression-less faces, wearing head-sets with personal music playing throughout the talk. They would also collect their children from school linked up to their IPods and appeared to show little reciprocal emotion when with their children in public.

Use of electronic devices plugged into the ear affects spatial awareness during the period of use. Whereas vision tells us what is happening ahead and to the side, hearing and balance inform us about what is happening behind and beyond the scope of vision. When a sound is heard, the difference in the distance from each ear to the source of sound enables us to locate where the sound is coming from. This orientation to auditory stimuli provides part of our spatial map of the world in which we live from moment to moment. When the ears are occupied by synthetic sounds transmitted through headsets, this part of the orientating system is partially blocked.

Not only is attention distracted, but there is a lack of sensory awareness of the immediate environment outside of the field of vision which affects far more than simply hearing. When people wear headsets in the street, there is an alteration in the way that they walk: the rhythm of movement alters and they tend to lose the natural spring in the step. The face takes on a mask-like appearance, similar to a person with Parkinson's disease or on certain anti-schizophrenic medications – they tend to look 'spaced out'.

From a purely social point of view, use of headsets in public affects general spatial awareness. Without the sensory input of external sound, users tend to be unaware of other people or traffic behind them, making them more likely to step out on to a busy street or block the pavement, oblivious of other people trying to get past them.

Have we reached such a stage of sensory overload in our modern environment that it has become necessary to use one electronic device to shut out the noise and visual stimuli of others, as well as the intrusion of the outside world? Or is the real physical world with the demands of human interaction such an alien place to some young adults that it is more comfortable to shut themselves inside the comfort of a smaller, less-demanding world of their own choosing?

As part of the same school initiative, young parents were encouraged to engage in physical play activities such as building a den or going through a miniature assault course. Once initial reticence to join in was overcome, the parents would enter the activity whole-heartedly and have a whale of a time, but did not include their children in the play. It was as if they were learning how to play for the first time, making up for lost time and having no room to include real children in their play.

There is much that parents can do to ensure that children have a rounded, first-hand experience of the physical world, as well as enjoying the entertainment provided by the virtual world of the electronic media.

In a Nutshell...

• Parents are the mediators between a child's needs and desires and society's expectations.

• Discipline surrounds a child with safe boundaries, helping them to learn to regulate their behaviour, develop good habits, learn from mistakes, and to take other people into account. The aim of effective disciplines is to teach.

• Children learn best when expectations and adult behaviour is consistent.

• Children benefit from routine.

• Mealtimes matter.

• Adults act as sounding-boards for different types of behaviour.

• Play is an essential part of learning.

Endnotes

1 Baumrind, D., 'Parenting styles and adolescent development', in: R.M. Lerner, A.C. Peterson, and J. Brooks-Gunn (Eds), *The encyclopedia of adolescence,* Garland. New England. Weiss, B., Dodge, K.A., Bates, J.E., and Pettit, G.S., 'Some consequences of early harsh discipline: child aggression and a maladaptive social information processing style', *Child Development,* 63/6, 1992: 1321-35.

2 Healy, J.M., *Endangered minds: Why children don't think and what we can do about it,* Touchstone, Simon and Schuster, New York, 1990.

3 Christakis, D.M., Zimmerman, F.J., DiGiuseppe, D.L., and McCarty, C.A., 'Early television and subsequent attentional problems in children', *Pediatrics,* 113/4, 2004: 708-13.

4 Lister, S., cited in: 'Ban TV to save toddlers' minds say scientists', *The Times,* 6 April 2004.

5 'Understanding TV's effects on the developing brain', *Care Network Today,* 7 September 2001. International child and youth care network.

6 Krugman, H.E., 'Brain wave measures of media involvement', *Journal of Advertising Research,* 11/1, 1971: 3–9.

7 Large, M., 'Switch on the kid's telly, switch off their brains', *Parliamentary Brief* (London), 10 (11), December 2006.

8 Emery, M., 'The social and neurophysiological effect of television and their implications for marketing practice', unpublished doctoral dissertation, Australian National University, Canberra.

9 Gentzkow, M. and Shapiro, J.M., Abstract for: 'Does television rot your brain? New evidence from the Coleman study (with Jesse M. Shapiro)', *National Bureau of Economic Research (NBER) Working Paper* # 12021 (last updated, February, 2006).

10 Krugman, H.E., 'Memory without recall, exposure without perception', *Journal of Advertising Research,* 40, 2000: 49-54.

11 Winn, M., *The plug-in drug,* Viking, New York, 1985.

12 Sigman, A., *Remotely controlled,* Vermilion Press, London.

13 Olds, J. and Milner, P., 'Positive reinforcement produced by electrical stimulation of septal area and other regions of rat brains', *Journal of Comparative and Physiological Psychology,* 47, 1954: 419-27.

14 Amen, D., Healing ADD: *The breakthrough program that allows you to see and heal the 6 types of ADD,* G.P. Putnam, New York, 2001.

15 Skeffington, A.M., Optometric Extension Programme Continuing Education Courses, Optometric Extension Programme, Santa Ana, 1928-1974.

11.

From Toddlers to Teens: Why Parenting Matters

Rough-and-Tumble Play

Physical or rough-and-tumble play is important because it recruits and exercises many brain areas and abilities from the brainstem at the base of the brain right up to the somatosensory cortex at the top. Rough-and-tumble play helps to develop physical fitness, sensory awareness, regulation of strength, and self-control within social settings.

Physical play affects the body's neuro-chemistry, possibly by increasing brain opioids that create feelings of social strength similar to the effects of oxytocin in forming social bonds between mother and child. Through the exercise of these circuits, rough-and-tumble play affects the cortex because it involves regulation, problem solving, and seeking and innovative behaviour. Jaak Panksepp[1] describes how, during play, 'animals are especially prone to behave in flexible and creative ways', and that in addition to the effects on muscular development, this type of play probably also 'promotes the generation of new ideas and has a major adaptive function in generating a powerful positive emotional state'.

Play is different from formal learning because it seems to lack any clear goal other than the process of play itself. Rough-and-tumble play often involves movements borrowed from other behaviours, such as chasing, fleeing, play-fighting, stalking, and so on. Play engages in dangerous pursuits within a relatively safe setting – a practice ground for the regulation of survival behaviours and risk taking, which will need to be adapted to social settings later on.

Rough-and-tumble play occurs most intensely in early life when the brain is developing and neural connections are being formed. It is pleasurable and uses considerable energy; it is also social. Social play (other than formal games such as board games) usually involves practice of movement, agility, and skill in space, or control of strength. Animals will chase, catch, and tussle with each other. Birds will play as a flock, diving from the branches of trees to breakfast from a shrub of berries in the autumn, engaged in an elaborate race to see who can get there first, collect their booty, and get out of the way before the next one arrives. Most of all, play should be *fun,* and one of the hallmarks of play circuitry in action is laughter. The importance of laughter for life is greatly under-estimated in the modern world, especially in the upbringing and education of children.

Laughter is a form of release, freeing us to expand and become more of ourselves. It promotes physical and emotional well-being, increasing muscle tone, respiration, and the cardiovascular system. The initial effects of laughter are stimulatory, followed by a brief relaxation phase. Laughter has been found to have positive effects on the immune system by affecting the activity of natural killer cells, which engulf viral or cancerous cells, and by reducing serum levels of the stress hormones cortisol, dopac, and epinephrine, as well as growth hormone. Laughter also changes brain-wave activity, arouses different brain areas, and facilitates communication between the left hemisphere, the occipital lobe (an area involved in processing sensory information), and the frontal lobes.[2] As a form of exercise for the nervous system, laughter literally tickles the brain.

Fry[3] also found that there is an increase in catecholamine levels during laughter. One theory is that this may have an effect on mental functions such as increasing interpersonal responsiveness, alertness, and memory. It is well known that children and adults tend to remember things better if they have connected physically and emotionally to the event or facts in some way. Laughter does both.

Rough-and-tumble play helps to develop control of strength. Masters of the martial arts teach that the strong man does not need to exercise his skill to exert power. His authority comes from possessing skill and self-control. Education of boys in ancient Greece involved many varieties of wrestling requiring agility, endurance, inventiveness, and *control of temper.* My husband, who boxed for a while in the navy, said that the first match he lost was when he lost his temper! In other words, developing physical strength is one thing, but it is the exercise and control of strength that really matters.

Fathers are particularly good at this type of physical play, carried out within safe boundaries with father acting as the control. Biting, kicking, and pinching are not acceptable when 'rough-housing' with Dad; so as Mum acts as an external regulator of emotional affect in the early years, Dad teaches the basis for fair play and self-control. The other side of the coin is fathers who use bullying and abusive tactics with their sons, which can be damaging to their sense of self-esteem and understanding of fair play later on.

Whereas mothers tend to soothe and cuddle their babies, fathers will bounce their babies, throw their children in the air, chase, tickle, and wrestle with them, using larger movements which children love, because it takes them beyond the boundaries of their own motor capabilities.

Vestibular stimulation can be soothing (if slow and gentle) or arousing if the movements are larger and faster. Arousal that takes us to the edge of feeling scared is experienced as excitement. Children who are bounced and swung through the air usually peal with laughter, wake up, and, if over-done, become over-excited. Freedom of movement is experienced as joy: 'When there is joy, children learn'.[4] The English word 'joy' is similar to the French words 'joie' and 'jouer', the latter meaning 'to play'. The French talk about 'joie de vivre', the English refer to a person 'jumping for joy'. Hence, within our languages there is a fundamental understanding that movement, joy, and play are all important components of learning.

Why Children Need Fathers

The fact that it is relevant to include a section on the importance of father love is a reminder of how much and how quickly the world has changed in the last 60 years. As the process of conception can be carried out without the father being present, with more couples electing to live together and start families without formalizing their parental relationship in marriage, and with same-sex couples starting families, the concept that children need a parent of each sex not only in their creation but in their daily lives is treading on sensitive territory.

Organisms that reproduce through sexual as opposed to asexual reproduction are generally complex organisms whose complexity is in part due to the sharing of a wide gene pool at the time of their conception. This is one of the reasons behind the taboo of incest, that if sexual relations occurred between close relatives, the replication of shared genes greatly increased the risk of congenital abnormalities in the child. In the same way, by the very fact that they are *different,* men and women bring special attributes to the process of being parents, which as individuals they cannot provide.

As every woman knows, men are different from women in how they process sensory information, understand and express emotions, use language, deal with problems, set priorities, and how they view the outside world. Some women have more masculine brains in the way they handle information and vice-versa. There is a growing body of literature available on the differences between the male and female brain and how hormones affect these gender differences. The point is that, rather than being divisive, these differences *compliment* each other, providing the growing child with a wider and richer range of vocabulary for understanding emotions and behaviour. Fathers are important because they are *not* the same as mothers.

While mothers tend to be more nurturing and attentive to emotional distress in their children, fathers tend to be more practical, helping their child to overcome negative or 'childish' emotions. Mothers tend to provide security and avoid risk, while fathers encourage their children to extend the scope of security, to explore, to discover, and to become self-reliant. Risk is an element of discovery, and a society that does not allow its children to take risks not only deprives them of the joy of discovery but also prevents them from learning how to take care of themselves. Fathers tend to be more willing to stretch boundaries of safety and teach their children how to master new situations and life skills. This is important for developing self-confidence. The child who is never allowed to take risks can become a fearful child, afraid of trying new situations, or a child who is 'cavalier' when let loose, taking extraordinary risks because he has never learned to sense danger for himself. Mothers tend to be more tolerant and understanding of childish behaviour, whereas fathers bring a more 'worldly' response, being less accepting of the reasons behind the behaviour and expecting the child to conform. This is closer to how a child is treated when he is outside the home, not only at playgroup, school, and when out shopping but also when he grows up and moves into the workplace.

Boys need fathers to teach them how to be men and how to be competent at manly activities. When I separated from my first husband, although our children continued to see their father regularly, I became acutely aware that as my sons grew up they missed out on the daily rough-and-tumble play which tends to be a part of the father-son relationship. For several years, there was no one to take them out and kick a ball around, or take them out for bicycle rides if I was busy with jobs in the house – not because I couldn't also ride a bike or kick a ball, but because the single parent cannot do *every*thing. When there is only one parent there is no sharing of daily tasks, and therefore some activities simply have to go on the shelf.

Just as, ideally, girls need a woman to help them deal with the onset of periods, sexuality, learning how to dress, apply make-up, and so on, boys need a man to help them know when it is time to start shaving, how to groom themselves, and deal with their sexual development. The norms for gender differences vary across cultures, but each parent plays a part in helping their child to identify with the gender expectations of the cultural milieu in which they live.

Men and women tend to function and communicate in different ways. This is in part due to different organization within the brain. In women the functional differences between left and right sides of the brain are less clearly defined, whereas male brains are more specialized. The more feminine the brain, the more diffuse the brain functions and vice-versa.[5] Structural and functional differences between the male and female brain (the corpus callosum is up to 40 per cent larger in women) have led a number of authors to write books about how these differences affect our daily lives (why men don't iron and women don't read maps). Although there is significant individual variation across both sexes in these traits, nevertheless the male and female parent does contribute different communication and thinking styles to their child's development.

Women tend to modify their language when talking to young children, raising the pitch of the voice and simplifying words and sentences to fit their child's level of understanding. Men are less likely to modify their language. Male talk tends to be more direct, brief, and content based. Father language is more likely to use the 'imperative', which is clearer and more commanding. For example, a mother might say to her five year old child, 'would you go and turn off the TV for Mummy?'. A father is more likely to say, *'turn* off the TV'. When a child grows up he will encounter both styles of communication. The child who has never experienced 'command language' is more likely to become offended, upset, or rebellious when he comes across 'father' language at school or in the workplace for the first time.

Boys need mothers to nurture their emotional side to help them relate to others and form loving relationships later on, but they need fathers to grow into their masculinity with confidence, to learn strength, self-control, and fair play in the world beyond the home.

Girls need fathers to teach them that they are valuable as women, to be proud of their femininity, and to be loved as women without the involvement of sex. When a girl has had a good relationship with her father, she is less likely to seek love purely through sex to affirm her own self-worth or buy affection.

Sex is fun; sex as part of a loving relationship brings joy and pleasure as well as helping to cement and nourish the relationship, and nature designed sex for the procreation of children. Sex used as currency to procure love or to feel loved and wanted has limited success. Love obtained purely through sex is like the paper and kindling wood for making a fire. It flares up and burns brightly with great intensity for a short time: it is exciting; it makes a person feel wanted, special, and attractive. In an era where adults and children are discouraged from touching each other outside the boundaries of immediate family, touch provides warmth, reassurance, and the feeling of being cared for. Good sex increases the body's production of endorphins, creating a warm, relaxed feeling for a short time afterwards. But as with all opiates, the feeling wears off with time. The level of excitement starts to decline after several months, and in order to derive the same level of satisfaction, a new element or new relationship must be introduced. Sex in itself can be addictive. If, on the other hand, sex takes place within the context of growing affection, security, and love, love acts like the ingredient which stokes logs or coal on to the fire to keep it burning, sustaining it for many years ahead.

Girls who have grown up in a family in which they have felt alienated, neglected, or unappreciated tend to seek love and approval through sex.

Children who have grown up in regular contact with secure and loving parents have a good start when they have children of their own. This does not necessarily mean that the transition into parenthood is easy, but the elements of parenting are part of the psyche. Children who have had poor parenting can also grow up to be excellent parents, deliberately rejecting the parenting styles of their own parents and consciously setting out to do things differently. Other children have no model of good parenting or available parents on which to develop their parenting skills in the future. As more children enter child-care from an early age and parents work longer hours, we are at risk of raising a generation of teenagers – the parents of tomorrow – who have had minimal experience of full-time parenting in the early years.

The school curriculum includes sex education from as early as five years of age. Most teenagers today have a good understanding of the mechanics of sex and of how to avoid conception and sexually transmitted diseases. It is my view that education should spend an equal amount of time teaching about the *product* of sex – children – what children need and how to be good parents in the future.

Earlier chapters of this book have covered factors before conception, during pregnancy, birth, and early feeding practices, which have an impact on the baby. These are as much a part of sex education as the sexual act and avoiding conception. How teenagers look after their bodies can affect their chances of conceiving and having a healthy pregnancy. Alcohol, binge drinking, drugs, and poor diet all have a potential effect on the health of the next generation. While teenagers will always experiment with danger, and launch their own individual rebellion against the constraints of childhood and authority – this is part of the process of finding their own way as individuals – in my view education should also spend time teaching them *why* self-care is important for their future and for the future of their children.

Ante-natal care has done much to safeguard the progress of pregnancy, but this is rather like shutting the stable door after the horse has bolted. Pre-conceptual factors mentioned in Chapters 2 and 3 such as maternal age, nutritional status, history of sexually transmitted disease, and use of alcohol and recreational drugs will also influence the course and possible outcome of each pregnancy. If youngsters are ignorant of these factors as they become sexually active, how can we expect them to begin to make responsible choices?

In a survey carried out for The Good Childhood Enquiry set up by the British Children's Society, children who were asked what was most important to them in their lives said their families were the most important thing.[6] Some 8,000 young people aged between 14 and 16 interviewed in the survey placed their families first in order of priority, followed by relationships and friends. The latest designer wear or gadget was not at the top of their list. Contrary to popular belief, and how many teenagers may appear to their families, family remains at the heart of their sense of security and stability. All groups placed a high priority on adults having the time to spend with them. The survey found that the quality of childhood in Britain in 2006 was the worst in Europe if measured in terms of well-being.[7]

The same survey found that 50 per cent of mothers of children under five in the UK were working outside the home. Government policy at the time of writing seems to be geared to encouraging women to go back into the workplace as soon as possible. Whereas in countries where maternity leave and good child-care provision has been provided by the state for many years, for example in Sweden, in the United Kingdom the costs of maternity leave must be borne by the employer rather than the state, making it extremely difficult for small employers to extend maternity leave, or even to meet the demands of the current six-month period. This in turn puts more pressure on women to return to work, and place their child in child-care, in spite of the fact that numerous studies have found that the most effective way of building independence in children is to secure their need for dependence first. This was explained by the anthropologist Margaret Mead, who wrote, 'we do not know – man has never known – how else to give a human being a sense of selfhood and identity, a sense of the worth of the world'. 'The path to the sturdy self lies directly across the lap of mother and father. There is no other route.'[8]

The same idea of independence growing out of secure dependence was explained by Dr E. R. Matthews as playing a part in successful loving relationships between adults, in a series of lectures on sex and marriage given to sixth formers at a boys' public school in the 1960s. He said that the emotional needs of men and women are different. While man has a need for stability and closeness, he also has a need for freedom; woman needs security in order to become independent within a chosen relationship of inter-dependency. In other words, only when she becomes secure within a relationship does she cease to need constant reassurance.

When looking at successful models for child-care in other parts of Europe, Sweden is often held up as the gold standard. Sweden has an excellent record as a welfare state: it has the highest percentage of public employees and public expenditure, but also higher tax rates than any of the Western economies. Every citizen is guaranteed a job or an income, but such security comes at the price of high taxation. The level of taxation necessary to support such a welfare state has had an enormous impact on the family. With taxes so high, women must work. This reduces the time available for child-rearing, thus encouraging the expansion of a day-care system that takes a large part in raising nearly all Swedish children over age one. The massive Swedish welfare state has largely displaced the family as provider, in return for giving children back to the state. This in turn has had an effect on the stability of the family.

The lone teen pregnancies common in the British and American underclass are rare in Sweden, which has no underclass to speak of. Even when Swedish couples bear a child without being married, they tend to reside together when the child is born. Strong state enforcement of child support discourages single motherhood by teenagers. However, the discouragement of lone motherhood has only a short-term effect. Due to the efficiency of the welfare state, mothers and fathers can survive financially alone with the result that, although children born outside of marriage are raised, initially, by two cohabiting parents, many later break up. The state replaces the family as the unit of stability.

This may seem an attractive alternative in an era in which family break-up is at a record level, but the state is a large impersonal concept, which does not care about the personal needs or the emotional life of the individual. However imperfect or impermanent, the family is the heart of society, and family pressures just like blood pressure provide a measure of the health of both.

Teenagers – the Chrysalis Period

The term 'adolescence' is derived from the Latin verb 'adolescere', which meant 'to grow into adulthood'. It begins with the onset of puberty (the phase when sexual maturation becomes evident) and ends with the assumption of adult responsibilities. 'Adolescence begins in biology and ends in culture.'[9]

Brain development does not stop at the end of the primary school years but continues through the teen years and well into the twenties. Just as there is a major spurt of development between 6½ and 8 years of age involving proliferation, pruning, and myelinization, so a similar process takes place though adolescence, as the structure of the brain is redesigned by the triple sculptors of maturation, the chemical effect of hormones, and environmental opportunity:

> Hormones have a dual effect on the brain. While the brain is developing in the womb, the hormones control the way the neural networks are laid out. Later on, at puberty those hormones will revisit the brain to switch on the network they earlier created. Their action is like the process of photography; it is as if a negative is produced in the womb, which is only developed when these chemical messengers return in adolescence.[10]

MRI images have revealed that during this second major period of myelinization the amount of grey matter in the brain decreases as it is replaced by white matter (myelinized tissue).[11] New skills are learned best when grey matter is increasing, for example between 7 and 11 years of age, but improvement and perfection of skills occurs with myelinization (increasing development of white matter). Thus, it would appear that the teen years, when the brain is pruning and insulating neural circuits, are the years for consolidating existing skills such as learning to play a musical instrument or develop expertise in sport.

The teenage brain is like the building site of a motorway under construction. In the early teen years it resembles the stage when the countryside has been ripped up, and just the rough track has been laid. Many parents will recognize this image as being reminiscent of their son or daughter's bedroom at this stage in development. The point is that many of the changes in mood and behaviour that take place through the teenage years reflect the reorganization that is taking place within the brain. Not only is your teenager having to learn to deal with the effects of hormones on the body and a major reorganization of neural pathways, but also the chaos of living inside a construction site that will take several years to complete. These changes were summarized in four key points following a meeting of the New York Academy of Sciences in 2003, on the subject of Adolescent Brain Development: Vulnerability and Opportunity:

- Much of adolescent behaviour is rooted in biology, intermingling with environmental influences to cause teens conflicts with their parents, take more risks, and experience wide swings in emotion.
- Lack of synchrony between a physically mature body and a still-maturing nervous system may explain these behaviours.
- Adolescents' sensitivity to rewards appears to be different from adults, prompting them to seek higher levels of novelty and stimulation to achieve the same feeling of pleasure.
- With the right dose of guidance and understanding, adolescence can be a relatively smooth transition.

Girls' brains tend to mature more quickly than boys. In the early years, girls' speech and fine motor skills were in advance of boys, giving them an advantage in the first years at school. Similarly certain aspects of brain development occur more quickly for girls in adolescence, one of the reasons why teenage girls often seek the company of older boys, because at this stage in development their own age-group seem immature, although this levels off by the mid-twenties, when boys catch up. These differences in the rate of brain development provide substance to support the argument that boys often perform better in single sex schools where teaching is aimed more specifically at their level of development.

The frontal lobes of the brain also undergo a lot of development during the teen years. This is the part of the brain that controls social activity, and it is also the time of life when youngsters start to care more about friends and what other people think of them. This can be a time of conflict if peer influences are in direct opposition with parental values and each child within a family can challenge parental values in different ways.

What has Changed in the Environment in which Teenagers Grow up?

Seventy years ago the concept of the teenage years was unknown. Parents and educators knew that the second decade of a child's life brought certain 'moral' temptations and risks, and it was expected that the parent or the educational establishment would set standards and provide an environment which would contain behaviour and minimize risks until the young adult was considered mature enough to be set free.

The 'coming of age' at 21 meant that parents retained legal responsibility and a degree of control for longer than is the case with the current age of majority at 18. The brain development of the 21 year old is significantly closer to the mature adult brain than at 18, although it will continue up until age 25 and in some cases even longer.

Before the contraceptive pill became available, sexual activity carried a much higher risk of resulting in pregnancy. Fear of unwanted pregnancy combined with social disapproval of pregnancy outside marriage meant that the fear of pregnancy alone acted as a deterrent to precocious sexual activity for many (not all!). In other words, the prospect of having to face the consequences of actions helped to instil a greater sense of personal responsibility and self-control.

A lower school leaving age and less economic prosperity meant that there was a clearer division between those youngsters who left school at 14 (later 15) to go out into the workplace or serve an apprenticeship, and those who would go on to higher education. Although this division helped to perpetuate class boundaries and make upward mobility more difficult, it also meant that teenagers who were not naturally academic could go out and start a useful occupation with a wage packet at the end of the week, and a sense of pride and responsibility. In poorer families, this wage packet was an essential contribution to the family income.

Apprenticeships provided an opportunity for the non-academic to learn a skill and a trade, a means to earning a fair wage and develop a sense of pride and responsibility. Only in the last 20 years have educators woken up to the fact that children have different learning styles, and not everyone is 'wired' to succeed through formal education. Some people excel when they are shown physically rather than taught theoretically how to do something, and are motivated when they see an immediate reward or product for their efforts. These youngsters, who may have been disaffected and under-achievers at school, do much better when placed in an environment where they are taught a practical skill leading on to a secure job with the reward of a regular wage packet. The discipline of the workplace also helps them to develop life skills, responsibility, and self-respect.

Prolonging the educational process extends the period of childish dependence on parents for financial support. Whilst today's teenagers are given the freedom to vote and to drink at 18, if they stay in formal education they are unlikely to be financially independent and therefore truly responsible for themselves until they are at least 22; and if they enter a profession which requires post-graduate training, 24 years of age. For those who have had to borrow money to finance higher education, they start their adult life with a burden of debt which can take up to 10 years to pay off.

We do not need a society top heavy with graduates and post-graduates. We need a society which nurtures and *values* an eclectic mixture of skills – people who can mend, build, fix, grow things, take care of the land, and are willing to provide nursing *care* as opposed to medical treatment for an increasingly aging population – in other words, people who are good at *doing*. Increasingly we rely on migrant workers from other countries to carry out many of these jobs which traditionally have been lower paid, do not carry *status*, but which are just as important to society as selling stocks and shares or making boardroom decisions.

If you cannot shine at school, you are too young to leave school, and you have no prospects after school, it is very difficult to maintain self-esteem and self-respect. Respect for others begins with self-respect, hence the commandment to 'love thy neighbour as thyself'. If you have no sense of achievement, hope of achievement in the future, or self-worth, it is very difficult to understand why others should be treated with dignity, respect, and generosity.

The concept of status as a separate entity from financial reward seems to be particularly undervalued in British society. This was brought home to me a number of years ago, when we were holidaying on one of the Greek islands. As we walked down to the village one evening, a local man who spoke no English gestured us to follow him into a house he was building. First of all he showed us the olive and lemon groves he had planted, the terraces, and the outline for the garden; then he took us into the house and showed us the rooms. It seemed he wanted us to let him know whether we liked what he had done. The next day we asked the owner of the villa where we were staying what it had all been about. I have always remembered his choice and emphasis of words – He said:

> you have to understand that this man's **profession** was a gardener to wealthy people in Athens. He has recently retired, but his government pension is not sufficient for him to live on it for the rest of his life. This piece of land is his retirement fund and he is building a villa with holiday apartments, which he will rent out to see him through the winter months. But, the important part for him is the garden – the olive and lemon groves – this is where his pride and his heart is. He wanted to know from you, if as tourists, you would like to stay in his apartments, but he also wanted you to see his garden.

The same element of pride, efficiency, and self-respect was evident in all the jobs that local men and women did on the island. One waiter would manage a restaurant of 20+ tables on his own; orders were taken without delay, food arrived promptly, and everything was served with an air of panache. People were *proud* of what they did; *every* job was a *profession*. Money was not the sole source of pride and self-respect.

Raising the academic qualifications for entry into the various professions may have improved the standard of education within the professions but it has not always resulted in better practice. The nursing profession is one case in point. In the 1960s and early 1970's entry into nursing required 5 GCE 'O' Levels, of which at least one had to be a science subject. Nursing is now a graduate profession, but the standards of patient care and hygiene have not necessarily improved for the patient despite higher entry requirements into the profession and higher standards of training. The effect has been to remove the most highly qualified further away from the daily tasks of nursing, and put routine tasks such as emptying bedpans, washing and feeding patients, regular observations and cleaning, into the hands of people employed under new job descriptions who do not have full nursing qualifications. When entry requirements into the profession were lower, nurses were responsible for every aspect of a patient's care and standard of care from the patient's point of view was higher.

In January 2007 the Daily Mail[12] carried an article covering the results of a survey that showed that half of major employers were unable to fill graduate vacancies because students lacked basic work skills. Employers reported that even graduates with first- and second-class degrees had such poorly developed communication skills that they had concerns about letting them answer the 'phone, attend meetings, or give presentations. One example cited was of an interviewee at an investment bank starting his meeting with, 'You all right mate?'. I remember being struck by a similar lack of communication skills amongst the most highly educated some 30 years earlier when I was reading history at a Scottish university. When one of the students in a tutorial group was asked what he thought about Martin Luther and his ideas, his reply was, 'Pretty good bloke, really'. Apparently two years of 'A' levels and a year at university do not guarantee the development of good oral communication or the basic manners expected in the work place.

The Association of Graduate Recruiters went on to say that, 'candidates are normally academically proficient but lacking in soft skills such as communication as well as verbal and numerical reasoning'. Employers are struggling to find candidates with good general educational standards in spelling, punctuation, and grammar and advanced skills in science and technology. Clearly education alone is not enough. Work placement and training of work-related skills are just as important to success in the workplace. Often, youngsters who move into work at a younger age develop these skills ahead of their more academic peers.

In a funeral sermon, a seventeenth-century clergyman compared youth to 'a new ship launching out into the main ocean without a helm or ballast or pilot to steer her'[13] While this statement is how many adolescents feel and appear at times, it need not be entirely the case. Parents who are involved with their teenage children can still act as the pilot when needed, as the teenager attempts to steer his or her own way through the uncharted territory of the teen years. Adolescents still need the active involvement of their parents, not in telling them what to do but in being available to listen, to suggest, and at times to say 'no'. At this stage in development, youth is still searching for ways to fit in with peers without simply following the crowd, establish a sense of identity, explore the impulses that come with burgeoning sexuality, and develop skills and abilities in preparation for adult life. If a teenager is to develop the reasoning powers of an adult, he or she first needs to internalize the voice of reason. This means that the disciplinary boundaries set in early childhood act as a framework. Parents need to relax some of those boundaries in the teenage years while supporting others.

This is similar to Freud's concept of developing the 'parent within', the concept that the voice, advice, and discipline of parental and adult influences during development eventually become the parent to the child within the self. The inner voice of reason prevents the child within from carrying out acts which might hurt himself or others, helps him to look ahead and foresee possible consequences of future actions. The parent within should never become so dictatorial that the child within is never allowed to play, but the gradually emerging self or ego should be learn to modify and fit the desires of the child to the requirements of the adult world. This is where a background of authoritative parenting appears to be the most successful in helping teenagers to make the transition from child through the chrysalis period of adolescence to mature adult. Although testing parental boundaries (and this is an essential part of developing personal identity) is a normal stage of adolescence, most young people still care what their parents think and need continued parental involvement in their daily lives.

We see examples of where parental influence has been insufficient every day. In the first decade of the twenty-first century there has been an explosion of 'reality TV' programmes, which take out-of-control youngsters and place them in a disciplined environment. One such experiment placed young men with a history of trouble with the law and/or alcohol and drug abuse into a 1950s-style National Service army camp for several weeks. One young man found it almost impossible to fit in with his peers or conform to the demands of the non-commissioned officers. The result was a miserable existence for the first few weeks of the experiment. While most of his peers received weekly letters from girlfriends and family, no one wrote to him, until one week he received a letter from the company sergeant encouraging him not to give up. This small act of kindness coupled with consistent discipline and paternalistic support was enough to help him turn the corner.

The early twenties is rather late to start to learn the basic laws of cause and effect. This is something that many of today's parents seem to find it very hard to teach. I regularly see families where parents complain that their child constantly interrupts, will not do as he is asked, and reverts to inappropriate babyish behaviour when he is not the centre of attention. These parents love their children very much but have never established regular routines or household rules. As a result the child rules the roost, parents are exhausted from continuous nagging, and the child is not a happy child because most of the time spent in the company of his parents is with two weary, stressed people. More serious are the longer term implications for a child who has never learned to fit in with the needs of the people around him or established a degree of self-discipline. How could he, when he has had no model of discipline from which to learn?

I can think of two recent examples of boys of 10 who came to see me with mild problems at school. Each was very bright, articulate, and charming, but they would take hours to get dressed in the morning, complete a meal, or do their homework. In exasperation, their mothers would sometimes dress them for school or end up spoon-feeding them, and doing a proportion of their homework for them despite the fact that they were perfectly capable of doing both for themselves. On further investigation, it emerged that the families did not sit down together to eat as a family, and in one of the cases the boy would sit at the table with his feet on the chair reading a book. He was far more interested in the book than the contents of his plate, and meals did not take place within the milieu of 'social' environment, which carried certain expectations and codes of behaviour.

It was suggested that the family should start eating together at least three evenings a week, and good table manners were required. This meant never having a book at the table, and sitting properly. His parents were concerned that he would continue to take hours over his food, with the result that they would all still be at the table some two hours later. They looked appalled when it was suggested that there should be a time limit for completing the first course; and if it was not finished in that time, the remainder should be thrown away and nothing offered to replace it until breakfast the next morning. It was also suggested that there should be a set time for homework to be completed, and if he had not finished his homework in that time, the homework should be removed and he would have to explain to his teacher the next day why it had not been done. In other words, it was time that the boy learned to deal with the consequences of his behaviour in the real world, rather than relying on his parents' love to protect him. This would present him with a choice – to carry on as he was; or to learn to conform. Even as adults we sometimes need unpleasant reminders that certain behaviour may not be appropriate in order to be motivated to modify it. The earlier we learn this, the easier life becomes.

If the bases for understanding cause and effect and good habits have been established in the pre-adolescent years, it does not *guarantee* easy and safe passage though the teens, but the foundations for self-discipline are in place and can be accessed when required. Belinda Barnes, founder of the Foresight organization, described the physiological equivalent of this process as, 'in the teen age years the hormones switch on anew all the problems that were left behind in toddlerhood'! Parental love does not mean giving in to your children at all times. It means helping your children to learn how to modify and regulate their own behaviour to adapt to the requirements of the environment so that they can 'fit in' and feel at home almost anywhere.

While manners can be taught in individual situations, the essence of good manners in a more general sense is consideration for other people. Consideration for others transcends the boundaries of culture, creed, and race. It is a way of living that can be transferred to any place or situation in the world, but it begins in the home and is developed in a society which also looks after its neighbours and takes care of its surroundings. When a society becomes afraid of standing up for its codes of behaviour, of helping someone in trouble, or intervening when someone is doing something wrong, it is a society that has already started to destroy itself and one in which, lacking secure boundaries of behaviour, its youth struggles to find its identity.

Speaking on the 'Thought for the Day' programme on BBC Radio 4, the Anglican Bishop of Liverpool recounted how he was part of an inter-religion discussion group, set up to discuss where the different religions had common ground. When covering the topic of what being British meant, there were many different views, but eventually they all agreed that they shared three things in common: landscape, language and the monarchy. Surprising, perhaps, within a country devoted to the ideal of democracy with freedom to change governments, laws, and policies, that it was longer-term stable factors that bind us together. This is what effective parenting should do – provide a long-term stable background – which provides consistency from childhood into adulthood until a child becomes secure enough in who he is and is able to stand on his own two feet.

You are the bows from which your children as living arrows are sent forth.
The archer sees the mark upon the path of the infinite, and He bends
    you with His might that His arrows may go swift and far.
Let your bending in the archer's hand be for gladness;
For even as he loves the arrow that flies, so He loves also the bow that
    is stable.

From: *Of Children, The Prophet.*
by Kahlil Gibran.

In a Nutshell...

- Children need rough-and-tumble play. The electronic media are no substitute for physical play and human interaction.

- Mothers and fathers bring different attributes to parenting.

- The teenage brain is like a building site under construction. Many of the characteristics of the teen years are directly connected to neurological and hormonal changes. Parents are particularly important during these years.

- As society has concentrated on raising the level of education, it has marginalized the less academic, or those who do not want to pursue higher education. Society needs to nurture and value skills and training schemes that will enable the less academic to earn a living and have a sense of pride in their achievements.

Endnotes

1   Panksepp, J., *Affective neuroscience: The foundations of human and animal emotions,* Oxford University Press, New York, 1998.

2   Derks, P., Gillikon, L., Bartolome, D.S., and Bogart, E.H., 'Laughter and electroencephalographic activity', *Humor,* 10, 1997: 283–98.

3   Fry, W.F., Jr., 'The physiologic effects of humor, mirth, and laughter', *JAMA, Journal of the American Medical Association,* 267/13, 1992: 1857.

4   Kiphard, E.J., 'Psychomotor therapy in Germany and the importance of body control for learning', 12th European Conference of Neuro-Developmental Delay in Children with Specific Learning Difficulties, Chester, March 2000.

5   Moir, A. and Jessel, D., *Brainsex: The real difference between men and women,* Mandarin Paperbacks, London, 1991.

6   **www.goodchildhood.org.uk**

7   Bradshaw, J., Hoelscher, P., and Richardson, D., *An Index of Child Well-Being in the European Union,* Social Indicators Research, Springer, USA, 2006.

8   Mead, M., cited in: Zinsmeister, K., 'What's the problem with day care?', *The American Enterprise,* 5:1. 1998 (May/June) 1998 (The American Enterprise online).

9   Mussen, P.H., Conger, J.J., Kagan, J., and Huston, A.C., *Child development and personality,* Harper& Row, New York, 1990.

10 Moir and Jessel, *Brainsex.*

11 Thompson, P., Lee, A., Hayashi, K., and Toga, A., UCLA Laboratory of Neuro Imaging; Nitin Gogtay and Judy Rapoport, Child Psychiatry Branch, NIMH.

12 'Unskilled graduates aren't worth hiring say British bosses', *Daily Mail,* 30 January 2007.

13 Smith, S.R., 'Religion and the conception of youth in seventeenth century England', *History of Childhood Quarterly: The Journal of Psychohistory,* 2, 1975: 493-516.

12.

What Needs To Be Done?

As technology advances, so does the pace of life and the pace of change. Organisms must be able to adapt to the changing needs of the environment if they are to survive; small organisms such as viruses and bacteria are particularly good at doing this, but the larger and more complex the organism, generally speaking, the slower the process of adaptation and evolutionary change.

The infant brain has a remarkable capacity to mould itself to the needs of the environment, hence the richness and diversity of cultural differences seen in the peoples that cover the earth. However, within this diversity and potential for growth are certain biological factors that are common to all human beings. Every child has the right to a good biological beginning.

Even with the development of IVF techniques (leaving the shadow of human cloning aside), nature still requires a healthy egg, sperm, and uterine environment for the creation of a new and viable life. Normally a woman's immune system would reject any outside organism invading her body, but when natural fertilization takes place, the ovum allows a single sperm to penetrate the thick outer wall and stimulate a complex process of cell division. In this way, nature has ripened a suitable egg, accepted a sperm with good motility compatible with the host, and provided a uterine environment, which will enable the new organism to develop. Even after all of this, the woman's body can still reject the embryo at any time in the first few weeks, usually because there is a problem with either the host (the mother) or the visitor (embryo).

The health of both parents *before* conception can therefore influence the chances of conception, the course and successful outcome of pregnancy, and the health of the resulting child. This includes the age of the mother as well as physical health and social circumstances. We know that risk factors increase in teenage mothers and mothers over the age of 35, but as a society, we make it increasingly difficult for young women in their twenties to be in a financial position to produce a family.

Many of the sicknesses of the modern world are preventable and result as much from lifestyle as from true disease. As the nineteenth-century German physician Virchow said, it is not the virus that makes you ill – the virus flourishes because you are already ill; the mosquito does not make the swamp – the mosquito exists because the swamp provides it with a rich habitat. Diseases of the Western world such as diabetes, heart disease, obesity, eating disorders, sexually transmitted diseases, infertility, and drug-induced psychosis, many of these can be prevented through changes in lifestyle and life pressures. A doctor recently said to me that in his opinion, more had been done in the past to improve health through public health initiatives than through 'cures' for specific diseases.[1] We see this all too clearly when natural disasters or wilful human demolition of society take place such as in times of war. It takes only a few days without shelter and clean water for disease to take a hold and ravage people in a shocked and destitute state.

Through sanitation, vaccination, improved nutrition, and anti-biotics we have the ability to save and preserve life beyond the wildest dreams of our ancestors, but we are at risk of taking these things for granted and forgetting that each of us has a responsibility to take care of ourselves. This responsibility is the beginning of becoming an adult, and of parenting in particular.

As the demands on government to sustain and improve public services increases, so government seeks to extract through taxation additional sources of revenue to support the expectations of its people. As the percentage of women in the workplace increases, so the revenue derived from taxation also increases. Whether we like it or not, women are now major contributors to the Exchequer through taxation. When a woman gives up work to have a baby, the Exchequer loses money. Laying the burden of extending paid maternity leave on the employer is not the solution either, as small companies cannot afford to pay for long periods of time both for an employee who is not working and for a temporary replacement. We need to acknowledge as a society that in the first year(s) of life, babies need their mother. Government needs to take a greater share in the financial responsibility of making it possible for parents to choose to stay at home.*

A Litany of Needs for the Parents of Tomorrow and the Children of Today

- We need to find ways to enable women to take a career break in the years of maximum fertility and brain maturity. This combination occurs from the early twenties to the early thirties, just the time when men and women who have persisted through higher education are trying to secure a place on the career ladder, pay off debts accrued during the years of higher education, and take on new ones to set up a home. Providing initiatives to get mothers back into the workplace as soon as possible is not in the best interests of mother, child, or ultimately society. A society which really cares for its children makes it possible for a mother and child to be together for at least the first 2-3 years, because these are crucial years for secure attachment and emotional development. It is not just quality time that matters but also the amount of time spent in physical interaction and engagement every day.

In order to do this, there has to be a change in the way that the politics of society views the place of women in the workplace. There has to be a means of financially supporting the family through these years. There needs to be greater accessibility to *returning* to the workplace after a few years' absence and *flexibility* to *start* a career after the first phase of motherhood. A gap of a few years may result in a woman being out of date with current working practices and developments within the specific career field, but she will also bring back to the workplace a new set of skills. It may seem very old fashioned to suggest that the skills of a mother running a home

---

* One solution might be to reduce the tax burden on fathers for the first two years after a child is born, with the benefit being paid directly to the full-time parent. This would enable women to spend the first year at home, encourage fathers to support their children, and give an incentive for women to begin to return to the workplace in their child's third year.

include, planning, financial management, multi-tasking, time management, negotiation, and other finely honed 'people' skills. It also brings
with it a permanent sense of responsibility. These are transferable
skills which are not acquired through the process of formal education
but come through living.

- We need to make the young people of today aware that the
  lifestyle choices they make in their teens and early adult lives may
  have a lasting influence on whether they are able to conceive. It is
  possible through improved awareness to prevent some of the
  heartache of miscarriage, premature births, non-essential surgical
  intervention at birth, and birth abnormalities. This is what the
  Foresight organization was set up to do, to minimize preventable
  risks in the pregnancies of tomorrow.

- We need to make young people aware of the advantages of
  breast-feeding, to celebrate breasts not primarily as sexual objects
  but also as nature's gift to every child. Organizations such as the
  National Childbirth Trust and the La Leche League do an
  enormous amount of work in this respect, but it is only a
  relatively small percentage of the parents of tomorrow who come
  into contact with these organizations.

From a purely fiscal point of view, the National Health Service
could probably be saved millions of pounds in the future simply by
encouraging mothers to breast-feed for a few months (even a few
days is better than none) at the beginning of every child's life. As
Belinda Barnes and Suzanne Bradley write at the end of their book,
Planning for a healthy baby,

> natural feeding means less crying, sounder sleep, eventual slow
> gentle weaning, less likelihood of allergies and better assimilation of
> food. A well nourished brain means a bright, curious, conversational
> child who finds life a rewarding experience, and sees 'grown ups'
> as quite friendly and reasonable! Relationships and learning hold
> great potential when the developing brain is free from biochemical
> aberration.[2]

Various studies have shown improved reading and problem solving amongst children given daily supplements of Omega 3 and Omega 6 fatty acids. Professor Basant Puri, a visiting professor at Imperial College, London carried out an investigation of four children aged between 8 and 13 who were overweight. Brain scans carried out before and after supplementation, combined with reduced intake of fizzy drinks and junk food, showed significant increase in the gray matter of the brain. The scans revealed the equivalent of three years increase in gray matter over a period of just three months of supplementation and improved diet. One of the most abundant sources of Omega 3 and Omega 6 fatty acids in an easily absorbed form is human breast milk. Simply by improving the diet of women prior to and during pregnancy and encouraging breast feeding for the first few months of life, we could reduce the risk of obesity, behavioural and learning problems. The incidence of allergies and dietary related illnesses could also be reduced.

We need to make space and time to follow the instincts of our nature. To give children adequate time for touch, for movement, for physical interaction and conversation; to develop the senses through play, to jump for joy, to hear music in the sound of running water and language in song; to experience the physical world in as many ways as possible and to enter the world of imagination and infinite possibility; only then can the formal process of education really start to inform.

We need to make sure that parents and children have *time* to spend together, from early physical contact with Mother to rough-and-tumble play with Dad, and the camaraderie of daily shared experience. Just as young animals seek close physical contact with their mother, so the human infant develops the capacity to love through love received and love returned in a physical as well as an emotional sense. Parents are the first mirror through which a child sees his own reflection.

Michel Odent suggested that many of today's mental illnesses, from suicide and eating disorders to social problems of addiction and anti-social behaviour, are a direct result of an impaired capacity to love, stemming from an impaired capacity to love the self and therefore take care of the self.[3]

- We need to make space for children to belong and be welcomed into the adult world every day: at mealtimes, in our city centres, and our places of public entertainment. Although fast-food outlets are now a global fact of life, other European countries are not as ready to wean their children on a diet of chips, burgers, and chicken nuggets. Restaurants adapt their menus to make miniature portions of adult meals. Children learn to eat from a wide range of the national cuisine, eating out in adult restaurants where good behaviour is expected. In other words, the adult world needs to welcome children into society and 'take children up into the culture'.[4]

Mediterranean countries are generally much better at including children in the adult world than we are in the United Kingdom. Partly helped by the climate and different working hours, children are a part of the village, town or city in the evening. Piazzas are closed to traffic and children play freely while adults have a drink or dine together. Children do not dominate adult time, but they are an important part of it. This is very different from the child who isolates himself in the bedroom to play with the latest computer game or TV programme.

- We need to persuade politicians to influence local planning policy to enable small independent shops to survive amongst the might of the multiple outlets. Much could be done to reduce the rates and rents of small independent retailers. Policies could set out to insist on a certain number of spaces being allocated at a reduced price to independent retailers for every giant that graces our High Streets. In this way we could bring back to our town and city centres independent butchers, greengrocers, bakers, and specialist food shops whose greatest asset is that they sell *fresh, local* produce, and can be accessed by pedestrians who want to buy fresh food to eat later the same day.

In Japan, where kitchens are small, men and women have to shop several times a week for fresh produce because there is less storage space available at home. When we buy fresh ingredients we are more likely to cook a traditional meal from scratch and not to fall back on 'ready-made' meals.

Fridges, freezers, and supermarkets have made life easier, but not necessarily healthier or climate friendly. 'Fresh' foods are flown in refrigerated containers from all parts of the world so that we can still eat peas and exotic fruits in winter and sprouts in the middle of summer, if we wish. We have almost forgotten the wisdom of the land in which we live, which produces root vegetables in the frosts of winter, rich in carbohydrates to provide the body with warmth and energy through the winter months; the taste of the fresh fruits of summer, grown on local soil containing the minerals of the region and full of vitamin C to boost the immune system for the winter months ahead, as well as the arts of bottling and preserving.

Flying and shipment of goods from one part of the world to another releases emissions into the atmosphere and contributes to the process of man-made global warming. Whilst refrigeration and freezing is useful in the short term for preserving perishable foods, infrequent shopping in bulk, the addition of preservatives to food and modern packaging techniques have combined to mean that much of the food we eat has been immortalized on the shelves of the supermarket, or in the drawer of our freezer. The goodness of perishable foods comes in their freshness. When city centres lose their small specialist food shops, they lose some of the instant access to fresh, locally grown food as well as the daily exercise of shopping for the meals of today and tomorrow.

- We need to make ample space for children to play freely and safely in our towns and cities. This does not only mean municipal playgrounds with equipment which pre-suggests the type of play activity the child will carry out, but also spaces with trees and 'natural' areas in which to play. The value of land, and commercial and financial interests, tend to overshadow environmental and aesthetic considerations when regeneration of city areas is being planned; but a city that is pleasant to live in is a city where there are regular open spaces with room for the senses to 'breathe'. Previous generations understood this. The squares and parks of London, designed and built in Georgian and Victorian times, made sure that the houses of the wealthy looked out on to an area of garden and trees. Prosperous mercantile cities such as Bristol and Liverpool were built with large green spaces and parkland as part of the design. As the fortunes of these cities have waxed and waned, buildings have been cleared and replaced, but the green and pleasant spaces between have not. Children need space in which to play – space in which to kick a ball, play tag, run races, roll down a grassy bank, and play hide and seek.

Enculturation begins with the development of self-awareness – the ability to identify oneself as an object, to react to oneself, and to be aware of the effect of one's actions on the world around. Self-awareness develops in concert with neuro-motor development: self-awareness is a product of physical interaction in space, which lays the foundations for stable perceptual awareness; perception – a general sensory awareness of the environment – precedes conception or cognitive awareness and understanding, which involves more specific knowledge of the interrelated needs, attitudes, and concerns and interests that define what one is. Abstraction – the ability to understand what is missing from a part of the environment – is the highest order thinking skill of all. All of the higher-order skills, including the sense of time, are built upon physical experience of the world around us.

• We need to ensure that parents know how to provide a secure and positive climate of discipline. The family is a tiny unit of society. Children grow up believing that their family and their experience of family life is normal and is representative of the world outside. Even if some of the values of the home are different from those of the greater society in which the child will live, as often occurs in families with strong religious beliefs and traditions, a secure base provides a framework from which it is possible to understand and make judgements about the world outside.

This last point was illustrated in the fictional world of Agatha Christie. Miss Marple, the heroine of many of Agatha Christie's detective stories, was described by one character as a little old lady whose entire life had been lived in the small fictitious village of St Mary Mead. From her knowledge of the minutiae of village life, human relationships and gossip, she was able to uncover the motives and actions of the criminal mind. In other words, by having a secure basis in a small world, she was able to understand the workings of the world in general. My father put it slightly differently. He described the experience of surviving boarding school from the age of 7-17 as 'giving you the ability to smell a cad from a mile off'. If, on the other hand, a child has had little experience of affection, reliable adults, or consistent discipline, the inner chaos of his small world tends to follow him when he goes out into the world beyond the home.

- We need to ensure that in our insatiable appetite for visual images we do not lose the oral tradition on which our written language and history are based. Paradoxically, when a society starts to document its history in written form, while it pays attention to the detail of the present and recent past, it can lose some of the knowledge previously passed down from one generation to the next through story, song and myth. Oral cultures transcend the detail of time lines to remember historical facts and events that precede recorded history. The Aborigines provide one example of this.

Within the mythical cycle of the 'dreaming', the aboriginal history, which is passed down from one generation to the next, is a story of a time when their land was submerged by a rising sea. People retreated to a mountain top taking with them their totem – an animal, plant, or symbol that acted as an individual talisman – and waited until the waters receded. Carrying remarkable similarity to the biblical story of Noah and the Ark, without written language, the Aborigines recall a time of flood, possibly also the result of an earlier period of global warming of which recorded history does not tell. The Eskimos tell a similar story of a time when the earth tilted and the climate changed (earthquake?). These oral histories do not tell us exactly *when* these events took place, but they are able to recall events from the far-distant past because they are carried within the mind of the narrator and passed from one generation to the next through the telling of stories. Computer games do not do this.

Stories from the past often contain what we would now consider to be stereotypes of good and bad, the wicked stepmother, the witch, and the big, bad wolf. When I was teaching in Germany a few years ago, I asked my host whether fairy stories were still an important part of German culture for children, or whether they had fallen victim to political correctness. He was astonished that I even needed to ask the question. Fairy stories, he said, are a vital part of childhood. They teach children how to understand the difference between good and evil; they are the nursery school for moral behaviour.

- We need to allow our children to take risks within reasonably safe boundaries. Everything in life carries an element of risk, but it is through learning to overcome risk that we learn a new skill and a new sense of self-confidence. Falling over is the first lesson in learning to balance, and we learn to walk and ride a bicycle by learning how *not* to fall over again. It is only through taking risks that children learn to take care of themselves, to anticipate danger, to find their way, and about how to handle themselves in new and difficult situations. There needs to be a healthy balance between keeping children away from dangers that they are not developmentally ready to deal with, and allowing them to explore and try new experiences that stretch their existing skills. Children do not learn a sense of responsibility by having everything done for them or by being over-protected from the dangers of the real world.

- We need to make parents and politicians aware of how different child-rearing practices foster different strengths and characteristics, which ultimately affect the nature of society. Two general trends were identified by John and Beatrice Whiting and Irvin L Child[5] as dependence training and independence training.

Dependence training describes children who grow up in families and groups where there is close physical contact in the early years followed by involvement in group and family welfare, such as being involved in domestic tasks and making contributions to the daily life of the group tends to nurture individuals who are more obedient, supportive, non-competitive, generally responsible, and unwilling to be disruptive. Their sense of 'self' is strongly bound to their affiliation within the group and consideration for group members.

Independence training describes children who are reared in an environment where the independence of the individual, self-reliance, and personal achievement are the goals. This type of upbringing tends to discourage physical closeness between children and parents from an early age: 'In the United States, people have gone to the extreme of turning the biological functions of infancy – eating, sleeping, crying and elimination – into contests between parents and offspring.'[6] At 15 weeks of age, the average infant at home in North America is in contact with its mother about 20 per cent of the time; infants of the same age in the traditional Ju/'hansi society of South Africa's Kalahari Desert are in close contact with their mothers for 70 per cent of the time. They also have extensive physical contact with other adults and children at times when they are not with their mothers. In societies where physical contact time is as little as 20 per cent, 80 per cent of the infant's time is alone or in less close physical contact with secondary care-givers.

Children growing up in technological societies are generally not encouraged to spend much time engaged in domestic chores or contributing to the welfare of the family. Children are encouraged to become independent and to ask for help and attention when they need it, rather than giving it. Success is usually derived through a process of selection, and therefore comes at someone else's expense. In short, extreme independence training tends to promote selfish behaviour which, if it is the norm, fosters a selfish society.

Societies in which the interests of money and the money market predominate tend to encourage independence training in the upbringing of their young.

- We need to ensure that parents realise how necessary they are in their children's lives, from attending to the basic physical needs of the young baby, to reading bedtime stories, attending school plays, football matches, and concerts, to being a willing 'listener' without necessarily giving advice when things go wrong in the teenage and the adult years. One of the most important aspects of parenting is the silent one of simply 'being there'. Parenting does not stop when your children leave home for university or to set up their own home. It does not stop when your children become parents. It simply changes. The nature of the parenting relationship changes through every phase of your child's development, once a parent, always a parent. Parenting is for life.

Charter for Childhood

In 2006, on the initiative of Sue Palmer, author of the book *Toxic Childhood*, I was invited to join a group of women to discuss what we thought were important issues for the future of childhood. Each one of us was asked to write down four key points as the basis for a new '**Charter for Childhood**'. My points are summarized in the list below:

1. *Nutrition* – the biochemical basis for life.
2. *Affection, nurture, and engagement* – the origins of affect, communication, and emotional security.
3. *Physical interaction with the environment* – entrainment for sensory motor development through the process of play, which develops the physical foundations for perception, conception, and later abstraction.
4. *Discipline* in its true sense meaning, 'instruction, correction, training in action, and control', rather than the modern interpretation of punishment. Discipline of this kind has as much to do with parental *self*-discipline in setting routines, *consistent* standards such as regular bedtimes, mealtimes, and rules of the house.

The four main pillars of child development should be emphasized in different ways at different stages in development:

1. Pre-conceptual Care
This is the time when nutrition, health, and emotional well-being of the mother-to-be can have a lasting effect on the child's subsequent development. Mothers and motherhood *matter*.

2. Children's Needs in the First Year of Life
- Early attachment – 'the first love affair of life', reflected in the physical care the child receives from adults;
- Feeding choices – the long-term benefits of breast- vs bottle-feeding, and implications for feeding choices when women feel forced back into the workplace too soon; and
- The importance of sensory experience and motor opportunity in the first year of life. Tummy time, physical play, songs and rhymes, the music of language, and conversation.

3. Exploring the Physical World: 1-3 and Pre-School Years
- Nutrition;
- Stimulating the senses through physical play;
- The importance of rough-and-tumble play for social development (fathers have a place!);
- Extending the child's world through reading stories, singing songs, and preparing the ear and the brain for the sounds of literacy; and
- The value of simple fairy stories, heroes, adventures, and heroines – they help children to understand the difference between right and wrong. More advanced versions of these stories follow the child through the middle years of childhood.

4. School Years: Primary
- Nutrition;
- Ensuring children have the physical skills in place to be able to achieve in the classroom. Developmental Testing of all Children at rising 5, 7-8, and 11 years of age to ensure physical readiness is in place, and offering appropriate remedial intervention and referral;
- Using physical experience to support literacy;
- Teaching with concrete examples;
- Time for 'sounding out'. Children learn to read silently when they develop an 'inner voice' with which to read. Before they can internalize, they need sufficient practice in reading and reciting aloud;
- Teaching with development – certain stages of neurological development are more receptive to one type of teaching than another;
- Making parents aware that the time they spend sharing activities and chores with their children are as important as 'quality' time. This is how children learn to parent the next generation; and
- The inclusion of sex education instruction in what babies need.

5. Secondary School
- Increased instruction in sex education and drugs awareness on *the outcomes* of sexual activity, not just the prevention of conception and sexually transmitted diseases. Developing awareness in teenagers of the responsibilities of parenting and the needs of children;

- Instruction in the effects of poor diet, alcohol, and drug abuse during pregnancy, lactation, brain development, and behaviour;
- Teaching of life skills, cooking, fixing, and mending; and
- Need for more apprenticeship and job training schemes for less academic youngsters from 16 years of age.

6. Adults

Greater flexibility in career and work choices for women during the optimum child-bearing years and afterwards.

Finally, if childhood is to be valued, as a society we also need to value parents, in particular mothers. The social status of motherhood needs to be seen as being as important as, and carrying equal social status to, any other job. Motherhood is not a temporary break from more intellectually or financially rewarding employment; it is a vocation for life. The first love affair of life is a child's unquestioning love for its mother. The ways in which that love is returned will have a major influence on how the child views him- or herself and will treat others in later life.

The first A, B, C, is not the one that children learn when they go to school and begin the process of formal education. The first A, B, C, is the one they learn at home, the alphabet for life.

The A, B, C, of Children's Needs – Only a Beginning:

A is for Affection, Attachment, and Attention
B is for Bonding, Breast-feeding, and Balance
C is for Communication, Coordination, Consistency, Cherishing
D is for Developmental opportunity and Discipline
E is for Emotional Education
F is for Fathers, Fun
G is for Games, Gentleness
H is for Hugs and having the safety, security and comfort of Home
I is for Interaction and Imagination
J is for Joy
K is for Kindergarten
L is for Love, Laughter, Listening

M is for Mother, Movement and Music in the early years
N is for Nourishment and Nurture
O is for Opportunity
P is for Play
Q is for Quantity and Quality of time spent together, Quietness, Quest
R is for Rough and tumble, Risk, Reading to your child
S is for Sensory experience, Space, Stability, Story-telling,
T is for Touch, Time
U is for Understanding
V is for Values, Verity
W is for Wonderment
X is the hidden factor which makes every child different
Y is learning to be Yourself
Z is for Zest and Zeal for life

A child's capacity to love begins with its mother through love received and love returned.

Every new life is nature's individual miracle and society's opportunity to learn from the mistakes of the past. Despite all the advances in modern technology and the complexity of the modern world, the greatest miracle of all is still the creation of new life itself. With the birth of each child, parents have the chance to begin life again.

> Life is a clown, hiding a million hurts. A dancing, happy clown, born with the gift of laughter. This clown came to earth one day and danced naked through empty lands. Civilisation clothed him, but he is dancing still.[7]

If we want our children to carry laughter – the gift of life – into adult life, we do not need a Nanny State. We need a state that gives children their parents and, most of all, gives babies their mothers back.

My grandmother believed that a nation's women were the measure of its greatness. The report produced by UNICEF in 2006 examining the lives and well-being of children and adolescents in the economically advanced nations began by declaring:

> The true measure of a nation's standing is how well it attends to its children – their health and safety, their material security, their

education and socialization, and their sense of being loved, valued, and included in the families and societies into which they are born.[8]

The hand that rocks the cradle may not rule the world, but it does have a profound influence on future generations.

'The Hand that Rocks the Cradle'

Blessings on the hand of women!
Angels guard its strength and grace,
In the palace, cottage, hovel,
Oh, no matter where the place;
Would that never storms assailed it'
Rainbows ever gently curled;
For the hand that rocks the cradle
Is the hand that rules the world.

Verse 1 of 4.
William Ross Wallace (1819-1881)

Endnotes

[1]   Fieldhouse, D., personal communication, 2007.

[2]   Barnes, B. and Bradley, S.G., *Planning for a healthy baby*, Ebury Press, London, 1990.

[3]   Odent, M., *The scientification of love*, Free Association Press, London, 2001.

[4]   Clouder, C., Summary following debate on the UNICEF Report at The Alliance of Childhood Forum, British Association for Early Childhood Education Centre, London, March 2007.

[5]   Whiting, J.W.M. and Child, I.L., *Child training and personality: A cross cultural study*, Yale University Press, New Haven, CT, 1953.

[6]   Haviland, W.A., *Cultural anthropology*, Harcourt Brace College Publishers, Fort Worth, TX, 1996.

[7]   Eichler, L., *The customs of mankind*, William Heinemann, London, 1924.

[8]   UNICEF, *An overview of child well-being and rich countries*

Appendix

Towards a Holistic Refoundation for Early Childhood: The Hawthorn Press 'Early Years' Series

by Richard House, *Series Editor*

'...the magical thinking of the right brain is what allows us to see beyond what is, and create a better world. Imagination is the mother of creativity...'

Sally Goddard Blythe,
What Babies and Children Really Need

A 'Paradigm War' in – and for – the Heart of Early Childhood Experience

Hawthorn Press's highly successful 'Early Years' series – to which the present book is the latest addition – is providing much-needed inspiration in the face of modern culture's over-active, prematurely intellectual intrusion into the very being of young children. For more than a decade now, a quasi-formal schooling ideology has been surreptitiously colonizing early childhood policy-making and practice – with the relentless bureaucratization of early learning environments stemming from, in England's case, overly mechanistic developmental assessments, centrally defined 'Early Learning Goals', and the imposition of what is a 'curriculum' in all but name on to children as young as 3. Most worryingly, these trends are widely observable in the educational systems of the Western world, caught up as they are in what some have called the 'death throes of modernity', and a pervasive cultural anxiety which, when uncontained by the policy-making process, is disowned and unwittingly projected out, and perhaps especially on to children.

In England in 2003, for example, we had to pinch ourselves when reading that reception teachers were having to work their way through no less than *3,510 boxes* to tick, as they were forced to assess every child against a staggering *117 criteria*. At the time, David Hart, the general secretary of the National Association of Head Teachers, was quoted as saying that 'I cannot think of another Government intervention which has caused so much anger among teachers of the early years, and it must be addressed urgently'.

More recently, the new Early Years Foundation Stage (EYFS) is causing mounting concern at the developmental assumptions that underpin it, with (for example) children in their fourth year being required to recall in the correct sequence a story that has just been read aloud, with four year olds being asked to *analyse* 'Humpty Dumpty'! Later, we read in the same EYFS documentation that as 'Cinderella' is being read, 'we will discuss the story as we go along'. The practitioner's feedback on this was that 'The 4 year olds needed quite a lot of prompting to discuss the story. They were happy to sit and listen to it.' From the standpoint of the kind of holistic child-development theory supported in Sally Blythe's new book, the demand to 'recall, discriminate and describe' taxes a child's memory and analytical intellect at far too early an age. We are also told that 4 year olds will be required to write 'a shopping list, a doctor's prescription and instructions for a game'. Oh, and 'a party invitation using a computer programme' for good measure. Then, by school starting age (4-5 years of age in England), the expectation is that children will 'use their phonetic knowledge to write simple regular words and make phonetically plausible attempts at more complex words' and 'use developing mathematical ideas and methods to solve practical problems'... – and all this laid down as a compulsory statutory framework to which all early years settings, irrespective of status and source of funding, will be subject.

In response, the recently formed 'Open EYE' campaign (**www.savechildhood.org**), of which the author of this book Sally

Blythe and I are both founding supporters, is challenging this ideology that – albeit with the best of intentions – treats children as 'mini-adults', and encourages cognitively biased early learning at the expense of the kind of *physicality-centred* holistic development and learning which is essential in early childhood, and which is championed in this book (on which, more later). Professor David Elkind, among many others, has pointed out that children are not 'mini-adults', and are positively harmed through having to cope with age-inappropriate demands. This was also one of the many crucial developmental insights that Rudolf Steiner emphasized, and on which his original pedagogical indications for Steiner (Waldorf) education are based – and it also recurs throughout Sally Blythe's earlier and acclaimed 'Early Years' series book *The Well Balanced Child*.

Nobel Prize-winning physicist Murray Gell-Mannis is quite specific about the harm caused by unbalanced educational experience:

> an elementary school program narrowly restricted to reading, writing, and arithmetic will educate mainly one hemisphere [of the brain], leaving half of an individual's high-level potential unschooled. Has our society tended to overemphasize the values of an analytical attitude, or even of logical reasoning? Perhaps in our educational system we lay too little emphasis on natural history.

Recent brain research by F. Ostrosky-Solis and colleagues at the National Autonomous University in Mexico is corroborating these concerns, with their finding that learning to read and write requires inter-hemispheric specialization, with preliterate subjects showing patterns of brain activation that are significantly different from those of literate subjects. A clear implication of these findings is that *the forced, 'adult-centric' imposition of early literacy (and numeracy) learning on to the developing brains of young children is something that should only be pursued with extreme caution.* At the very least, a strict 'precautionary principle' should be followed in this field, such that the onus of proof is on those who advocate early formal learning to demonstrate that it is not harmful to the neurological and related development of young children, rather than the burden of proof lying with those who argue against the 'too much too soon' ideology. There seems to be sound scientific-experimental evidence emerging, then, that *premature intellectual (left-brain) development is acutely harmful to young children's development* – a view long held in Steiner Waldorf educational circles.

In a letter written to the 'Open EYE' campaign members on 8th December 2007, Children's Minister Beverley Hughes stated quite explicitly that the six areas of development in the EYFS framework 'are equally important' (her phrase). Ms Hughes' department is therefore assuming that (for example) literacy, problem-solving, reasoning and numeracy are *of equal importance* **for this age-group** as are (for example) physical, and social and emotional development. Yet there exists no research evidence whatsoever to show that the EYFS's six developmental competencies are 'equally important' for the age-group covered by EYFS. Indeed, to the contrary, there is plenty of empirical and anecdotal evidence – much of it quoted in Sally Blythe's new book – to suggest that for young children, certain kinds of development are far more important and developmentally appropriate than are others. On this view, then, the British government's EYFS developmental injunctions assume an erroneous view of child development, and there certainly exists no research evidence to support it.

All this should also be seen in the context of a managerialist, so-called 'surveillance culture' ideology now cascading down the education system, right to the earliest of ages. As a whole range of factors continues to reinforce the cognitive 'hot-housing' and overly utilitarian atmosphere pervading modern mainstream education, the Hawthorn Press Early Years series is just one cultural manifestation of a widespread disquiet about the manic politicization of early-years learning which has recently occurred with breathtaking rapidity – and with virtually no informed public or political debate.

One common effect of these disturbing trends – and this is a recurring theme throughout the series – is what we might call t*he dismembering and the 'toxicity' of childhood experience* in modern technological society. Yet as the books in this series compellingly demonstrate, there are tried and tested, viable alternatives to the aforementioned developments, grounded in a potent combination of perennial wisdom and cutting-edge research and understanding about child development, care, and learning. Certainly, there is a growing 'counter-cultural' public mood which is clamouring for a humane and demonstrably effective alternative to the deeply unsatisfactory fare currently on offer in 'mainstream society' – which fact throws much light on just why this series has been so well received since its first book appeared seven years ago, and why there is now a growing cacophony of voices being raised from many quarters challenging the prevailing *Zeitgeist* and its arguably toxic practices.

The books in this series, then, have an overriding focus which is **holistic, informed, and practical** – offering readers state-of-the-art information for those who are involved in early-childhood settings (i.e. from birth to about 6 years), be they familial or professional. The books offer practical, theoretically informed insights into a whole range of early-years-related questions and issues – thereby making a major contribution to the global cultural movement of concerned parents that educationalist Neil Postman was referring to when he wrote:

> There are parents... who are defying the directives of their culture. Such parents are not only helping their children to have a childhood... Those parents... will help to keep alive a human tradition. [Our culture] is halfway toward forgetting that children need childhood. *Those who insist on remembering shall perform a noble service.*

Indeed, Postman's inspiring championing of childhood could hardly provide a more fitting epigraph for the Early Years series.

Books in the 'Early Years' Series

There are certain themes which recur throughout the books in the series. The distorting *effects of anxiety* on healthy development and learning constitutes one such theme; and another is the crucial role of *free creative play*, with all our authors no doubt agreeing that freely and unintruded-upon imaginative play is vital for healthy child development (and notice that we are speaking here of *free*, child-led play based on imitation, not the adult-centric strain of 'directed' or 'structured' play beloved of the mainstream policy-makers). The young child, then, needs an unintruded-upon 'space' (in the physical, emotional, and the spiritual sense) in which to play with, elaborate, and work through her deepest wishes, anxieties, and unconscious fantasies; and in turn, the child will thereby gain competence in healthily managing – with her own freely developed will – her curiosities and anxieties about human relationship. Sally

Jenkinson's seminal 'Early Years' book, *The Genius of Play*, develops these arguments at much greater length.

As already intimated, another consistent theme in the series is the pernicious deforming effects on young children of *premature cognitive-intellectual development*. There are now convincing *neurological* as well as social rationales which argue against the one-sidedness of 'left-brain', over-intellectually *unbalanced* learning, particularly at young ages. As Professor Patrick Bateson and Paul Martin have written, 'Children who are pushed too hard academically, and who consequently advance temporarily beyond their peers, may ultimately pay a price in terms of lost opportunities for development'; and the important research of Professor Lilian Katz of Illinois University, amongst others, is now bearing this out. Certainly, at least some Western governments seem to be narrowly preoccupied with a control- and development-obsessiveness – leading to a child 'hot-housing' ideology which may well be harming a whole generation of children.

Tell-tale signs of the harm being done by a one-sidedly consumerist culture in general, and by the current early years educational regimes in particular, are increasingly coming to prominence. A study by the British National Health Foundation, for example, has recently reported record levels of stress-related mental health problems in children. It was for this overriding reason that author and educational consultant Sue Palmer and I co-organized the Open Letter on 'toxic childhood' published in the *Daily Telegraph* in September 2006, with Sally Blythe joining over 100 authorities from across the fields of education and psychology to challenge the negative impacts that many aspects of modern life are arguably having on childhood experience.

Symptoms of so-called 'attention deficit disorder' and the like are surely far better understood as children's understandable response to, and unwitting commentary on, technological culture's ever-escalating manic overstimulation (cf. see Martin Large's book, *Set Free Childhood)* – and not least, its cognitively-biased distortions of early child development and assault on young children's vulnerable senses by an increasingly pervasive televisual technology – a theme which Sally Blythe also emphasizes in her new book (see her Chapter 10).

Re-membering Childhood: The 'Early Years' Series

The 'Early Years' series is very much driven by the experience of parents themselves, rather than being primarily professionally or 'expert'-driven, as is much of the early-years literature. The distinctive approach represented in these books is strongly, but not exclusively, informed by the flourishing world-wide network of approaching 2,000 Steiner (Waldorf) Kindergartens, with over 80 years of accumulated wisdom on child development that this global movement has built up – founded on the original indications of the educationalist and philosopher Rudolf Steiner. The series freely draws upon the wisdom and insight of other prominent holistic approaches, including Froebel, Montessori, and other respected holistic early-years specialists – thus embracing the emerging 'company of like-minded friends' working together in their distinct yet complementary ways for healthy child development.

A defining feature of each book is its focus on a specific topic or question for which parents, teachers, or other early-years workers commonly require sound information and effective practical input. Books are based on up-to-date research and practice, and are written by a prominent authority in the field in question. Sally Blythe's new book is especially impressive in this regard – being a model of the way in which the full range of mainstream research evidence can be convincingly adduced to make a compelling case for a *scientifically informed* holistic approach to early childhood experience.

Each book contains 'Resources' and Further Reading sections so that interested readers can follow up their interest in the field in question. Titles published to date are already proving to be ideal study-texts for reading, study, and support groups, as well as authoritative sources for holistic perspectives on early-years training courses of all kinds. A number of books in the 'Early Years' series promise to become *the* definitive works in their particular fields for many years to come, and have already received very favourable reviews and widespread acclaim from a range of sources across the globe.

In her earlier book for the series, Sally Blythe placed equal emphasis and value upon both science and perennial wisdom, and *The Well Balanced Child* demonstrated a mature understanding of the holistic nature of learning, and the subtle interrelationships entailed in healthy early learning that transcends by far the crassly mechanistic approaches that dominate modern mainstream thinking and practice. As she put it in her earlier book,

Whilst science – the testing of observations and ideas – constitutes an essential part of civilization and progress, intuition is the spark that lights the fire of scientific investigation. In looking at child development, I wanted to marry the processes of science and intuition, to find an explanation as to why certain social traditions and child-rearing practices have been consistently successful, despite a vastly changing world and a diversity of cultural ideals.

Love and early learning – or cultivating the 'pedagogy of love'

The unambiguous conclusion to which working with young children surely leads the sensitive practitioner is this: that *non-possessive love and warmth are crucial and perhaps even decisive factors in whether or not young children develop healthily and fully.* One need only look at the burgeoning clinical literature in psychology, child psychotherapy, and infant massage to witness the manifold negative influences that the absence of love or nurturing physical touch can have on child development. It was the great paediatrician and psychoanalyst Donald Winnicott who emphasized the core role of the mother's attuned *physical holding and handling* of her baby in children's early healthy development.

It is surely testimony to the mechanistic utilitarianism that is now informing early-years policy-making and praxis that it can almost feel *revolutionary* to speak of love in this way. It seems to take courage even to dare to mention the crucial developmental role of love in 'professional' discussions of 'scientific' pedagogy; yet as Rudolf Steiner and, more recently, Sue Gerhardt (amongst others) have clearly recognized, there is a quite literal way in which love can decisively influence healthy development – and not just emotionally and spiritually, but physically too.

That love is indeed a central factor in successful early learning is also consistent with recent findings of the British Effective Provision of Pre-school Education longitudinal research project, led by Professor Kathy Sylva of Oxford University. In their study of 141 randomly selected pre-school settings, the researchers found that the best settings actually combine care [for which read 'love'] and education – or in other words, that love is a necessary condition of early (and perhaps all?) healthy learning. In addition, a recent welcome book by psychoanalytic psychotherapist Sue Gerhardt – *Why Love Matters* – shows how the young child's earliest relationships actually shape the child's nervous system – yet another example, then, of the way in which modern science is only now beginning to catch up with and confirm the indications laid down by Rudolf Steiner almost a century ago.

What Babies and Children Really Need

[It is] as if thought must be translated into action before it can be uttered as sound....

Sally Goddard Blythe,
What Babies and Children Really Need

All this sits very easily with the central theme in Sally Blythe's new book. In the author's own words, 'The new book examines the science behind why a child's physical development, together with physical interaction and social engagement in the early years, are so important, in the hope that parents, teachers, politicians, educators, and trainee teachers of the future will have a better understanding of why physical development, educational progress and social integration go hand in hand and have their origins in the early years.' Forworded by distinguished best-selling author of *Toxic Childhood* and *Detoxing Childhood*, Sue Palmer, the book looks in turn at just why early development matters, the importance of pre-birth experience, and the events surrounding and following birth, including breast-feeding. The heart of the book then examines in detail what Sally Blythe calls the 'movement instinct' and the 'language instinct'; and we read about the key developmental role played by the reflexes, and how, for example, *movement is a child's first language,* enabling information received by the senses to be integrated. Children clearly need plenty of opportunity for free movement and exploration in the early years; and space, time, opportunity to play, and human interaction are vital to a baby's and a young child's healthy all-round development.

The latter parts of the book then consider the neuroscience behind the regulation of the emotions, and the factors parents can influence in their children's development – like the role of discipline, parenting styles, consistency, mealtimes, children's play, and impact of the electronic media. The book ends with wide-ranging discussions of 'the needs for the parents of tomorrow and the children of today', including the 'Charter for Childhood'.

Sally Blythe's book and the arguments therein have profound policy relevance in relation to the incursion of quasi-formal learning into early-years education, referred to earlier in this essay. Not least, Sally Blythe's important work shows just how crucial is the enabling of greater flexibility in matching developmental readiness to the time when children are entering formal education. As she has written elsewhere, there exists a lamentably poor understanding of the reasons why physical development, play, song etc. are important in partnership with more formal preparation for formal early childhood education. As she points out, probationary teachers' experience of the role of early physical development in learning is limited if not non-existent.

Sally Blythe follows a long tradition of early education based on Rudolf Steiner and Margaret Macmillan's pedagogy, that *physical development should be of primary import in early learning,* as it is through physical development that a child expresses his/her experience, understanding, and knowledge of the world, with physical development also underpinning all communication and social skills. Based on her own research, it appears that possibly more than a third of Britain's school children may be developmentally immature in terms of their physical skills at school entry, and that these physical immaturities have a profoundly deleterious impact upon educational achievement.

Sally Blythe gives us hints at at least some of the mechanisms underlying the growing 'adultization' of children that many have observed. At the end of Chapter 7, for example, we read that 'all of these physical actions have a corresponding verbal connection'. Immaturity in the functioning of balance and reflex pathways has cognitive and emotional consequences because the reflex, vestibular, and cerebellar systems should act as 'secretary' to the thinking brain. *If these lower centres cannot fulfil their functions at a subconscious level, the 'boss' or thinking brain ends up doing much of their work for them.*

We are told, further, that in the first year of life, the infant brain recapitulates its own evolutionary history, aiding motor and sensory development, both facilitating and reflecting maturity in the functioning of the brain. She continues, 'If as parents we seek to rush through these stages, minimize, or eliminate certain movement experiences in order to fit in more easily with the demands of modern living, we potentially deprive our children of vital building blocks for learning and emotional development. Space, time, opportunity to play, and human interaction are as vital to a baby in the first year of life as food, sleep, and a clean nappy'.

The first three years of life also constitute the sensitive period or 'window of opportunity' for learning to understand and use the sounds of language. Major periods of what she terms 'neural housekeeping' take place at 2-3 years of age, at ages 6-7, and again around puberty, enabling increased functional specialization, but at the cost of reduced generalization. This is one of the reasons why establishing the basis for language in the first three years of life is so important, with the brain's ability to 'hear' becoming less sensitive and flexible over time.

We also learn about how interaction in *real human relationship* is a vital part of every child's language development. Thus, we read that

A child learning its first language also needs time to listen, to practise, and to hear again. This means time spent with parents, being willing to talk to their child, wait while the child processes the information, listen to the response, and then be willing to reflect back. This is a uniquely human skill, and cannot be substituted with electronic media. Television doles out a surfeit of speech, but does not *listen* to what the child has to say back. It is a passive process. It omits the motor-sensory integration stage of the child responding to what is on the screen. It provides stimulation and arousal but no physical outlet for that arousal....

Research which investigated the effects of visual cues on children's language has also confirmed how important it is to be able to see the face of a person whilst being spoken to.

Conclusion: Finding a Better Way

There is little empirical research being carried out – and certainly not by government – into the medium- and long-term effects on children's overall development of the dangerously mechanistic educational 'regimes', with their one-sidedly materialistic values and physicality-deprived experience, to which young children are being unforgivingly subjected. This is nothing short of a national scandal, at which future, more enlightened generations will surely look back aghast at our crass immaturity and almost wilful neglect of what really matters in living a healthy life.

Yet there is now an increasingly tangible sense that the tide is turning against those pernicious cultural forces that have been systematically dismembering childhood – and towards a *re*-membering of a holistic vision of childhood which recognizes the damage that is being wrought by modern culture, and which offers practical and effective alternatives. Sally Blythe's path-breaking work, as enunciated in this new book, lies at the heart of these developments. To the extent that the Hawthorn 'Early Years' series can buttress and reinforce this mounting sea-change in attitudes to childhood, it will have more than served its purpose.

In sum, the key to building a better world surely lies in just how successfully we can facilitate our children's healthy development. Hawthorn Press's 'Early Years' series is making available a rich range of books which will 'help parents defy the directives of modern culture' (Neil Postman), and *find a better way* to raise their children and help them realize their full potential. These books are helping parents and professionals alike to *reinvigorate* the rapidly disappearing art of *understanding children and their developmental needs,* which modern materialist culture has done so much to undermine; and both of these countervailing trends are illuminatingly illustrated in Sally Blythe's new book.

Above all, the authors in this series would all agree that education should nourish and facilitate, rather than subvert, children's innate *love of learning.* By way of closing, we invite you, the reader, to support this important series – and in so doing, to join the rapidly growing body of parents and educators who are determined to reinstate 'the pedagogy of love' and *informed developmental appropriateness* at the heart of the learning environments we create for this and future generations of children.

Richard House
London, Christmas 2007

Select Indicative Bibliography

Note: 'Early Years' Series books are set in **bold** type.

Alliance for Childhood (2000) *Fool's Gold: A Critical Look at Computers in Childhood,* College Park, Md

Baldwin Dancy, R. (2000) *You Are Your Child's First Teacher,* 2nd edn, Celestial Arts, Berkeley, Calif.

DeGrandpre, R. (2000) *Ritalin Nation: Rapid-Fire Culture and the Transformation of Human Consciousness,* W. W. Norton, New York

Elkind, D. (1981) *The Hurried Child: Growing Up Too Fast Too Soon,* Addison-Wesley, Reading, Mass.

Elkind, D. (1987) *Mis-education: Pre-schoolers at Risk,* A. A. Knopf, New York

Evans, R. (2000) *Helping Children to Overcome Fear: The Healing Power of Play,* Hawthorn Press, Stroud

Gerhardt, S. (2004) *Why Love Matters: How Affection Shapes a Baby's Brain,* Brunner-Routledge, London

Goddard Blyth, S. (2004) *The Well Balanced Child: Movement and Early Learning,* Hawthorn Press, Stroud

Healy, J. M. (1990) *Endangered Minds: Why Children Don't Think and What We Can Do about It,* Touchstone/Simon & Schuster, New York

Healy, J. M. (1998) *Failure to Connect: How Computers Affect Our Children's Minds – for Better and Worse,* Simon & Schuster, New York

Hirsh-Pasek, K. and Golinkoff, R.M. (2003) *Einstein Never Used Flash Cards: How Our Children Really Learn – and Why They Need to Play More and Memorize Less,* Rodale

Hirsh-Pasek, K., Michnick Golinkoff, R., Berk, L.E., and Singer, D.G. (2007) 'All work and no play: a call for evidence-based preschool education', submitted/in press

House, R. (forthcoming) *The Trouble with Education: Stress, Surveillance and Modernity,* Ur Publications, Montreal

Jaffke, F. (2000) *Work and Play in Early Childhood,* Floris Books, Edinburgh

Jenkinson, S. (2001) *The Genius of Play: Celebrating the Spirit of Childhood,* Hawthorn Press, Stroud

Large, M. (2003) *Set Free Childhood: Parents' Survival Guide to Coping with Computers and TV,* Hawthorn Press, Stroud

Medved, M. & Medved, D. (1998) *Saving Childhood: Protecting Our Children from the National Assault on Innocence,* HarperCollins, Zondervan

Mellon, N. (2000) *Storytelling with Children,* Hawthorn Press, Stroud

Mills, D. and Mills, C. (1997) 'Britain's Early Years Disaster: Part 1 – The Findings', mimeograph

Moore, R. S. & Moore, D. N. (1975) *Better Late than Early: A New Approach to Your Child's Education,* Reader's Digest Press (Dutton), New York

Oldfield, L. (2001a) *Free to Learn: Introducing Steiner Waldorf Early Childhood Education,* Hawthorn Press, Stroud

Ostrosky-Solis, F., Garcia, M. A., and Pérez, M. (2004) 'Can learning to read and write change the brain organization? An electrophysiological study', *International Journal of Psychology,* 39 (1), pp. 27-35

Patterson, B.J. and Bradley, P. (2000) B*eyond the Rainbow Bridge: Nurturing Our Children from Birth to Seven,* Michaelmas Press, Amesbury, Mass.

Peck, B. (2004) *Kindergarten Education – Freeing Children's Creative Potential,* Hawthorn Press, Stroud

Postman, N. (1994) *The Disappearance of Childhood,* Vintage Books, New York

Rawson, M. and Rose, M. (2002) *Ready to Learn: From Birth to School Readiness,* Hawthorn Press, Stroud

Sanders, B. (1995) *A is for Ox: The Collapse of Literacy and the Rise of Violence in an Electronic Age,* Vintage Books, New York

Schweinhart, L.J. and Weikart, D. P. (1997) *Lasting Differences: The High/Scope Preschool Curriculum Comparison Study through Age 23,* High/Scope Press, Ypsilanti, MI; Monographs of the High/ Scope Educational Research Foundation No. 12

Thomson, J. B. & others (1994) *Natural Childhood: A Practical Guide to the First Seven Years,* Gaia Books, London

A fuller bibliography can be obtained from the author on request – from **richardahouse@hotmail.com**

Resources

Useful addresses

The Institute for Neuro-Physiological Psychology
1 Stanley Street, Chester CH1 2LR
Tel/Fax: 00 44 (0)1244 311414
E-mail: mail@inpp.org.uk
www.inpp.org.uk

Association of Breastfeeding Mothers
ABM
PO Box 207, Bridgwater, Somerset TA6 7YT
Tel: 08444 122949
www.abm.me.uk

Foresight – The association for promoting pre-conceptual care
178 Hawthorn Road, West Bognor, West Sussex PO21 2UY
Tel: 00 44 (0)1243 868001
Fax: 00 44 (0)1243 868180
www.foresight-preconception.org.uk

La Leche League
La Leche League (Great Britain)
PO Box 29, West Bridgford, Nottingham NG2 7NP
Tel: 0845 456 1855
www.laleche.org.uk

National Childbirth Trust
Alexandra House, Oldham Terrace, London W3 6NH
Tel: 0870 444 8707
Fax: 0870 770 3237
www.nct.org.uk

Primal Health Research Centre
www.birthworks.org/primalhealth

SONATAL – Music for babies from pregnancy to 7 years of age
www.sonatal.ru

Toddler Kindy GymbaROO – Activities for mothers and babies
Cotham
PO Box 3095, Kew, Victoria 3101, Australia
Tel: 00 61 (0)3 9817 3544
Fax: 00 61 (0)3 9817 5902
E-mail: office@gymbaroo.com.au
www.gymbaroo.com.au

Bibliography

Agid, O., Kon, Y., and Lerer, B. (2000) 'Environmental stress and psychiatric illness', *Biomedicine and Pharmacotherapy,* 54: 135-41

Ahnert, L. and Lamb, M.E. (2003) 'Shared care: establishing a balance between home and child care settings', *Child Development,* 74/4: 1044

Aisien, A.O. and others (1994) 'Umbilical cord venous progesterone at term delivery in relation to mode of delivery', *Int. J. Gynaec. Obstet.,* 47/1: 27-31

Alhazen, cited in: Arnheim, R. (1969) *Visual thinking,* University of California Press, Berkeley

Amen, D. (2001) *Healing ADD: The breakthrough program that allows you to see and heal the 6 types of ADD,* G.P. Putnam & Sons, New York

Anderson, U.M. (1967) 'Progress and virtue of non-adjustment: an historical insight into the origins of public health', *Journal of International Health,* Spring: 2-16.

Anderson, U.M. (2007) *Personal communication*

Anon (n.d.) Medical References: Drinking alcohol during pregnancy, **www.marchofdimes.com**

Anon (2007) 'Unskilled graduates aren't worth hiring say British bosses', *Daily Mail,* 30th January

Antonov, A.N. (1947) 'Children born during the siege of Leningrad in 1942', *Journal of Pediatrics,* 30: 250-9

Apgar, J. (1992) 'Zinc and reproduction: an update', *J. Nutrit. Biochem.,* 3: 266-78

Arvedson, J.C. (2006) 'Swallowing and feeding in infants and young children', GI Motility online, doi:10.1038/gimo17

Aslin, R.N. (1985) 'Oculo-motor measures of visual development', in G. Gottlieb and N. Krasnegor (eds), *Measurement of audition and vision during the first year of life: A methodological overview,* Ablex, Norwood, NJ, pp. 391-417

Ayres, A.J. (1978) 'Learning disabilities and the vestibular system', *Journal of Learning Disabilities,* 11: 18-29

Bagnoli, F. and others (1990) 'Relationship between mode of delivery and neonatal calcium homeostasis', *Eur. J. Pediatr.*, 149/11: 800-3

Bainbridge, B. (2000) *A visitor within: The science of pregnancy*, Weidenfeld and Nicolson/Orion, London

Barnes, B. (2006) Personal communication

Barnes, B. and Bradley, S.G. (1990) *Planning for a healthy baby*, Ebury Press, London

Barnes, D. and Walker, D.W. (1981) 'Prenatal ethanol exposure permanently alters the rat hippocampus', cited in *Mechanisms of alcohol damage in utero*, CIBA Foundation Symposium, 105, Pitman, London

Barnett, S.B. (2001) 'Intracranial temperature elevation from diagnostic ultra-sound', *Ultrasound Med. Biol.*, 27/7: 883-8

Barr, R.G. and Elias, M.F. (1988) 'Nursing interval and maternal responsiveness: effect on early infant crying', *Pediatrics*, 81: 529-36

Barrett, S.E., Spence, M.J., Abdi, H., and O'Toole, A.J. (2003) 'Psychological and neural perspectives on the role of motion in face recognition', *Behavioural and Cognitive Neuro-science Reviews*, 2/1: 5-46

Barsch, R.H. (1968) *Achieving perceptual-motor efficiency: A self-oriented approach to learning. Volume 1 of a perceptual-motor curriculum*, Special Child Publications, Seattle

Basic Skills Agency (2002) *Summary report of survey into young children's skills on entry to education*, London

Baumrind, D. (1991) 'Parenting styles and adolescent development', in R.M. Lerner, A.C. Peterson and J. Brooks-Gunn (eds), *The encyclopedia of adolescence*, Garland, New England

Beech, B.L. (1993) 'Ultrasound unsound?', talk delivered at Mercy Hospital, Melbourne, Australia, April

Bel, B. Cited in W.R. Trevathan, O.E. Smith, and J.J. McKenna (eds), *Evolutionary obstetrics: Evolutionary medicine*, Oxford University Press, New York, 1999, pp. 183-207

Bellis Waller, M. (1993) *Crack affected children: A teacher's guide*, Corwin Press, Newbury Park, Calif.

Bellis Waller, M. (2003) Personal communication

Bellis Waller, M. (2006) Personal communication

Bender, M.L. (1976) *The Bender-Purdue Reflex Test and training manual*, Academic Therapy Publications, San Rafael, Calif.

Bennett, R.V. and Brown, L.K. (1989) *Myles textbook for midwives*,

Churchill Livingstone, Edinburgh

Berard, G. (1993) *Hearing equals behaviour,* Keats Publishing, New Canaan, Conn.

Biagini, G. and others (1998) 'Postnatal maternal separation during stress hyporesponsive period enhances the adrenocortical response to novelty in adult rats by affecting regulation in the CA1 hippocampal field', *Int. J. Dev. Neurosci.,* 16/3-4: 187-97

Binney, R. and Janson, M. (eds) (1976) *The atlas of the human brain,* Mitchell Beazley, London

Bird, J.A. and others (1996) 'Endocrine and metabolic adaptation following caesarean section or vaginal delivery', *Arch. Dis. Child Fetal Neonatal Ed.,* 74/2: F132-4

Birth Choice UK website, **www.BirthChoiceUK.com**

Blaffer Hardy, S. (1999) *Mother Nature,* Chatto and Windus, London

Blauvelt, H. (1956) 'Neonate-mother relationship in goat and man', In B Schaffner (ed.), *Group Processes,* Josiah Mary Jr Foundation, New York, pp. 94-140

Blythe, P. (1974) *A somatogenic basis for neurosis and the effect upon health,* The Institute for Psychosomatic Therapy, Chester

Blythe, P. and McGlown, D.J. (1979) *An organic basis for neuroses and educational difficulties,* Insight Publications, Chester

Boksa, P. and El-Khodor, B.F. (2003) 'Birth insult interacts with stress at adulthood to alter dopaminergic function in animal modes: possible implications for schizophrenia and other disorders', *Neurosci. Behav. Rev.,* 27/1-2: 91-101

Bourne, G. (1979) *Pregnancy,* Pan Books, London

Bradshaw, J., Hoelscher, P., and Richardson, D. (2006) *An Index of Child Well-Being in the European Union,* Social Indicators Research, Springer, USA

Brotherson, S. (2006) 'Keys to building attachment with young children', **www.ag.ndsu.edu**

Broughton Pipkin, F. and Symonds, E.M. (1977) 'Factors affecting angiotensin 11 concentrations in the human infant at birth', *Clin. Sci. Mol. Med.,* 52/5: 449-56

Brown, P. (2004) *Eve: Sex, childbirth and motherhood through the ages,* Summersdale Publishers, Chichester

Buckley, S.J. (2005a) *Gentle birth, gentle mothering,* One Moon Press, Brisbane

Buckley, S.J. (2005b) 'Leaving well alone – a natural approach to third stage', *Medical Veritas,* 2/2: 492-9

Burne, J. (2006) 'IVF: why we must be told the truth over birth defects', article featured in 'Good Health' section, *Daily Mail,* 12th December

Butler Hall, B. (1998) 'Discovering the hidden treasures in the ear', paper presented at the 10th European Conference of Neuro-Developmental Delay in Children with Specific Learning Difficulties, Chester

Caldwell, D.F., Oberleas, D., and Prasad, A.S. (1976) *Trace elements in human health and disease. Vol. 1. Zinc and copper,* Academic Press, New York

Capute, A.J., Accardo, P.J. (1991) *Developmental disabilities in infancy and childhood,* Paul Brookes Publ. Co., Baltimore

Capute, A.J., Pasquale, J., and Accardo, P.J. (1978) 'Linguistic and auditory milestones during the first two years of life: a language inventory for the practitioner', *Clinical Pediatrics,* 17/11: 847-53

Chasnoff, I.J., Burns, K.A., Burns, W.J., and Schnoll, S.H. (1986) 'Prenatal drug exposure: Effects of neonatal and infant growth development', *Neurobehavioral Toxicology and Teratology,* 8: 357-62

Chasnoff, I.J., Schnoll, S.H., Burns, W.J., and Burns, K.A. (1985) 'Cocaine use in pregnancy', *New England Journal of Medicine,* 313: 666-9

Christakis, D.M., Zimmerman, F.J., DiGiuseppe, D.L., and McCarty, C.A. (2004) 'Early television and subsequent attentional problems in children', *Pediatrics,* 113/4: 708-13

Christensson, K. and others (1993) 'Lower body temperatures in infants delivered by caeserean section than in vaginally delivered infants', *Acta Paediatr.,* 82/2: 128-31

Clarke, E., Reichard, U.H., and Zuberbühler, K. (2006) 'The syntax and meaning of wild gibbon songs', *PLoS One,* 1(1): e73

Cleeland, L. (1984) 'Vestibular disorders – learning Problems and Dyslexia', *Hearing Instruments,* 35/8

Clouder, C. (2007) Summary following debate on the UNICEF Report at The Alliance of Childhood Forum, British Association for Early Childhood Education Centre, London, March

Collishaw, S., Maughan, B., Goodman, R., and Pickles, A. (2004) 'Time trends in adolescent mental health', *Journal of Child*

Psychology and Psychiatry, 45/8: 1350-62

Commons, M.L. and Miller, P.M. (1998) 'Emotional learning in infants: a cross-cultural examination', paper presented at the American Association for the Advancement of Science, Philadelphia, February

Cook, P.S. (1999) 'Rethinking the early childcare agenda: who should be caring for very young children?', *MJA,* 170: 29-31

Coryell, J. and Henderson, A. (1979) 'Role of the asymmetrical tonic neck reflex in hand visualization in normal infants', *American Journal of Occupational Therapy,* 33/4: 255-60

Cuomo, V., La Sapienza University, Rome

Darwin, C. (1872) *The expression of the emotions in man and animals,* New York

Davidson, R.J. (1992) 'Anterior cerebral asymmetry and the nature of emotion', *Brain Cog.,* 20: 125-51

deMause, L. (1982) *Foundations of psychohistory,* Creative Roots, New York

de Quirós JB, Schrager OL, 1979. *Neuropsychological fundamentals in learning disabilities.* Academic Publications. Novato.CA.

Delacato, C. (1970) *The diagnosis and treatment of speech and reading problems,* Charles C. Thomas, Springfield, Ill.

Demyer, W. (1980) *Technique of the neurological examination,* McGraw-Hill, New York

Department for Education and Skills (DfES) (2006) *Foundation Stage Profile 2005,* National Results (Provisional), National Statistics Office

Derks, P., Gillikon, L., Bartolome, D.S., and Bogart, E.H. (1997) 'Laughter and electroencephalographic activity', *Humor,* 10: 283–98

Diamond, M.C. (1988) *Enriching heredity,* The Free Press, New York

Dickson, V. (1989) Personal communication

Anon... 'Ecstatic birth: the hormonal blueprint of labour' (2002) Online Mothering Magazine, issue 111, March/April **www.mothering.com.articles.**

Eggesbø, M., Botten, G., Stigum, H., Samuelson, S., Brunekreef, B., and Magnus, P. (2005)' Cesarean delivery and cow mild allergy/intolerance', *Allergy,* 60/9: 1172

Eichler, L. (1924) *The customs of mankind,* William Heinemann, London

Ekman, P. (2003) *Emotions revealed: Recognising faces and feelings to improve communication and emotional life,* Times Books, New York

Ekman, P., Davidson, R.J., and Friesen, W.V. (1990) 'The Duchenne smile: emotional expression and brain physiology II', *J. Person. Soc. Psych.,* 58: 342-53.

Ekman, P. and Friesen, W.V. (1977) *Manual for the Facial Action Coding System,* Consulting Psychologists Press, Palo Alto, Calif.

El-Chaar, D. (2007) 'Fertility treatment raises birth defect risk', presented at conference hosted by the Society for Maternal-Fetal Medicine, San Francisco, 9th February

Emery, M. (1985) 'The social and neurophysiological effect of television and their implications for marketing practice', unpublished doctoral dissertation, Australian National University, Canberra

Endo, A. and others (2001) 'Spontaneous labour increases nitric oxide synthesis during the early neonatal period', *Pediatr. Int.,* 42/1: 340-2

EPPE Study **www.dfes.gov.uk/research**

Eustis, R.S. (1947) 'The primary origin of the specific language disabilities', *Journal of Pediatrics,* 31: 448-55

Fachinetti, F. and others (1990) 'Changes in beta-endorphin in fetal membranes and placenta in normal and pathological pregnancies', *Acta Obstet. Gynaecol. Scand.,* 69/7-8: 603-7

Faxelius, G. and others (1983) 'Catecholamine surge and lung function after delivery', *Arch. Dis. Child.,* 58/4: 262-6

Fenig, E., Mishaeli, M., Kalish, Y., and Lishner, M. (2001) 'Pregnancy and radiation', *Cancer Treatment Review,* 27/1: 1-7

Fernald, A. (1984) 'The perceptual and affective salience of mother's speech to infants', in L. Feagans, C. Garvey, R. Golinkoff and others (eds), *The origins and growth of communication,* Ablex, Norwood, NJ

Fernald, A. and Simon, T. (1984) 'Expanded intonation contours in mothers' speech to newborns', *Develop. Psychol.,* 20: 104-13

Field, T. (2005) *Touch therapy,* Churchill Livingstone, Edinburgh

Fieldhouse, D. (2007) Personal communication

Finnegan, J. (1993) *The vital role of essential fatty acids for pregnant and nursing women,* Celestial Arts; **http://www.thorne.com/townsend/dec/efas.html**

Fitzgibbon, J. (2002) *Feeling tired all the time,* Gill & Macmillan.

Foresight: **www.foresight-preconception.org.uk**

Freudigman, K.A., Thoman, E.B. (1998) 'Infants' earliest sleep/wake organization differs as a function of delivery mode', *Dev. Psychobiol.,* 32/4: 293-303

Fry, W.F., Jr. (1992) 'The physiologic effects of humor, mirth, and laughter' *JAMA, Journal of the American Medical Association,* 267/13: 1857

Fujimura, A. and others (1990) 'The influence of delivery mode on biological inactive rennin level in umbilical cord blood', *Am. J. Hypertens.,* 3/1: 23-6

Gale, C.R. and Martyn, C.N. (2004) 'Birth weight and later risk of depression in a national birth cohort', *British Journal of Psychiatry,* 184: 28-33

Gallese, V., Fadiga, I., and Rizzolatti, G. (1996) 'Action recognition in the pre-motor cortex', *Brain,* 119: 593-609

Gentzkow, M. and Shapiro, J.M. (2006) Abstract for: 'Does television rot your brain? New evidence from the Coleman study' (with Jesse M. Shapiro), NBER Working Paper # 12021, last updated February 2006

Gershon, M.D. (1998) *The Second Brain,* HarperCollins, New York

Gibran, K. (1972) *The Prophet,* Heinemann, London

Goddard Blythe, S.A. (2003) *The well balanced child,* Hawthorn Press, Stroud

Goddard Blythe, S.A. (2005) 'Releasing educational potential through movement', *Child Care in Practice,* 11/4: 415-32

Goddard Blythe, S.A. and Hyland, D. (1998) 'Screening for neurological dysfunction in the specific learning difficulty child', *British Journal of Occupational Therapy,* 61/10: 459-64

Goddard, S.A. (2001) *Reflexes, learning and behaviour,* Fern Ridge Press, Eugene, Ore.

Gronlund, M.M. and others (1999) 'Fecal microflora in healthy infants born by different methods of delivery: permanent changes in intestinal flora after caesarean delivery', *J. Pediatr. Gastroenterol. Nutr.,* 28/1: 19-25

Gruenwald, P., Funakawa, H., Mitani, T., Nishimura, and Takeuchi, S. (1967) 'Influence of environmental factors on fetal growth in man', *Lancet,* 1: 1026-8

Hagnevik, K. and others (1984) 'Catecholamine surge and metabolic adaptation in the newborn after vaginal delivery and caesarean section', *Acta. Paediatr. Scand.*, 73/5: 602-9

Hakansson, S. and Kallen, K. (2003) 'Cesarean section increases the risk of hospital care in childhood for asthma and gastroenteritis', *Clin. Exp. Allergy,* 33/6: 757-64

Hallstrom, M. and others (2004) 'Effects of mode of delivery and nectrotising enterocolits on the intestinal microflora in preterm infants', *Eur. J. Clin. Microbiol. Infect. Dis.,* 23/6: 463-70

Hambridge, K.M., Case, C.E., and Krebs, N.F. (1986) 'Zinc', in W. Mertz (ed.), *Trace elements in human and animal nutrition, Vol. 2,* Academic Press, New York, pp. 1-137

Harlow, H.F. (1965) 'Prolonged and progressive effect of partial isolation on.the behaviour of macaque monkeys', *J. Exp. Res. Pers.,* 1: 39-49

Haviland, W.A. (1996) *Cultural anthropology,* Harcourt Brace College Publishers, Fort Worth, Tx

Healy, J.M. (1990) *Endangered minds: Why children don't think and what we can do about it,* Touchstone/Simon and Schuster, New York

Heasman, L. and others (1997) 'Plasma prolactin concentrations after caesarean or vaginal delivery', *Arch. Dis. Child Fetal Neonatal Ed.,* 77/3: F237-8

Heinig, M.J., Nommsen, L.A., Peerson, J.M., Lonnderdal, B., and Dewey, K.G. (1993) 'Energy and protein intakes of breast-fed and formula-fed infants during the first year of life and their association with growth velocity: the DARLING study', *American Journal of Clinical* Nutrition, 58: 152-61

Hepper, P.G. (1988) 'Foetal "soap" addiction', *Lancet,* 11th June: 1347-8

Hepper, P.G. (1991) 'An examination of fetal learning before and after birth', *Irish Journal of Psychology,* 12: 95-107

Hepper, P.G. (1996) 'Fetal memory: does it exist? What does it do?', *Acta Paediatrica Supplement,* 416: 16-20

Hill, K. and Hurtado, A.M. (1996) *Ache life history: The ecology and demography of a foraging people,* Aldine de Gruyter, New York

Hills, F.A. and others (1996) 'IGFBP-1 in the placental membranes and fetal circulation: levels at term and preterm delivery', *Early Human Development,* 44/1: 71-6

Hofer, M.A. (1984) 'Relationships as regulators: a psychobiologic perspective on bereavement', *Psychosomatic Medicine,* 46: 183-97

Hollich, G., Rochelle, S., Newman, R.S., and Jusczyk, P.W. (2005) 'Infants' use of synchronized visual information to separate streams of speech', *Child Development,* 76/3: 598-613

Hollich G., cited in: Patterson Nueubert, A. (2005) 'Research: Noise, visual cues affect infants' language development', *Purdue University News,* 15th June

Horrobin, D. (2001) *The madness of Adam and Eve: How schizophrenia shaped humanity,* Corgi Books, London

Infant Feeding Survey 2005; www.ic.nhs.uk/pubs/breastfeed2005

International Child and Youth Care Network (2001) Understanding TV's effects on the developing brain, Care Network Today, 7th September

Isobe, K. and others (2002) 'Measurement of cerebral oxygenation in neonates after vaginal delivery and caesarean section using full spectrum near infrared spectroscopy', *Comp. Biochem. Physiol. A. Mol. Integr. Physiol.,* 132/1: 133-8

Jones, C.R. and others (1985) 'Plasma catcholamines and modes of delivery: the relation between catecholamine levels and in-vitro platelet aggregation and adrenoreceptor radioligland binding characteristics', *British Journal of Obstetric Gynaecology,* 92/6: 593-9

Kaada, B. (1986) *Sudden infant death syndrome,* Oslo University Press

Kaplan, H. and Dove, H. (1987) 'Infant development among the Ache of Paraguay', *Developmental Psychology,* 23/2: 190-8

Keen, C.L. and Gershwin, M.E. (1990) 'Zinc deficiency and immune function', *Annu. Rev. Nutri.,* 10: 415-31

Keen, C.L. and Hurely, L.S. (1989) 'Zinc and reproduction: effects of deficiency on foetal and post natal development', in C.F. Mills (ed.), *Zinc in human biology,* Springer-Verlag, London, pp. 183-220

Kelly, Y.J., Nazroo, J.Y., and McMunn, A. and others (2001) 'Birth weight and behavioural problems in children: a modifiable effect?', *International Journal of Epidemiology,* 30: 88-94

Kennell, J., Trause, M.A., and Klaus, M.H. (1975) 'Evidence of a sensitive period in the human mother', *Ciba Foundation Symposium,* 33: 87-101

Kennell, J.H. and Klaus, M.H. (1998) 'Bonding: recent observations that alter perinatal care', *Pediatrics in Review,* 19/1: 4-12

Kero, J. and others (2002) 'Mode of delivery and asthma – is there a connection?', *Pediatric Res.,* 52/1: 6-11

Kim, H.R. and others (2003) 'Delivery modes and neonatal EEG: spatial pattern analysis', *Early Human Development,* 75/1-2: 16-18

Kimmel, J. (2005) 'Are mothers necessary?', The Natural Child Project, **www.naturalchild,com**

Kiphard, E.J. (2000) 'Psychomotor therapy in Germany and the importance of body control for learning', 12th European Conference of Neuro-Developmental Delay in Children with Specific Learning Difficulties, Chester, March

Klaus, M.H. and Kennell, J.H. (1976) *Maternal-infant bonding,* Mosby, St Louis

Kohen-Raz, R. (1986) *Learning disabilities and postural control,* Freund Publishing House, London

Kohen-Raz, R. (2004) 'Posturographic correlates of learning disabilities and communication disorder', European Conference of Neuro-Developmental Delay in Children with Specific Learning Difficulties

Krugman, H.E. (1971) 'Brain wave measures of media involvement', *Journal of Advertising Research,* 11/1: 3-9

Krugman, H.E. (2000) 'Memory without recall, exposure without perception', *Journal of Advertising Research,* 40: 49-54

Kugiumutzakis, J.E. (1985) 'The origins of development and function of early infant imitation', unpublished Ph.D. thesis, Uppsala University, *Acta Universitatis Uppsaliensis,* 35

Lagercrantz, H. (1989) 'Neurochemical modulation of fetal behaviour and excitation at birth', in E. Euler, H. Forssberg, H. Lagercrantz (eds), *Neurobiology of Early Infant Behaviour,* Wenner-Gren International Symposium Series, Vol. 55, Stockton Press, New York

Lagercrantz, H. and Slotkin, T. (1986) 'The stress of birth', *Scientific American,* 254: 100-7

Large, M. (2006) 'Switch on the kid's telly, switch off their brains', *Parliamentary Brief* (London), 10 (11), December

Laubereau, B. and others (2004) 'Cesarean section and gastro-intestinal symptoms, atopic dermatitis and sensitisation during the first year of life', *Arch. Dis. Child.,* 89/11: 993-7

Lazarev, M. (2004) 'Foetal neurogymnastics', paper presented at the 16th European Conference of Neuro-Developmental Delay in Children with Specific Learning Difficulties, Chester, March

Leijon, I., Berg, G., Finnström, O., and Otamiri, G. (1988) European Congress in Perinatology, Abstracts, Rome

Leiner, H.C., Leiner, A.L., and Dow, R.S. (1987) 'Cerebro-cerebellar learning loops in apes and humans', Ital. J. Neurol. Sci., 8: 425-36

Levinson, H.L. (1984) *Smart but feeling dumb*, Warner Books, New York

Liebeskind, D. and others (1979) 'Diagnostic ultrasound: effects on the DNA and growth patterns of animal cells', *Radiology*, 131/1: 177-84

Liggins, G.C., Fariclough, R.J., Grieves, S.A., Forster, C.S., and Knox, B.S. (1977) 'Parturition in the sheep', in *The Fetus and Birth*, Ciba Foundation Symposium 47, Elsevier, Oxford

Lister, S. (2004) Cited in 'Ban TV to save toddlers' minds say scientists', *The Times*, 6th April

Locke, A. and Ginsborg, J., and Peers, I. (2002) 'Development and disadvantage: implications for early years', *IJCLD*, 27/1

Lorenz, K.Z. (1981) *The foundations of ethology*, Springer-Verlag, New York

Lucas, A., Sarson, D.L., Blackburn, A.A., Adrian, T.E., Aynsley-Green, A., and Bloom, S.R. (1980) 'Breast vs bottle: endocrine responses are different with formula feeding', *Lancet*, 1:1267-9

Lux Flanagan, G. (1962) *The first nine months of life*, Simon and Schuster, New York

MacLean, P. (1978) *A mind of three minds: educating the triune brain*, National Society for the Study of Education, Chicago

MacNeilage, P.F. and Davis, B.L. (2000) 'On the origin of internal structure of word form', *Science* magazine, 21st April: 527-31

Madaule, P. (1993) *When listening comes alive*, Moulin Publishing, Box 560, Ontario

Madaule, P. (2001) Workshop on 'The Audio-Vocal Feedback Loop' delivered to the Institute for Neuro-Physiological Psychology, Chester, November

Mahoney, D. (2003) Cited in *Pediatric News*, 31st July

Maier, R.A. (1962-3) 'Maternal behaviour in the domestic hen', *Laboratory Sciences*, 3/3: 1-12

Malamitsi-Puchner, A. and others (1993) 'Serum levels of creatine kinase and iso-enzymes during 1st postpartum day in healthy newborns delivered vaginally or by cesarean section', *Gynecol. Obstet. Invest.*, 36/1 25-8

Marchini, G. and others (1988) 'Fetal and maternal plasma levels of gastrin, somostatin and oxytocin after vaginal delivery and elective caesarean section', *Early Human Development*, 18/1 73-9

Marinac-Dabic, D. and others (2002) 'The safety of prenatal ultrasound exposure in human studies', *Epidemiology,* 13 (3 Suppl): S19-22.

Mason, W.A. and Berkson, G. (1975) 'Effects of maternal mobility on the development of rocking and other behaviours in the rhesus monkey: a study with artificial mothers', *Developmental Psychobiology,* 8/3: 197-211

Maurer, D. (1983) 'The scanning of compound figures by young infants', *Journal of Experimental Child Psychology,* 35: 437- 48

Maurer, D. and Maurer, C. (1989) *The world of the newborn,* Viking Penguin, New York

McGaha, C. (2003) 'The importance of the senses for infants', Focus on Infants & Toddlers, 16/1

McHugh, G.E. (1966) 'Auditory and vestibular problems in children', *The Laryngoscope*

Mead, M. Cited in Zinsmeister, K. (1998) 'What's the problem with day care?', May/June, American Enterprise online

Meltzoff, A.N. and Moore, M.K. (1977) 'Imitation of facial and manual gestures by human neonates', *Science,* 198: 75-8

Meltzoff, A.N. and Moore, M.K. (1983) 'Newborn infants imitate adult facial gestures', *Child Development,* 54: 702-9

Merck Manual of Diagnosis and Therapy (1999) General medicine, Merck Research Laboratories, Merck & Co. Inc., Whitehouse Station, NJ

Miclat, N.N. and others (1978) 'Neonatal gastric PH', *Anesth. Analg.,* 57/1: 98-101

Mitchell, M.D. and others (1979) 'Melatonin in the maternal and umbilican circulations during human parturition', *Br. J. of Obstet. Gynaecol.,* 86/1: 29-31

Moir, A. and Jessel, D. (1991) *Brainsex: The real difference between men and women,* Mandarin Paperbacks London.

Mongelli, M. and others (2000) 'Effect of labour and delivery on plasma hepatic enzymes in the newborn', *J. Obstet. Gynaecol. Res.,* 26/1: 61-3

Montagu, A. (1971) *Touching: The human significance of skin,* Columbia University Press, New York

Montgomery, S.M. and others (2006) 'Breast feeding and resilience against psychosocial stress', *Arch. Dis. Child.,* 000: 1-5

Mussen, P.H., Conger, J.J., Kagan, J., and Huston, A.C. (1990)

Child development and personality, Harper & Row, New York

Nathanielsz, P.W. (1996) *Life before birth: The challenges of fetal development,* W.H. Freeman and Co., New York

National Institute of Child Health and Human Development (1997) 'Early child care and cognitive outcomes associated with early child care: results of the NICHD study up to 36 months', NICHD, Research Network, Bethesda, Md., April

Naude, D. (2006) 'Cognitive visual therapy and creative learning', Paper presented at Vision, Basic Skills Development and Bridging the 'Skills Gap' Conference, London, November

New England Journal of Medicine (355: 992-1005) Cited in: **NewScientist.com.news service**, 22nd September 2006

Noble, S. and Emmett, P. (2006) 'Differences in weaning practice, food and nutrient intake between breast and formula fed 4 month old infants in England', *Journal of Human Nutrition and Dietetics,* 19/4: 303

O'Connor, T.G., Heron, J., and Golding, J. and others (2002) 'Maternal antenatal anxiety and children's behavioural/emotional problems at 4 years: report from the Avon Longitudinal Study of Parents and Children', *British Journal of Psychiatry,* 180: 502-8

O'Keane, V. and Scott, J. (2005) 'From obstetric complications to a maternal-foetal origin hypothesis of mood disorder', *British Journal of Psychiatry,* 18: 367-8

Odent, M. (1986) *Primal health,* Century Hutchinson, London

Odent, M. (1991) 'The early expression of the rooting reflex', paper presented at the European Conference of Neuro-developmental Delay in Children with Specific Learning Difficulties, Chester, March

Odent, M. (2001) *The scientification of love,* Free Association Books. London

Odent, M. (2002a) *The obstetrician and the farmer,* Free Association Books, London

Odent, M. (2002b) Lecture given to the Society for SEAL Conference, University of Derby

Okamoto, E. and other (1989) 'Plasma concentrations of human atrial natriuretic peptide at vaginal delivery and elective cesarean section', *Asia Oceania J. Obset. Gynaecol.,* 15/2: 199-202

Olds, J. and Milner, P. (1954) 'Positive reinforcement produced by electrical stimulation of septal area and other regions of rat brains',

328   WHAT BABIES AND CHILDREN REALLY NEED

Journal of Comparative and Physiological Psychology, 47: 419-27

Office of National Statisics (2005) *Mental health of children and young people in Great Britain,* Palgrave Macmillan, Basingstoke

Otimari, G. and others (1991) 'Delayed neurological adaptation in infants delivered by elective caesarean section and the relation to catecholamine levels', *Early Human Development,* 26/1: 51-60

Owen, G.C., Martin, R.M., Whincup, P.H, Davey Smith, G. and Cook, D.G. (2005) 'Effect of infant feeding on the risk of obesity across the life course: a quantitative review of published evidence', *Pediatrics,* 115/5:1 367-77

Palmer, G. (1993) *The politics of breastfeeding,* Pandora Press, London

Palmer, S. (2006) *Toxic childhood,* Orion Books, London

Palmer, S. (2007) *Detoxing childhood,* Orion Books, London, 2007

Panksepp, J. (1998) *Affective neuroscience: The foundations of human and animal emotions,* Oxford University Press, New York

Paynter, A. (2006) Cited in: Summary of reports from schools using the INPP schools' programme, INPP, Chester

Peiper, A. (1963) *Cerebral function in infancy and childhood,* International Behavioral Science Series, Consultants Bureau, New York

Pliszka, S.R. (2003) *Neuroscience for the mental health clinician,* Guildford Press, New York

Powell, A. (1998) 'Children need touching and attention, Harvard researchers say', *Harvard University Gazette,* April

Prechtl, H.F.R. (1956) Klin.Wschr, 281

Prescott, J.W. (1996) 'The origins of human love and violence', *Pre- and Perinatal Psychology Journal,* 10/ 3: 143-88

Profet, M. (1992) Cited in: J.H. Barkow and others (eds), *The Adapted Mind,* Oxford University Press, New York

Profet, M. (1995) *Protecting your baby-to-be: Preventing birth defects in the first trimester,* Addison-Wesley, Reading, Mass.

Ravelli, G.P. and others (1976) 'Obesity in young men after famine exposure in utero and early infancy', *New England Journal of Medicine,* 12th August: 349-53

Ravelli, A.C.J., van der Meulen, J.H.P., Osmond, C., Barker, D.J.P., and Bleker, O.P. (2000) 'Infant feeding and adult glucose tolerance, lipid profile, blood pressure and obesity', *Archives of Disease in Childhood,* 82: 248-52

Restak, R. (1986) *The infant brain,* Doubleday and Co., New York

Richardson, B.S. and others (2005) 'The impact of labor at term on measures of neonatal outcome', *Am. J. Obstet. Gynecol.*, 192/1: 219-26

Rigg, L.A. and Yen, S.S. (1977) 'Multiphasic prolactin secretion during parturition in human subjects', *American Journal of Obstetric Gynecology*, 128/2: 215-8

Righard, L. and Alade, M.O. (1990) 'Effect of delivery room routine on success of first breast-feed', *Lancet*, 3/336 (8723): 1105-7

Righard, L. (1995) 'Delivery Self-Attachment', DVD, Geddes Production Presents

Robinson, R. (1966) *Aboriginal myths and legends*, Sun Books, cited in: J.G. Cowan, The Aborigine tradition, Element Books, Shaftesbury

Rosenberg, K. and Trevathen, W.R. (2001) 'The evolution of human birth', *Scientific American*, November: 77-81

Rowe, N. (n.d.) *Personal communication*

Sangild, P.T. and others (1995) 'Vaginal birth versus elective caesarean section: effects on gastric function in the neonate', Exp. Physiol., 80/1: 147-57

Savan, A. (1997) A study of the effect of background music on the behaviour and physiological responses of children with special educational needs, research in progress

Schore, A.N. (1994) *Affect regulation and the origin of the self*, Laurence Erlbaum, Hove

Schrager, O.L. (1983) 'Postural adaptive reactions in one-leg position depending upon normal and abnormal vestibular-proprioceptive-oculomotor-visual integration', unpublished mimeo

Selye, H. (1956) *The stress of life*, McGraw-Hill, New York

Shayvitz, S. (1996) 'Dyslexia', *Scientific American*, 11: 77-83

Shonkoff, J. and Phillips, D. (eds) (2000) *From neurons to neighborhoods: The science of early childhood development*, Report of the National Research Council. National Academies Press, Washington, D.C.

Siegal, D.J. (1999) *The developing mind: Toward a neurobiology of interpersonal experience*, Guildford Press, New York

Sigman, A. (2005) *Remotely controlled*, Vermilion Press, London

Sills, F. (2004) 'Pre and perinatal psychology', draft extract from a paper on clinical issues related to pre and perinatal wounding, Karuna Institute, Widecombe in the Moor

Sims, M., Guilfoyle, A., and Parry, T.S. (2006) 'Children's cortisol levels and quality of care provision', *Child; Care, Health and Development,* 32/4: 453

Singhal, A. and others (2007) 'Infant nutrition and stereoacuity at age 4-6 years', *American Journal of Clinical Nutrition,* 85/1: 152-9

Skeffington, A.M. (1928-1974) Optometric Extension Programme Continuing Education Courses, Optometric Extension Programme, Santa Ana.

Small, M.F. (1999) *Our babies ourselves: How biology and culture shape the way we parent,* Anchor Books, New York

Smith, C.A. (1947) 'Effects of maternal undernutrition upon the newborn infant in Holland (1944-1945)', *Journal of Pediatrics,* 30: 229-43

Smith, S.R. (1975)' Religion and the conception of youth in seventeenth century England', *History of Childhood Quarterly: The Journal of Psychohistory,* 2, 493-516

Snowden, D. (2001) *Ageing with grace,* Fourth Estate, London

Sontag, L.W. (1944) 'War and the foetal maternal relationship', *Marriage and Family Living,* 6: 1-5

Stein, A., Gath, D.H., Bucher, J., Bond, A., Day, A. and Cooper, P.J. (1991) 'The relationship between post-natal depression and mother-child interaction', *British Journal of Psychiatry,* 158: 46-52.

Stein, Z,, Susser, M., Saneger, G., and Marolla, F. (1975) *Famine and human development: The Dutch hunger winter of 1944-45,* Oxford University Press, New York

Storr, A. (1993) *Music and the mind,* Harper Collins, London

Szmeja, Z., Slomko, Z., Sikorski, K., and Sowinski. H. (1979) 'The risk of hearing impairment in children from mothers exposed to noise during pregnancy', *International Journal of Pediatric Otorhinolaryngology,* 1: 221-9

Tallal, P. and Piercy, M. (1974) 'Developmental aphasia: rate of auditory processing and selective impairment of consonantal perception', *Neuropsychologia,* 12: 82-93

Teenage Pregnancy Report, **www.socialexclusionunit.gov.uk/publications.asp?=69**

Teenage Pregnancy, **www.dfes.gov.uk**

Tetlow, H.J. and Broughton Pipkin, F. (1983) 'Studies on the effect of mode of delivery on the renin-angiotensin system in mother and fetus at term', *Br. J. Obset. Gynaecol.,* 90/3: 220-6

Thompson, C., Syddall, H., Rodin, I., and others (2001) 'Birth weight and the risk of depressive disorder in late life', *British Journal of Psychiatry,* 179: 450-5

Thompson, P., Lee, A., Hayashi, K., and Toga, A. (n.d.) UCLA Lab of Neuro Imaging; Nitin Gogtay and Judy Rapoport, Child Psychiatry Branch, NIMH

Tong, S., Marjono, B., Brown, D.A., Mulvey, S., Breit, S.N., Manuelpillai, U., and Wallace, E.M. (2004) 'Serum concentrations of macrophage inhibitory cytokine 1 (MIC 1) as a predictor of miscarriage', *Lancet,* 363: 129-30

Trevarthen, C. (1989) 'Development of early social interactions and the affective regulation of brain growth', in C. Von Euler, H. Forssberg, and H. Lagercrantz (eds), *Neurobiology of early infant behaviour,* Wenner-Gren Center International Symposium Series, 55: 191-216, Macmillan, London

Trevarthen, C. (2006) 'Pleasure from others' movements: how body massage and music speak with one voice to infants and give meaning to life', paper presented at the GICM Professional Conference, Coventry, 7th October

Trevarthen, C. and Reddy, V. (2006) 'Consciousness in infants', in M. Velmer and S. Schneider (eds), *A companion to consciousness,* Blackwells, Oxford

Tuorman, T.E. (1994) 'The adverse effects of alcohol on reproduction', *International Journal of Biosocial and Medical Research,* 14/2; reproduced for Foresight, the Association for the Promotion of Preconceptual Care

UNICEF 2006. An overview of child well-being and rich countries. UNICEF Innocenti Research Centre. Report Card 7.

Urs, A., Hunziker, M.D., and Barr, R.G. (1986) 'Increased carrying reduces infant crying: a randomised controlled trial', *Pediatrics,* 77: 641-8

Verny, T. (1982) *The secret life of the unborn child,* Sphere Books, London

Violato, C. and Russell, C. (2000) 'A meta-analysis of the published research on the effects of non-maternal care on child development', in C. Violato, M. Genuis, and E. Paolucci (eds), *The changing family and child development,* Ashgate, London

Von Kries, R., Kolezko, B., Sauerwald, T., and others (1999) 'Breast feeding and obesity: cross sectional study', *British Medical Journal,* 319: 147-50

Wachsmith, I. (2006) 'Gestures offer insight', *Scientific American,* Oct/Nov

Weider, D., Sateia, M., and West, R. (1991) 'Nocturnal enuresis with upper airway obstruction', *Otolaryngology Head and Neck Surgery,* 105: 427-32

Weiss, B., Dodge, K.A., Bates, J.E., and Pettit, G.S. (1992) 'Some consequences of early harsh discipline: child aggression and a maladaptive social information processing style', *Child Development,* 63/6: 1321-35

West, J.R., Dewey, S.L., Pierce, D.R., and Black, A.C. (1984) 'Prenatal and early postnatal exposure to ethanol permanently alters the rat hippocampus', cited in *Mechanisms of alcohol damage in utero,* CIBA Foundation Symposium, 105, Pitman, London

Whiting, J.W.M. and Child, I.L. (1953) *Child training and personality: A cross cultural study,* Yale University Press, New Haven, Conn.

Wiles, N.J., Peters, T.J., Leon, D.A., and Lewis, G. (2005) 'Birth weight and psychological distress at 45-51 years', *British Journal of Psychiatry,* 187: 21-8

Winn, M. (1985) *The Plug-In Drug,* Viking, New York

www.goodchildhood.org.uk

www.merck.com

www.stokespeaksout.co.uk

Zanado, V., and others (2004) 'Neonatal respiratory morbidity risk and mode of delivery at term: influence of timing of elective caesarean delivery', *Acta Paediatr.,* 93/5: 643-7

Index

Other Titles

Reflexes, Learning and Behaviour: A Window into the Child's Mind

Sally Goddard Blythe

This unique book explores the physical basis of learning difficulties, Dyslexia, Dyspraxia, Attention Deficit Disorder (ADD) and Attention Deficit Hyperactive Disorder (ADHD), with particular focus on the role of abnormal reflexes and the effect upon subsequent development.

Sally Goddard, Director of The Institute for Neuro-Physiological Psychology, Chester, explains how the reflexes of infancy (primitive and postural) can affect the learning ability of the child if they are not inhibited and integrated by the developing brain in the first three years of life. Each reflex is described together with its function in normal development, and its impact upon learning and behaviour if it remains active beyond the normal period.

Simple tests for the reflexes that are crucial to education are described, together with suggestions for suitable remedial intervention. A brief history of how current methods of intervention designed to correct abnormal reflexes have evolved is included, together with a summary of some of the relevant research in the field.

This book is essential reading for parents, teachers, psychologists, optometrists, and anyone involved in the assessment, education, and management of children and their problems. It explains *why* certain children are unable to benefit from the same teaching methods as their peers, and why they remain immature in other aspects of their lives.

Published by Fern Ridge Press, USA; 182pp; 251 x 178mm; 978-0-961533-28-1; pb

Attention, Balance and Coordination: The A, B C of Learning Success

Sally Goddard Blythe

To be published by Wiley-Blackwell, August 2008; 224pp; 978-0-470516-23-2; pb

Wings of Childhood

A New CD of Nursery Rhymes for Modern Times

Wings of Childhood is a collection of songs written to inspire movement and development in young children from 3 to 7 years of age.

The songs have been written by Michael Lazarev, a Russian paediatrician and musician, who has developed a programme of musical stimulation to promote children's development from before birth up to 7 years of age. His method is being used in 140 cities in Russia including 1000 kindergartens in Turkestan. Studies following the progress of children whose mothers have used the programme have shown that the children have more advanced coordination and language skills and that there are fewer children suffering from bronchial asthma.

Wings of Childhood brings together for the first time the musical talent of **Michael Lazarev** with the developmental work undertaken by **Sally Goddard Blythe** at The Institute for Neuro-Physiological Psychology in Chester (INPP). Sally Goddard Blythe is Director of INPP and an internationally known author and lecturer on child development, her last book being *The Well Balanced Child* (Hawthorn Press).

INPP devises special movement programmes to improve children's attention, balance, and coordination, and help to get them 'ready' for school. INPP also offers individual programmes to help older children overcome problems at school.

The song collection can simply be enjoyed as a delightful collection of songs for children to sing along with their parents. It can also be used as the basis for Music and Movement programmes, encouraging children to act out through movement the 'characters' in the songs. The animal characters have been specially selected, based on developmental principles of movement. Practice of these early stages of movement can help to prepare children for more advanced skills later on.

The songs have been recorded using Bass and Soprano voices to provide a wide range of sound frequencies. Research has shown that a child's listening environment in the first 3-5 years of life provides the basis for speech, language, and reading later on. Children should be encouraged to sing along with the songs because use of the child's own voice helps to train sound discrimination. The second part of the CD contains a charming medley of piano improvizations on the songs, to which children and their parents can add their own words and movements. This is an activity for fathers as well as mothers.

Dr Michael Lazarev is a professor of medicine and Head of the Children's Rehabilitatory Medicine in Moscow. He is author of SONATAL (Sound and Birth).

Further information about the SONATAL programme can be found at **www.sonatal.ru**

Further information about The Institute for Neuro-Physiological Psychology (INPP) can be found at **www.inpp.org.uk**

Detoxing Childhood: What Parents Need to Know to Raise Happy, Successful Children

Sue Palmer

When Sue Palmer wrote her ground-breaking book *Toxic Childhood*, showing how problems of diet, education, fitness, and mental-health problems were all inter-related, she helped precipitate a national and international debate. Everyone from educationalists and scientists to politicians, religious leaders, and authors got involved in the ensuing dialogue. The problems seemed potentially overwhelming. Now, in this successor volume, Sue Palmer provides a guide on how to bring up children in a way that avoids the problems of a 'toxic' modern world. With practical, easy-to-follow advice, she explains what children need, in terms of food, play, sleep, and talk; what childcare and education will help most; how families can work together for the best, given the hectic pace of twenty-first century life; and how to turn the 'electronic village' of TV, computers, and mobile phones to our advantage. With so many pressures across so many parts of our lives today, this book serves as a one-stop solution to our multiple concerns about raising healthy, happy children in the modern world.

Published by Orion, UK; 176pp; 232 x 150mm; 978-0-752890-10-4; pb

Other Titles by Hawthorn Press

The Genius of Play
Celebrating the spirit of childhood
Sally Jenkinson

Imagine a teaching aid which enhanced a child's self esteem and social skills, enriched their imagination, and encouraged creative thinking. That teaching aid is play. Sally Jenkinson argues that even as a growing body of research helps us to understand the genius of play we are eroding children's self-initiated play with inappropriate toys, TV and consumerism.

224pp; 216 x 138mm; 978-1-903458-04-4; pb

Ready to Learn (2nd edition)
From birth to school readiness
Martyn Rawson and Michael Rose

Ready to Learn will help you to decide when your child is ready to take the step from kindergarten to school proper. The key is an imaginative grasp of how children learn to play, speak, think and relate between birth and six years of age.

224pp; 216 x 138mm; 978-1-903458-66-2; pb

The Well Balanced Child
Movement and early learning
Sally Goddard Blythe

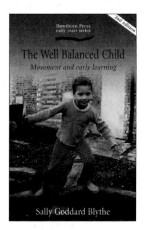

'Learning is not just about reading, writing and maths,' says Sally Goddard Blythe. 'A child's experience of movement will help play a pivotal role in shaping his personality, his feelings and achievements.' Her book makes the case for a 'whole body' approach to learning which integrates the brain, senses, movement, music and play.

The Well Balanced Child examines why movement matters; how music helps brain development; the role of nutrition, the brain and child growth; and offers practical tips for parents and educators to help children with learning and behavioural problems.

240pp; 216 x 138mm; 978-1-903458-63-1; pb

Set Free Childhood
Parents' survival guide to coping with computers and TV
Martin Large

Children watch TV and use computers for five hours daily on average. The result? Record levels of learning difficulties, obesity, eating disorders, sleep problems, language delay, aggressive behaviour, anxiety – and children on fast forward. *Set Free Childhood* shows you how to counter screen culture and create a calmer, more enjoyable family life.

240pp; 216 x 138mm; 978-1-903458-43-3; pb

Ordering books

If you have difficulties ordering Hawthorn Press books from a bookshop, you can order direct from:

United Kingdom

Booksource
50 Cambuslang Road
Cambuslang, Glasgow, G32 8NB
Tel: (0845) 370 0063
Fax: (0845) 370 0064
E-mail: orders@booksource.net

USA/North America

SteinerBooks
PO Box 960, Herndon
VA 20172-0960
Tel: (800) 856 8664
Fax: (703) 661 1501
E-mail: service@steinerbooks.org
Website: www.steinerbooks.org

or you can order online at **www.hawthornpress.com**

For further information or a book catalogue, please contact:

Hawthorn Press
1 Lansdown Lane, Stroud
Gloucestershire GL5 1BJ
Tel: (01453) 757040
Fax: (01453) 751138
E-mail: info@hawthornpress.com
Website: www.hawthornpress.com